By Lisa Damour

Under Pressure
Untangled

UNDER PRESSURE

LISA DAMOUR, Ph.D.

BALLANTINE BOOKS
New York

UNDER PRESSURE

CONFRONTING THE EPIDEMIC OF
STRESS AND ANXIETY IN GIRLS

Copyright © 2019 by Lisa Damour

Published in the United States by Ballantine Books, an imprint of Random House, a division of Penguin Random House LLC, New York.

BALLANTINE and the HOUSE colophon are registered trademarks of Penguin Random House LLC.

Translation of Horace from *Horace: The Satires* is by A. S. Kline, copyright © 2005, and is reprinted here by permission of the translator.

LIBRARY OF CONGRESS CATALOGING-IN-PUBLICATION DATA
Names: Damour, Lisa, author.
Title: Under pressure: confronting the epidemic of stress and anxiety in girls / Lisa Damour.
Description: First edition. | New York: Ballantine Books, [2019] | Includes bibliographical references and index.
Identifiers: LCCN 2018039456 (print) | LCCN 2018056183 (ebook) | ISBN 9780399180057 (hardcover) | ISBN 9780399180064 (ebook)
Subjects: LCSH: Stress in adolescence. | Anxiety in adolescence. | Teenage girls—Psychology. | Stress management.
Classification: LCC BF724.3.S86 (ebook) | LCC BF724.3.S86 D36 2019 (print) | DDC 155.5/33—dc23
LC record available at lccn.loc.gov/2018039456

Printed in the United States of America on acid-free paper

randomhousebooks.com

2 4 6 8 9 7 5 3

Title-page image: © iStock/ericsphotography
Book design by Simon M. Sullivan

To my daughters, and yours

It is not the presence or absence, the quality, or even the quantity of anxiety which allows predictions as to future mental health or illness; what is significant in this respect is only the ability to deal with the anxiety. Here, the differences between one individual and another are very great, and the chances of maintaining mental equilibrium vary accordingly.

The children whose outlook for mental health is better are those who cope with the same danger situations actively by way of resources such as intellectual understanding, logical reasoning, changing of external circumstances . . . by mastery instead of retreat.

—ANNA FREUD (1965)

Contents

. . . .

Introduction

. . . .

ON A CHILLY MONDAY AFTERNOON IN NOVEMBER, I FOUND MYSELF IN an emergency psychotherapy session with Erica, a seventh grader whom I'd seen on and off for a few years, and Janet, her very worried mother. Janet had called my practice that morning when Erica became so overwhelmed by anxiety that she refused to go to school.

"Erica had a rough weekend," explained Janet over the phone, "because a big group project that's due soon went off the rails over some social drama." She added that her daughter hadn't eaten breakfast for the last two weeks because she had woken up every morning with stomachaches that didn't let up until midday. Then, through tears I could hear over the phone, Janet added, "I can't *believe* that she's not at school today, but I couldn't figure out how to make her go. When I told her that I'd even give her a ride instead of making her take the bus, she looked at me like I was offering to drive her to a firing squad."

Feeling really concerned, I asked, "Can you come in today?"

"Yes, we *have* to," said Janet. "She's got to be able to go to school. I've got a meeting early this afternoon that I can't miss. Can we come in after that?"

"Of course. And don't worry," I offered earnestly, "we'll figure this out. We'll get to the bottom of what's going on."

Something has changed. Anxiety has always been part of life—and part of growing up—but in recent years for young women like Erica and so many others, it seems to have spun out of control. I've been a psychologist for more than two decades, and in that time I've watched tension rise in girls in my private practice and in my research. I also hear about the mounting pressures girls feel as I spend part of each week at an all-girls' school in my community and travel to talk with groups of students around the United States and around the world.

At work, I'm able to observe and learn from girls in so many ways, and when I'm home, I gain another perspective on them as the mother of two daughters. Girls are my world, and if I'm not with them, I'm often chatting about them with teachers, pediatricians, or fellow psychologists. In the last few years, my colleagues and I have spent more and more time discussing the scores of young women we've met who are overwhelmed by stress or who feel intensely anxious. And we talk about how it wasn't always this way.

Alarmingly, what we are observing on an intimate daily scale is confirmed by sweeping surveys. A recent report from the American Psychological Association found that adolescence can no longer be characterized as an exuberant time of life, full of carefree experimentation. Except for during the summer months, today's teens now, for the first time, feel more stressed than their parents do. They also experience the emotional and physical symptoms of chronic tension, such as edginess and fatigue, at levels that we used to see only in adults. Studies also tell us that the number of adolescents reporting that they are experiencing emotional problems and are highly anxious is on the rise.

But these trends do not affect our sons and daughters equally. It's the girls who suffer more.

As confirmed by report after report, girls are more likely than boys to labor under feelings of psychological stress and tension. A recent study found that a staggering 31 percent of girls and young women experience symptoms of anxiety, compared to 13 percent of boys and young men. Studies tell us that, compared to boys, girls feel more pressure, and that they endure more of the physical symptoms of psychological strain, such as fatigue and changes in appetite. Young women are also more likely to experience the emotions often associated with anxiety. One study found that the number of teenage girls who said they often felt nervous, worried, or fearful jumped by 55 percent from 2009 to 2014 while remaining unchanged for adolescent boys over the same time period. A different study found that anxious feelings are becoming more prevalent among all young people but are growing at a faster pace in girls.

These gendered trends seen in anxiety are also mirrored in the climbing rates of depression—a diagnosis that can serve as a proxy measure of overall psychological stress. Between 2005 and 2014, the percentage of teenage girls experiencing depression rose from 13 to 17. For boys, that same measure moved from 5 to 6 percent. While we hate to see emotional distress rise for our daughters *or* our sons, we should probably be paying attention to the fact that girls between the ages of twelve and seventeen are now nearly three times more likely than boys to become depressed.

The gender imbalance in stress symptoms that begins in middle school doesn't end after high school graduation. The American College Health Association found that undergraduate women were 43 percent more likely than their male counterparts to report feeling overcome by anxiety within the past year. Compared to male undergrads, college women also felt more exhausted and overwhelmed, and they experienced higher levels of overall stress.

When mental health professionals hear and read about statistics like these, we jump to attention. From there we typically adopt an appropriately skeptical stance and wonder whether there has *actually* been a dramatic change in the number of girls who are feeling pushed to the limit, or if we are simply getting better at detecting problems that have been present all along. Researchers who study these questions tell us that we haven't just pulled our heads out of the sand to discover a crisis that we have long ignored; the available evidence tells us that we are truly seeing something new. Nor does research indicate that girls are now simply more willing than they have been in the past to tell us that they are suffering. Rather, the situation for girls does actually seem to have gotten worse.

Experts point to a number of possible explanations for this emerging epidemic of nervous girls. Studies, for example, show that girls are more likely than boys to worry about how they are doing in school. While it's nothing new for our daughters to strive to live up to the expectations of adults, I now hear regularly about girls who are so fearful of disappointing their teachers that they skip sleep to do extra-credit work for points they don't need. Research also tells us that our daughters, more than our sons, worry about how they look. Though teens have always experienced moments of high anxiety about their physical appearance, we are raising the first generation that can, and often does, devote hours at a time to fretfully curating and posting selfies in the hopes that they will receive an avalanche of likes. Studies also suggest that girls are more likely than boys not only to be cyberbullied but also to dwell on the emotional injuries caused by their peers.

There are also sexual factors that apply uniquely to girls. Our daughters hit puberty earlier than our sons do, and the age of puberty for girls keeps dropping. It is now no longer unusual to see a fifth grader sporting an adult woman's body. To make matters worse, girls develop their grown-up bodies while being inundated by images communicating the strong and distinct message that women are valued mainly for their sex appeal. Making matters worse still, widely seen marketing content often exploits young girls—think of commercials with a "naughty school girl" angle—or targets them as consumers, as in advertisements now peddling thongs and push-up bikini tops for seven- to ten-year-olds. In years past, these images were at least limited to those put out through conventional media outlets. Today, girls are just as likely to come across a sultry selfie posted on Instagram by a sixth-grade classmate.

These prevailing explanations for why girls feel more pressure than boys are helpful, if not altogether surprising. But knowing about some of the particular difficulties girls face is not the same as knowing what we can do to address them.

If you are reading this book, then you have probably tried numerous ways to help your daughter feel less anxious and more joyful. You have reassured her that she should worry less about what she scored on that last quiz and do her best to ignore hurtful online chatter. You've already told her that she is beautiful or that looks aren't important. (Most loving parents, myself included, have said both!) You've taught her to question and critique cultural messages suggesting that a girl's worth hinges on how she looks, and you've worked to limit the amount of time she spends posting or scrutinizing digital images. Yet, despite your best efforts, you may still find yourself raising an absolutely terrific girl who spends far too much time feeling nervous or unhappy.

This book examines the forces that fray girls' nerves and suggests how we can help our daughters feel more at ease. I'll describe what I've learned from the growing research, my psychotherapy clients, my colleagues, girls at schools, and my own daughters about the steps we can take to shield young women from toxic stress and anxiety. At times, I illustrate my ideas with examples from my work, but I have altered identifying details and in a few cases presented composites in order to maintain the confidentiality of those who have shared themselves with me.

Under Pressure will start by building our understanding of stress and anxiety. From there, it will consider how tension finds its way into the many facets of girls' lives, examining chapter by chapter the difficulties that invariably arise for our daughters in their home life, in their interactions with other girls, in their dealings with boys, in their role as students, and in their participation in the broader culture. As parents, we may *wish* that we could clear our children's path of any source of discomfort, but there really are no stress-free routes from infancy to adulthood; even if we could make this happen, it would not serve our children well in the long run. That said, it's much easier to feel relaxed about the stressors that await our daughters when we know what to expect.

Anticipating the difficulties our girls will encounter as they age allows us to respond more helpfully when they become upset. And how we respond to a girl's worries and fears matters a lot. Every time your daughter scraped her knee as a toddler, she looked first at her knee and then at your face. If you remained composed, she felt better right away. Had you scooped her up and rushed her to the emergency room, she would have become unnecessarily terrified. Reacting with alarm to normal difficulties can make them worse and even contribute to a girl's unhealthy levels of stress and anxiety. With this in mind, *Under Pressure* won't simply itemize the concerns that arise for girls and young women, it will also offer strategies to help you reassure your daughter on the days that she feels she is falling apart and to help her manage on her own when she is ready.

Many of the stressors that come with growing up are age old, while others are new to the scene, such as the omnipresence of digital technology and the increasingly intense college admissions process. We'll consider how parents can help their daughters deal with both the old and new challenges effectively. This book should help your daughter to feel less anxious, but it cannot take the place of treatment for a diagnosable psychological disorder. If your daughter already suffers from crippling anxiety, you should consult with her medical provider or a licensed mental health clinician about the treatment options that make the most sense for her.

Under Pressure considers the burdens borne by girls, but don't be surprised if some of its guidance also helps with raising a son. It's true that our daughters are statistically more likely than our sons to be anxious, but plenty of boys struggle with feelings of tension and stress as well. And though *Under Pressure* looks at the topic of psychological pressure through the lens of gender, it will touch on ways that financial insecurity or minority status can add to the challenges that all girls encounter.

When it comes to reckoning with the mental and emotional pressures our daughters feel, there are no easy answers, nor quick fixes. But taking a detailed, comprehensive look at the problem opens a world of new approaches to solving it. We love our girls, we hate to see them suffer, and there is a great deal that we can do to help them feel happier, healthier, and more relaxed in the face of the challenges we know will come their way.

Let's get started.

UNDER PRESSURE

. . . .

CHAPTER ONE

Coming to Terms with Stress and Anxiety

I HAVE GOOD NEWS. ACTUALLY, I HAVE TWO PIECES OF REALLY GREAT news. First, stress and anxiety aren't all bad. In fact, you can't thrive without them. Understanding the difference between their healthy and unhealthy forms will change, for the better, how you help your daughter manage the tension she feels. Second, the field of psychology has a lot to say about how to alleviate stress and anxiety if they do reach toxic levels. Indeed, if I were to take an informal survey of my colleagues, the vast majority would agree that we have come to understand the root causes and inner workings of pathological stress and anxiety as well as we understand anything in our field. As a result, we have many ways to help people rein in psychological strain when it gets out of control.

Taken together, these two happy facts mean that you can already start to worry less about how stressed or anxious your daughter feels because, to a degree, these mental states are essential catalysts for human growth and development. And if you suspect that your daughter's unease far exceeds the healthy mark, then I'm here to reassure you that you and your daughter do not need to feel helpless. We're going to tackle unhealthy stress and anxiety, too.

Healthy Stress

Stress gets a bad rap. Though people don't always enjoy being stretched to new limits, both common sense and scientific research tell us that the stress of operating beyond our comfort zones helps us grow. Healthy stress happens when we take on new challenges, such as giving a speech to a large audience, or do things that feel psychologically threatening, such as finally confronting a hostile peer. Pushing ourselves past familiar limits builds our capacities in the same way that runners prepare for marathons by gradually extending the distances at which they train.

Learning to brave stressful situations is also a skill that develops with practice. Researchers actually use the apt term *stress inoculation* to describe the well-documented finding that people who are able to weather difficult life experiences, such as riding out a serious illness, often go on to demonstrate higher-than-average resilience when faced with new hardships. I can speak for myself in saying that being middle-aged doesn't seem to come with a lot of advantages, but it definitely has one particular benefit: problems don't bother me as much as they used to. Like most of my agemates, I've got enough life experience under my belt that I now take in stride events—such as having a plane flight canceled—that would have put me on the ceiling when I was younger. While the saying "What doesn't kill you makes you stronger" almost certainly overstates the point, it's not all wrong.

As parents, we should think of stress the way Goldilocks thought about making herself comfortable while trespassing. We don't want our daughter's stress level to be consistently too low or too high. But we can embrace reasonable levels of stress as a nutrient for our daughter's healthy development that will help her to grow into the strong and durable young woman we want her to be.

Much of what our girls learn about how to manage stress comes from observing how *we* manage it as parents. Our daughters watch us for cues about how alarmed they should be by life's difficulties. When we let our own inner Chicken Little take over and panic in the face of manageable challenges, we set a bad example. When we accept that stress often leads to growth—and help our girls do the same—we create a self-fulfilling prophecy for ourselves and for our daughters.

Obstacles, however, only make us stronger when we can surmount them. Accordingly, *Under Pressure* will address in its coming chapters how you can help your daughter master the challenges she will face as she moves from childhood to adulthood. With your help and over time, your daughter can come to appreciate that stress is a positive and growth-giving part of life.

Except for when it's not.

How Stress Becomes Unhealthy

Stress becomes unhealthy when it exceeds what a person can absorb or benefit from. There is no single yardstick for what constitutes unhealthy stress, because the volume of manageable hardship differs from person to person and can even differ for a single individual from day to day. Whether stress becomes unhealthy depends on two variables: the nature of the problem and the person upon whom the problem lands.

Psychologists consider stress to be unhealthy when it interferes with well-being in the short or long term. Whether or not a stressor harms well-being has surprisingly little to do with the source of the stress and much more to do with whether adequate resources—personal, emotional, social, or financial—are available to address the problem. For example, a broken arm could be a resilience-building hassle for a girl who writes with her other hand and has lots of friends to help carry her books. Or it could be a full-blown crisis for one who might lose a shot at a desperately needed athletics scholarship due to the injury. In the same way, if the primary breadwinner is laid off, that feels much worse for a family without a financial cushion than it does for one with a healthy savings account.

Knowing that stress becomes unhealthy only when its demands exceed our resources helps us to better support our girls. We can't always prevent calamities, but we can often summon reserves to help our daughter manage the challenges life puts in her path.

A terrific example comes from my work as a consulting psychologist to Laurel School, a local all-girls' school that runs from pre-kindergarten through twelfth grade. I've spent part of each week there for the past fifteen years, and in that time I've watched several high school girls and their families contend with the disease of mononucleosis, a particularly tenacious stressor. The course of the virus doesn't differ much from girl to girl, as sufferers usually miss classes for a few weeks and also need to suspend their extracurricular activities. But the illness turns out to be much more stressful for some students than for others.

Under ideal conditions, a girl's parents can surround their daughter with loving support to make the best of a bad situation. Her folks ensure that she gets lots of rest, they coordinate effectively with the Laurel faculty to keep their daughter reasonably up to date on her assignments, and they find ways for her friends to stop by for visits. One family of a dedicated soccer player happily drove their daughter to games so she could cheer on her beloved teammates from the bench. When parents have the wherewithal to marshal resources on their daughter's behalf, I've seen a bout of mono amount to nothing more than a bothersome blip in a girl's high school career.

Other families, especially those who may already be at the

limit of the stressors they can manage, can provide only minimal support. A girl who spends long hours alone at home can be inclined to choose social media over sleep, thus causing the virus to drag on longer than it should. She might fall far behind on her schoolwork or be dragged down by sadness about missing her friends or the fun parts of school. When students in this situation eventually get better, I've heard them ruefully remark, "Thanks to mono, my entire semester was messed up."

The Three Types of Stress

Of course, there are girls and families who do everything in their power to address the social and academic impact of mononucleosis yet still find themselves struggling to get back on track. We can better understand their challenges when we recognize that just as stress is not all bad, it is not all the same. When psychologists study stress and its impact on health, we sort it into three distinct domains, namely *life events, daily hassles,* and *chronic stress.*

Any life event that requires adaptation, such as a teenager catching mono, is inherently stressful. Even happy occasions, such as becoming a parent or starting a new job, come with the strain of adapting to abrupt change. There aren't many cardinal rules in psychology, but here's one: change equals stress. The more change a life event requires, the more taxing it will be.

Moreover, life events, both good and bad, often trigger daily hassles as well. For instance, parents who rearrange their schedules to care for an unhealthy teenager may have trouble getting around to their routine errands. Or they may not be able to clean up the sink full of dinner dishes that are usually loaded into the dishwasher by the teenager felled by mono. While daily hassles seem like they shouldn't be a big deal, they do add up. Quite remarkably, one research study found that it was the number of daily hassles triggered by a major stressor, such as the death of a loved one, that actually determined how much emotional difficulty people faced down the line. In short, the pain of losing one's wife is amplified by the stress of trying to figure out her system for paying the household bills.

Our instinctual understanding of the burden of daily hassles explains our impulse to cook for friends with new babies. We stock the fridges of those facing major life events to spare them the added nuisance of shopping and making meals. Appreciating that our own daily hassles really do compound stress can spur us to take steps to minimize them. Eating off paper plates for a few weeks won't cure a teenager's mono, but it can help to reduce the level of stress overall.

Apart from life events and daily hassles, there's also chronic stress. This is the kind that results when basic life circumstances are persistently difficult. Enduring chronic stress—such as living in a dangerous neighborhood or caring for a relative with dementia—has been found to take a grinding toll on both physical and emotional health. Yet even in the worst circumstances, relief can sometimes be found. Studies of how young people cope with two grave and persistent sources of stress—ongoing cancer treatment or being raised by a severely depressed parent—have yielded valuable lessons that apply to a wide range of chronically stressful situations.

I found myself relying heavily on what we know about helping children and adolescents manage stress, even in the context of unrelentingly difficult conditions, when working with Courtney, a bright seventeen-year-old whose parents were in a drawn out and contentious separation. Courtney and I started meeting weekly in the fall of her junior year after she announced to her folks that she could not bear another day of their fighting. Though they disagreed about many things, Courtney's parents both wanted to provide their daughter with some much-needed support.

Once we got to know each other, Courtney and I set our minds to figuring out how she could manage the problems at home. Our first step was to determine what she could and couldn't change.

"Honestly," she said, "I don't think that they'll ever get along." With an air of exasperation she added, "They say that they won't fight in front of me, but they can't seem to help themselves."

"I'm really sorry to hear that . . . and can only imagine how painful it must be to hear them go after each other."

Courtney looked at her hands and then back at me before replying wearily, "Yeah, it sucks."

I reflected a moment before saying, "With regard to the fighting, I think you're stuck. Your folks are the only ones who can make it stop, and it doesn't sound like they're ready to do so."

Courtney ruefully nodded her agreement.

"So, as much as I hate to say this, I think that you have to find a way to accept that reality for now."

Indeed, for difficulties that cannot be changed, research shows that practicing acceptance is the critical first step. If your nose wrinkles at the new-age aroma wafting from the suggestion to "practice acceptance" (true confession: that was my own first reaction), consider it pragmatically. Why expend energy fighting an immutable reality? Once we find a way to digest a hard truth, we can get on with adapting to it.

Courtney, however, was having none of it.

Simultaneously incredulous and annoyed, she replied, "How can I possibly accept their fighting? It's awful!"

"I hear you," I responded as nondefensively as I could. "And if I thought you had the power to help your parents come to a truce, I'd be encouraging you all the way. I do, however, think

that there are things you can control that will help your situation. Are you open to some ideas?"

Courtney reluctantly indicated her willingness to hear me out,
so I proceeded with more of what we know from the research on
chronic stress. Namely, that it's helpful for young people to seek
out happy distractions and enjoyable activities in order to take
cover, even briefly, from their monsoon of stress.

"Are there things you enjoy that their fighting can't disrupt?"

Courtney's face relaxed as she thought about my question.
"You know," she ventured, "there *is* something I really like to
do . . ."

I raised my eyebrows to let her know that I was eager for her to
continue.

"I have a car . . . we say it's my grandma's, but it's basically
mine . . . and I love to drive it out on Chagrin River Road." I
smiled to indicate my familiarity with the wooded, hilly route
that picks up about twenty minutes east of my office in the sub-
urbs of Cleveland. "I roll down the windows, even when it's cold
outside, and play my music loud. Even after one song, I feel better."

"Can you take that drive whenever you want?"

"Basically. Unless I have homework or something like that—
but it doesn't take me long to get there from my house."

"Then I think that should be part of our plan. You can't stop
your parents' fighting, but it sounds like you have a reliable way
to take a break from the stress of it."

Courtney bit her lip, letting me know that she remained un-
convinced.

"It's definitely an imperfect solution," I said gently, "but think
of it this way: the arguments make you feel bad, and driving
makes you feel better. Until your parents sort things out, taking
a drive when you need to gives you some control of your mood."

"That's true," she said slowly. She paused, then added, "I'll try it and let you know."

We can bring these lessons about coping with chronic stress home to our own girls by guiding them to think about what they can change and what they can't when they are stuck in difficult circumstances. Should your daughter find herself in a class dogged by unrelenting interpersonal strife (hello, seventh grade), you might help her to focus on what she can actually do about the situation, such as keeping ties with low-drama neighborhood friends. Beyond that, you can support her as she finds ways to distract herself from the social tempest until it dies down (fingers crossed, eighth grade). Given that unhealthy stress cannot always be avoided, we should take comfort in what the scholarship tells us about how to reduce psychological strain. Taking a strategic approach—fixing what we can and finding a way to live with what remains—makes it possible to feel less helpless and more relaxed, even in the face of substantial adversity.

From Stress to Anxiety

Stress and anxiety are like fraternal twins. They have a lot in common, but they're not the same. Stress and anxiety are alike in that they are both psychologically uncomfortable. But while *stress* usually refers to the feeling of emotional or mental strain or tension, *anxiety* usually refers to the feeling of fear, dread, or panic.

Though we can distinguish between stress and anxiety, in real life they often coil tightly around each other. For example, a girl who feels stressed by her academic workload may come to feel anxious about getting her assignments done. A girl who lives in a neighborhood where sporadic gun shots cause bursts of anxious panic will almost certainly suffer from chronic stress. We can't always tease stress and anxiety apart, and most of the time we don't need to. For practical purposes, we can treat the two concepts as nearly interchangeable (as this book will often do), focusing our efforts on helping our daughters to keep both their tension and their worries under control.

Stress and anxiety are also similar in that they can be good or bad. We've already taken a look at the difference between healthy and unhealthy stress. Now let's do the same for anxiety.

Healthy Anxiety

Anxiety is a gift, handed down by evolution, to keep humans safe. Every one of us comes equipped with a sophisticated alarm system programmed deep in our brains. When we sense a threat, that alarm system triggers anxiety. And the discomfort of anxiety compels us to take steps to reduce or avoid the threat. To put it another way, our prehistoric ancestors who sprinted for the cave when they spotted a saber-toothed tiger survived to pass down their anxiety alarm genes to us. The caveperson who casually remarked, "Hey, check it out, that's a really neat tiger" did not.

Our anxiety alarm now rings in response to a wide range of modern-day threats. It goes off when we nearly have an accident while driving, when we hear a strange noise while alone in the house, or when our boss calls an unexpected meeting in the midst of layoffs at work. In addition to warning us about the threats in our surroundings, anxiety also alerts us to dangers from within. You know that uncomfortable feeling that bubbles up right before we say something we later regret? That's anxiety trying to warn us to zip it. And you know that nagging sense that arises when we're binge-watching Netflix instead of doing our taxes? That's anxiety trying to keep us from having to pay the fines for filing late.

In short, anxiety works to protect us from the world and from ourselves.

Unfortunately, anxiety, like stress, has gotten a bad rap. Somewhere along the line we got the idea that emotional discomfort is always a bad thing. This turns out to be a very unhelpful idea. Psychological distress, like physical pain, serves as a finely tuned feedback system that helps us to course correct. Just as physical pain prompts us to stop touching a hot burner, emotional distress alerts us to pay attention to our choices. For example, if you always feel nervous before having lunch with a particular friend because you never know how she's going to treat you, it's probably time to reconsider that relationship.

So here's the first thing we can do to help our daughters take control of anxiety: we can teach them that anxiety is often their friend.

Several years ago I started working with a sixteen-year-old named Dana whose parents called me after she drank so much at a party that she landed herself in the emergency room. I had been practicing long enough to know not to come to any conclusions about Dana based on the single incident that brought us together, and indeed, when we met, my restraint was rewarded. In my waiting room I found a friendly teenage girl wearing jeans and a plaid flannel shirt. She stood up quickly and stuck out her hand as she introduced herself.

As we shook hands I said, "Hi, I'm Dr. Damour," to which she replied sincerely, "Thank you for meeting with me." I pointed the way to my office and followed her in as she walked, actually kind of bounced, ahead of me.

Once we were sitting down, I began. "Look, you don't know me and I don't know you," I said in a welcoming tone, "but I know that something really scary happened." Back in my early days as a psychologist, I used to make the rookie mistake of putting teenagers on the spot shortly after meeting them. In response, they usually clammed up. Experience has taught me that people (and teenagers are, of course, first and foremost people) feel much more comfortable broaching touchy topics when they're not cornered into doing so.

"Do you want to start with what happened," I continued, "or would you feel more comfortable if we just took some time to get to know each other?"

"I appreciate that," said Dana, "but I'm okay with talking about what happened. I'm actually super bothered about it," she began while tugging at a lock of her curly, shoulder-length hair. "A couple of weekends ago my friends and I went to a party at the house of a kid I've known for a long time, and that was fun. But then one of my friends heard about a party at another house, so for some reason we decided to go over there. I didn't know the kid hosting the second party, but I knew a bunch of his friends. But there were also tons of kids I had never seen before, which was kinda weird."

I nodded as she spoke but didn't interrupt. Dana almost seemed as if she felt eager to unburden herself as quickly as possible. "I was really uncomfortable, just nervous. I drank one beer at the first party and I was totally fine, so I thought it would be okay if I had another beer at the second party." She continued, "I just wanted to calm down a bit because my friends were having a good time so I figured we'd be there a while.

"While I was drinking that beer, someone offered me a shot, which I wouldn't normally do, but I thought that would help me relax fast. So I drank it." As she spoke, I found myself mentally cringing at two things: the free-flowing alcohol, which I hear about way too often, and Dana's total certainty that she needed to find a way to quiet her nerves. "After that," she said, "I don't really remember. My friends said that I kept drinking. When I passed out, one of my friends got really scared and called her mom, who called my mom."

"That's a good friend," I said, to which Dana nodded her solemn agreement. Then I asked, "Can you take me back to when you arrived at the second party?" She nodded again, so I continued, "Do you have a sense of what was making you feel so uncomfortable?"

"Oh, yeah," she said quickly, "it was nuts. I couldn't believe how many kids were there and some of them were definitely sketchy. Not to be unfair," she said in the same offhanded tone teens use when they say "no offense" before expressing an unvarnished opinion, "but they were definitely way too old to be at a high school party."

"Got it," I said, "so let me run an idea by you. I'm wondering if part of what went wrong is that you treated your anxious feelings as your *enemy*, when I actually think they were acting as your *ally*." Dana looked at me quizzically. I continued, "My hunch is that you felt really uncomfortable because you are smart enough to know that it was probably a risky party and you wanted to leave."

"Definitely," she replied emphatically, "it wasn't a good scene. But I knew my friends wanted to stay, so I didn't know what to do." She paused, then added sheepishly, "Obviously, I shouldn't have done what I did."

"True," I said. "And I'm sure you're not surprised to hear that I think you should lay off drinking." She tilted her head to acknowledge my perspective. "I also think that you'll feel much better, and worry much less about something like this happening again, if you can get to know your anxiety." Once more, Dana gave me a puzzled look. "Adults often talk about anxiety as if it were a bad thing, but it's not," I said. "It can get out of control, and we don't want that. But most of the time it's a really useful emotion." I could see from Dana's face that she now understood completely.

"Instead of trying to calm myself down with that shot," she

reflected out loud, "I probably should have paid attention to how nervous I felt and found an excuse to go home."

"Yep," I agreed, "you've got a sophisticated warning system that works well for you. Let's put it to good use."

Try this at home. The next time your daughter tells you that she's feeling really nervous about a test for which she has yet to study, cheerily reply, "Good! I'm glad you're worried. That's the ideal reaction, because right now you know you're not ready. As soon as you start studying, your nerves will calm down." As she heads out with friends on a Friday night, you might say, "Have fun. Take good care of yourself, and if you find yourself in a situation that makes you uncomfortable, pay attention to that feeling! We're always happy to spring you if things go south."

In sum, when a girl gets anxious we want her to take that emotion seriously and wonder, "Why is my alarm going off? And what's the best way to get it to quiet down?" Given that our culture has slapped a bad name on anxiety and all of the other uncomfortable feelings, we need to go out of our way to help girls attend to and appreciate anxiety as the protective mechanism it is.

The Mechanics of Anxiety

Fear is a powerful emotional experience that can feel alarmingly out of control. But psychologists have come to recognize that anxiety is, in fact, a highly predictable and systematic reaction that activates the cascading involvement of four different systems. First, stress hormones trigger a biological reaction known as the fight-or-flight response. Adrenaline and its chemical side-kicks crank up the heart rate, slow the digestive system, and widen the airways to the lungs in order to direct more oxygen to our punching and running muscles. In response to messages sent to our lungs from our central nervous system, breathing speeds up and becomes more shallow. Our pupils dilate so that we can see at greater distances. Once the perceived danger passes, an equally complex system resets the body to its pre-anxiety state. This is why moments of panic are often followed by an urgent trip to the restroom as the digestive system gets going again. Whatever else we might say about anxiety, it's hard to deny that it puts on a pretty spectacular biological show.

Almost simultaneously, our emotions get in on the action. We tend to experience nervousness, fear, or dread, though some people also feel edgy or irritable when anxious. When our emotions are affected, our cognitive—or thought—system jumps in. Deep thinking goes out the window as we vigilantly scan our surroundings for information about the perceived threat. Upon hearing an unexpected noise while home alone, we prick up our ears while fretfully asking ourselves, "Did I remember to lock the door? Could someone be trying to break in?" At other times, anxiety simply causes the mind to go blank, or to have exaggerated, irrational thoughts such as, "An ax murderer is at the door!"

Last of all, our action system kicks in. Someone who feels truly frightened by a strange sound in the night might stiffen up so as not to make any noise, reach for the phone to dial 911, or stalk around household corners wielding a baseball bat.

Even when anxiety serves a useful purpose—perhaps helping us discover an outside door flung open by the wind—it's a biological, emotional, mental, and physical workout. If this elaborate alarm system malfunctions and spins out of control, we are run absolutely ragged. At these times, clinicians are likely to diagnose an anxiety disorder.

Anxiety Disorders and Their Treatments

The many different ways our alarm systems can become faulty is illustrated by the variety of anxiety disorders clinicians diagnose. When the alarm rings persistently—sometimes quietly, sometimes loudly—but far too much of the time, we apply the diagnosis of generalized anxiety disorder (GAD). Children (and adults) who suffer from GAD are beset by worries they cannot control, their minds racing from one concern to the next: Will I be picked last when we choose teams in gym? Will the teacher call on me unexpectedly? Will our car pool leave without me at the end of the day? This constant ringing of the anxiety bell can undermine sleep, concentration, and, of course, the ability to feel calm or happy.

In other disorders, the alarm is less indiscriminate, but rather blares at unreasonable decibels in response to particular threats. For example, separation anxiety disorder, social phobia, and specific phobia cause debilitating distress when their sufferers are, respectively, parted from caregivers, exposed to the possibility of social scrutiny, or faced with an object or situation of which they are mortally afraid. Given that young children often miss their parents when separated from them, and that most adolescents have moments of feeling uncomfortably "onstage," and that all humans have fears, we diagnose an anxiety disorder only when a person's worries are entirely out of proportion to the perceived threat or if they hamstring daily functioning. For example, it's one thing to dislike spiders and quite another to skip an important meeting in a musty old building for fear of encountering one.

When anxiety comes on like a horrific siren that may blare for no clear reason at all, we call that a panic attack. These attacks are no joke. They are acute bursts of terror in which the physical symptoms of anxiety are so powerful that sufferers often think they might be losing their minds or about to die. Indeed, studies find that roughly a quarter of all visits to emergency rooms for chest pain are prompted by a panic attack, not a cardiac event. Panic attacks peak and recede quickly—often within twenty minutes. They can occur in the midst of an obviously stressful situation such as a high-stakes job interview, or can happen out of the blue.

Interestingly, panic attacks are common. At some point in our lifetimes, nearly 30 percent of us will be hit by a wave of anxiety so intense that it includes some combination of nausea, dizziness, numbness, tingling, a feeling of detachment from reality, chills, sweating, and, as already noted, fear that one is losing control or dying. Though having a panic attack is miserable, we diagnose panic disorder only when recurrent, unexpected attacks sow the constant fear of having another attack or cause people to rearrange their lives. Sometimes sufferers will start to avoid situations or places where they've had a panic attack—such as staying away from the gym or parties—in the hope of preventing another one.

A few summers ago, a friend whom I've known since childhood called me from the side of a highway somewhere in southern Colorado. She and her seventeen-year-old daughter were halfway into a six-hour road trip from our hometown of Denver to Santa Fe, New Mexico, where her daughter would be spending the summer in a long-coveted job with Santa Fe's chamber music festival.

After filling me in on the background, my friend continued, "We were in the middle of this beautiful drive, and then out of nowhere, my daughter lost it. She started shaking, said she felt like she was suffocating, and explained that she'd never been more terrified in her life, but she didn't know why. One minute she was completely fine, and the next she said she felt like she was losing her mind. She's okay again now. But she's really wigged out."

After asking my friend a few more questions, I weighed in. "What you're describing sounds like a classic panic attack. They feel completely awful," I empathized, "but they're basically harmless." My friend was relieved to hear this but wanted to know what to do next.

"I'm wondering if we should tell her boss that she'll have to start late and head back to Denver to get this checked out."

"No," I said, "I think that the best thing will be for you to get back on the road to Santa Fe. Panic attacks happen, but we don't want to give a single attack more power than it deserves." I then told my friend about the one panic attack I've had in my lifetime. It happened in graduate school when I found myself sharing intelligence test results with a shoot-the-messenger parent who was not at all happy to hear that his really quite charming son hadn't tested stratospherically. I encouraged my friend to tell her daughter that I remembered the panic attack vividly. I felt terrified and couldn't end the meeting and get out of the consulting room fast enough. Luckily, however, it has yet to happen again.

"Okay," said my friend before adding tentatively, "you know, I think that my aunt used to have really bad anxiety. Are you *sure* we shouldn't get it checked out?"

"Panic attacks can run in families," I said, "but I still think it's better to stay on the road to Santa Fe. If it happens again, call me and we'll see about connecting her with a clinician in New Mexico."

I didn't hear from them again that summer. When I was recently back in Denver to visit my folks, I caught up with my friend and asked how things had turned out. She shared that her daughter had a great start to the summer, but then had another attack while out jogging in late August shortly before it was time to come home. "She got through it okay," my friend explained, "because she knew what was happening. After that, she looked up some information about relaxation techniques but thankfully hasn't had another attack since."

When a girl's nerves do interfere with her day-to-day life, it's time to seek help from a clinician who specializes in treating anxiety. Cognitive-behavioral therapy (CBT) takes a tailored and systematic approach to treating the four components of anxiety we've addressed. CBT practitioners use advanced techniques to help clients manage their physiological reactions, cope with distressing emotions, challenge anxiety-provoking thoughts, and gradually confront their fears.

Psychodynamic psychotherapy, which focuses on thoughts and feelings that may be outside of our awareness, can be especially helpful when there's a reason for the ringing anxiety alarm that needs to be uncovered. That was the case for Simone, a high school sophomore whose mother found me through the counselor at her daughter's school. On the phone, Simone's mother explained that her daughter felt constantly on edge, but no one could figure out why. Things at home were good, Simone was doing well academically, she had a manageable schedule, and she had several close friends. When I asked how Simone felt about meeting with me, her mother replied that she was "really nervous about it and wants me to be there with her." I explained that I was glad to do whatever was needed to ease Simone into therapy. We found a time when they both could come in.

In our first meeting, Simone and her mother sat beside each other on my couch so closely that their legs touched from hip to knee. It struck me as somewhat surprising that a fifteen-year-old would allow her mom to sit so near, but Simone had an unusual quality. She seemed at once to require the comfort of the physical contact with her mother, while also being utterly her own person. Our initial meeting was remarkably unremarkable. I learned that Simone was the oldest of three children, that her mom was a successful entrepreneur who traveled every few weeks for work, and that they had lived in the same home in Beachwood, a suburb near my practice, for nearly twenty years.

At our next session, Simone felt ready to come into my office alone. She sat at the far end of the couch, reached for a bowl of colorful magnetized toy rods and silver ball bearings that I keep on a small table, nestled the bowl into her lap, and constructed a pyramid that rose with a series of satisfying clicks as the rods and balls connected. As she worked, Simone comfortably answered my questions about her day (she had lots of homework waiting for her at home), her friendships (they were happy and reliable), and her current level of anxiety (heightened, thanks to her impending midterms). She talked about her close relationship with her mom, saying, "We get along well . . . not all the time but mostly. And even though I don't tell her this, I really admire her," and her dad, whom Simone described as "kinda hard to read—distant, I guess—but a really good dad, and a really good person."

After our second session I found myself puzzling over why Simone was meeting with me at all. None of what I knew so far seemed to explain her constant edginess, nor did Simone seem to be in a rush to get to the bottom of what was causing it. But in our third session, the problem quickly came into focus. Simone entered my office quietly, returned to her pyramid-building, and worked silently for several minutes before asking, "How much do you tell my mom about what we talk about?" I assured her, as I had in our first meeting, that our conversations were private unless she gave me a reason to think that she, or someone else, might come to harm.

"My mom had an affair," Simone said bluntly, "and she doesn't know I know." From there she went on to explain that, several months past, she had overheard her parents talking about the fact that Simone's mother had used some of her work travel to arrange trysts with a former college boyfriend. She added, "From what I heard, I guess that my mom ended the affair and told my dad about it. I'm sure that was hard on my dad, but I think that they're in therapy together and things seem to be okay at home. So I'm not sure what to do."

"That's a heavy secret to carry," I said. Simone closed her eyes, perhaps to hold back tears, and bowed her head in agreement. We could both appreciate that harboring the secret of her mom's affair helped explain Simone's edginess. Together, we considered some of her options. She could tell her parents what she knew, or keep the news to herself for now and decide what to do later on. As she left, Simone seemed relieved. In fact, she seemed visibly lighter having shared the burden she had been shouldering alone.

"There's something else," said Simone, at the start of our next meeting. "I know that this affair doesn't really involve me, but I'm not sure how I'm supposed to feel about my mom." She explained how much she liked and counted on her mom, and how proud she was to have a mother who was the main breadwinner in the family. "I really respect her," Simone continued gingerly, "so it's hard to know what to think."

I asked tentatively, "Is there any chance that you're feeling sort of frustrated with her?" In truth, I suspected that Simone was far more than frustrated, but I've learned to tiptoe toward any feeling that is being kept at bay. Asking, "Are you enraged?" only shuts clients down, especially when they have built ramparts around their anger.

Tears, twin currents of them, suddenly streamed down both of Simone's cheeks. We had hit an emotional jackpot, but we weren't celebrating. "Listen," I said warmly, "it's really painful to be mad at someone you love and need so much." After we sat together quietly for a long time I spoke again. "Your frustration makes a lot of sense," I said, "and I think that it also helps explain some of your anxiety." Simone now held me in her gaze. "Perhaps your edgy feelings are actually the third step in a hidden emotional sequence.

"Step one," I explained, "might be that somewhere deep inside you feel very frustrated with your mom. Step two is that you don't want to feel that way. And step three, the one that brought you here, was that you became filled with worry. Perhaps you worried that your angry feelings might damage your good relationship with your mom."

Simone tightened her lips in concentration. "Maybe . . . I don't know," she said, "that *could* be it. But I'm not really sure."

Over our next several sessions Simone's worries started to ease as we weighed the possibility that her anxiety was actually fueled by anger. Our work was slow going, but at least we were headed down the right path.

Not all anxiety can be chalked up to a hidden cause, but we should bear in mind that anxiety works to alert us to threats both from without and *from within*. Sometimes a girl feels tense because she's dealing with an external threat, such as being in trouble with a parent. And sometimes everything looks okay on the outside, but the girl faces a powerful internal threat, as was the case for Simone, who felt frightened of her anger toward her mom.

When therapy doesn't provide sufficient relief, or work quickly enough, anxious feelings can also be managed with medical help. It's important to note that being female may increase the biological vulnerability to anxiety. Beginning in childhood and for the duration of adulthood, girls and women are at least twice as likely as boys and men to be diagnosed with an anxiety disorder. Overwhelmingly, we attribute this massive gender disparity to nonbiological factors that we'll be tackling in the rest of this book, but there are nonetheless a few physiological forces at work that fray girls' nerves more than boys'.

You're probably not surprised to hear that premenstrual hormonal shifts routinely leave many girls and women feeling more tense, irritable, or uneasy than usual. Furthermore, for those who suffer from panic attacks, some research indicates that the premenstrual drop in estrogen and progesterone levels can temporarily ramp up the frequency and intensity of panic attacks for girls and women who have them. Several experts suggest that the emotional ups and downs of the menstrual cycle may contribute to the development of anxiety disorders or help to sustain or exacerbate disorders that are already under way. Studies show that anxiety can also be conferred genetically, but the jury is still out regarding whether it is more likely to be passed down to daughters than to sons.

Whether anxiety results from a genetic predisposition or not, prescription drugs can help to muffle it. Though I rarely suggest medication as a first line of approach, I don't hesitate to recommend a consultation with a psychiatrist when psychotherapy isn't putting a dent in persistent anxiety, or to clients who are paralyzed by unrelenting panic attacks. Indeed, antidepressants often provide fast relief to individuals with panic disorder—the diagnosis we give when overwhelming fears of having a panic attack undermine everyday living. The symptoms of anxiety are usually warded off so long as the medication is in use, which allows clients to capitalize on the anxiety cease-fire to explore hidden, difficult feelings in therapy or to learn relaxation techniques, thinking strategies, and routines that may give them the option of ultimately managing their distress without medication.

In recent years, mindfulness practices have emerged as a highly effective way to counter anxious emotions and ideas. Mindfulness, an approach rooted in ancient Buddhist meditation techniques, involves learning to observe—but not judge—one's own feelings and thoughts. Anxiety stirs up trouble when it convinces our daughters that they're facing insurmountable threats and then prompts them to imagine dreadful outcomes. Mindfulness addresses anxiety by teaching its practitioners to carefully observe their emotions, ideas, and sensations, but not to get carried away by them.

Mindfulness practices aren't necessarily a substitute for psychotherapy, but they share key principles with established Western approaches to managing difficult feelings. Indeed, early on in my career, one of my favorite colleagues pointed out to me that psychologists have a very strange job. On the one hand, we aim to help people learn precisely what they are feeling and what they are thinking. We want our clients to become intimately familiar with the landscape of their inner lives. Then, once the people we care for are in close touch with their own painful, upsetting, or frightening internal worlds, we step back to reassuringly point out that what they have discovered is *only* a thought or *only* a feeling—and that they have options for how they might respond to their ideas and emotions.

If you suspect that your daughter is very high on the anxiety continuum but remain unsure about whether a visit to a specialist makes sense, there's a half step to consider. Alongside the guidance provided in *Under Pressure*, you and your daughter might explore one of the many excellent workbooks and guides available on how to regulate the anxiety response system or those on how to practice mindfulness. Several suggestions can be found in the list of *Recommended Resources* at the back of this book.

Dealing with Ordinary Anxiety

While there's no definitive line that separates "normal" anxiety from its unhealthy extremes, clinicians usually feel that a diagnosis becomes warranted only when a person's anxiety becomes so pervasive or potent as to spoil daily life. Unfortunately, many young people (and sometimes, their parents) now treat even the slightest whiff of anxiety as grounds for concern. Indeed, it is not at all unusual for a girl to say to me, "I have anxiety," as if she were describing a grave and permanent congenital defect.

Given that anxiety is an adaptive factory setting provided to all humans, you can imagine that I sometimes have to stop myself from responding enthusiastically, "Well, of course you do! That's how you are able to cross streets safely and not get hit by cars!" Instead, I usually ask a lot of questions about the situations that trigger her anxiety. More often than not, I find myself making the point that anxiety is usually a good thing, as I did regarding the worries that arose for Dana when she found herself at a strange party.

Put another way, informed adults can help girls and young women feel far less worried about the fact that they feel any anxiety at all. To do this, we can teach girls that their nerves may occur on a continuum that ranges from the usefully protective to annoyingly disruptive. And even when a girl finds herself on the miserable end of that continuum, there's a great deal that can be done to return her worries and fears to healthy levels.

To help girls manage their jitters, we address the same four response systems that serve as a safeguard in healthy anxiety and misfire when anxiety is out of control: physical reactions, emotional responses, thought patterns, and behavioral impulses. A few years ago I found myself coaching a close colleague of mine through these steps over lunch at Laurel School. We were chatting in the cafeteria line when she asked, "Can I get your help on something we're dealing with at home?"

"Sure," I said, "what's up?"

"My eleven-year-old has herself completely tied up in knots about an upcoming sleepover at her cousin's house. She's dying to go because she loves her cousin and the other two girls who will be there, but she's terrified that she won't be able to fall asleep. When she thinks about going to the sleepover, she practically starts hyperventilating."

"I'm so glad you asked," I replied, "because there's *a lot* that you can do to help her manage the sleepover." We got some silverware and carried our plates to a relatively quiet corner of the lunchroom.

"For starters," I said, "you should help her understand that her body goes into overdrive when she gets nervous—that's why she's hyperventilating."

My friend cocked her head.

"Explain to her that her brain is telling her heart and breathing to speed up so that she can get ready to deal with danger. Her job—which she can do—is to let her brain know that nothing's really wrong."

"How?"

"Well . . . you know how everyone talks about taking deep breaths to calm down?"

"Yeah," my friend said gamely.

"It really does work, but I've found that it's most effective when girls know *why* it works."

I shared with my colleague that, just as nerves run from the brain to the lungs to tell the body to speed respiration, nerves also run from the lungs *back* to the central nervous system to tell the brain to calm down. The brain is particularly interested in dispatches arriving from the respiratory system because, if a person is suffocating, the brain needs to tell the body to start freaking out. When we deliberately deepen and slow our breathing, stretch receptors in the lungs pick up the message that all is well and send that high-speed, high-priority, and highly reassuring dispatch back to the brain.

"Tell your daughter that she can use her breathing to hack her own nervous system and calm it down when she starts to tense up about the sleepover. You guys can look up different breathing techniques online to see what the options are. My favorite is called square breathing."

"Explain," she said between bites.

I told my friend that she could coach her daughter to inhale slowly for a count of three, hold that breath for a count of three, exhale slowly for another count of three, and then pause for a final count of three before repeating that cycle a few more times.

"That sounds easy enough," said my friend as a gaggle of third graders entered the lunchroom.

"It is," I agreed, "and it's most effective when girls practice it before they need it. Any time I teach it to one of the girls here at Laurel I offer the analogy of tennis players who smash dozens of lobs in practice to find a rhythm they can count on in the middle of a game. Using a breathing technique to relax works the same way. Square breathing is easy to do, but it's most effective if it's a well-worn groove that a girl can slip into when she's feeling afraid."

"So," my friend said, "I can help her get her body to settle down, which is good, but I still think she'll be upset."

"Then find out about her fears. In general, anxiety happens when we overestimate how bad something is going to be and underestimate our ability to deal with it."

"Well, she's totally terrified that she'll be awake all night."

I paused a moment to think of a suggestion. "You might say to her, 'It's true that it will probably be harder for you to fall asleep at your aunt and uncle's house than at home, but I'm guessing that you'll get tired enough that you zonk out before too long.' Or something like that. You'll want to validate her concerns while helping her see that they're probably exaggerated."

"Right," she said, "but then I know that she'll tell me she's worried that if she doesn't get enough sleep, she'll be a total mess the next day."

"We call that catastrophizing—imagining the worst possible outcome."

"Oh, yes," my friend replied with a smile, "she can be *very* good at that."

"Let her know that, even if she stays awake all night, she'll just be tired the next day and can go to bed early. Be matter-of-fact about it so that she can tell you don't think it's a big deal."

"Honestly, I'm not sure that she'll buy that, but I'll give it a try."

"Fair enough," I said.

"I've got one more question . . . I know that when she gets there, she'll want to call me a lot so that I can tell her that she'll be okay. Should we do that?"

"No," I replied quickly, "that's not a great idea."

I explained that anxiety can get us to do things that provide immediate relief—such as seeking reassurance or compulsively checking on something we're worried about—but these nervous habits don't help in the long run because they only reinforce the idea that something's really wrong.

"Tell her that she can call you at bedtime if she wants to say good night but, other than that, you're going to count on her to use her square breathing to help herself relax if she's feeling upset."

The look on my colleague's face darkened. "She's probably not ready to bite that bullet, but I know how badly she wants to go."

"Not to worry," I said. "If she doesn't make it to this sleepover, there will be others. In the meantime, she'll stop feeling at the mercy of her anxiety if you teach her how to calm herself down and question her own worries and anxious ideas."

Stemming the Worrisome Tide

When we allow girls to view all stress and anxiety as harmful, they feel stressed about getting stressed and anxious about getting anxious. Instead, we can help our daughters take control of stress and anxiety by teaching them that both serve as normal and healthy parts of life. And if stress and anxiety do grow out of control, we can draw on our large body of knowledge about how to put them in check.

It's important to remember that stress and anxiety can accumulate, and that their overall volume in our lives rises and falls like a water level. Even under the best conditions, every one of us sloshes around in at least a shallow puddle. We wade through our typical daily hassles and have moments when the waters rise quickly, such as when we receive an unexpected call from the school nurse, and lower again almost as fast, such as when we learn that she was phoning simply to alert us that our daughter bumped heads with a classmate in gym class but has no signs of a concussion, only a goose egg, to show for it.

For too many girls the floodwaters of anxiety have risen from their ankles up to their necks. *Under Pressure* is about the sources of that deluge and how we can bail our daughters out or keep them from becoming swamped in the first place. The chapters that follow consider five different wellsprings of stress for girls: their interactions at home, with other girls, with boys, at school, and with the broader culture. Tributary by tributary, we'll address what we can do as loving adults to ease the feelings of stress and anxiety that sometimes threaten to drown our daughters.

CHAPTER TWO

· · · · · · · · · · ·

Girls at Home

WHEN THINGS GO WRONG, OUR DAUGHTERS ARE OFTEN ABLE TO hold it together while at school or with their friends before falling apart in the privacy of our homes. How parents respond to a girl's distress has the power to make things much better, or much worse.

This chapter will unpack the common, everyday exchanges that occur between well-meaning adults and their overwrought daughters. It will address what doesn't work, and why, and describe tested and effective strategies for helping girls manage their nerves and worries in both the short and long term.

Avoidance Feeds Anxiety

On a recent Tuesday at Laurel School, I was pulled into an interaction with a student that highlights a dynamic that often unfolds between parents and their anxious daughters. As I carried a plateful of food from the cafeteria back to my office, I heard a student trotting up behind me. Turning around, I found Jamie, a usually chipper sophomore, who was clearly in a panic.

"Dr. Damour! Do you have a minute?"

"Sure. Of course." I was more than happy to ditch my plan to answer email while eating lunch at my desk. Jamie followed me around a corner and down a few steps into what the Laurel girls call my Harry Potter office. Like Harry's bedroom at the Dursleys', my office is wedged under the school's central staircase in what used to be a large utility closet. As odd as it sounds, the space is perfect. It sits in the center of the building on the school's main hallway and yet is tucked out of sight so that girls or their parents can meet with me discreetly.

When I set my plate down and asked, "What's going on?" Jamie burst into tears. She put one hand on her stomach, gripped the arm of her chair with the other hand, and started to hyperventilate. Though I am used to sitting with girls who are very upset, I was surprised by how quickly and completely Jamie fell apart. It became clear that she had been barely holding herself together until we got to the privacy of my office. Once there, her levee broke and dammed-up emotions poured forth.

"I can't take my chemistry test today," she said in a rush, "I'm not ready, I'm gonna fail, it's gonna wreck my grade, I can't do it." She then paused to take a heaving breath before begging, "Can you get me out of it? Can you write me a note or something?"

I was stuck. I don't have the power to waive tests at Laurel; I'm there to support the girls, not to alter the academic program. At the same time, I fully agreed that Jamie was, at that moment, in no state to take a test.

"What period is chemistry?" I asked, while trying to figure out how I could insert myself between Jamie and her teacher.

"It's not until last period." Jamie paused and her breathing started to slow to its normal rhythm. Then I watched her tension seem to drain away as she added hopefully, "Maybe my dad can come get me before then and I can go home."

The instant I heard the relief in Jamie's voice as she imagined her escape from school, a central tenet from my training as a psychologist came back to me. I pushed my protective instincts to the side as soon as I remembered that helping Jamie avoid the test was probably the least helpful thing I could do.

Primitive instincts tell humans to run from threats. Dashing away can be a great idea, especially if the threat is a burning building, an obviously unsafe keg party, or an aggressive sales clerk brandishing a loaded atomizer. Often, however, running off is actually a terrible idea, because everything we know in academic psychology tells us that avoidance only makes anxiety worse.

Avoidance doesn't just feed anxiety. It serves up a two-course meal. First, dodging a perceived threat actually feels good. In fact, avoidance works like an incredibly powerful and fast-acting drug. Jamie felt better as soon as she even *thought* about having her dad rescue her from her chemistry test. The short-term relief gained from avoiding her chemistry test would have soon given way to her fears about the next test on her calendar and how bad *that* one would be. Second, sidestepping our fears effectively prevents us from discovering that they're overblown. Had Jamie found a way to skip the test, she would have robbed herself of the chance to learn that it wasn't so bad after all.

In fact, full-blown phobias can develop when people routinely evade the things they fear. Imagine a woman, we'll call her Joan, who is afraid of dogs. When Joan walks down the street, she feels a burst of dread every time she sees a dog coming her way. Naturally, Joan crosses the street to remove herself from the dog's path. She always feels immensely better when she gets to the opposite sidewalk, which makes her that much more likely to cross the street the next time she spies a canine. And in doing so, Joan never has a chance to meet a friendly dog. She remains convinced that all dogs should be avoided and knows that staying away from them will reliably deliver an immediate sense of relief.

Psychologists know a lot about how to treat phobias. And

what we know about helping people like Joan master her irrational fear translates perfectly to helping girls confront overblown
anxieties. To address fears, we address fearful avoidance.

Treating Joan's dog phobia would be a fairly straightforward
process. We'd teach Joan some basic relaxation techniques and
assess how near she could get to a dog while remaining calm.
Using a system called graduated exposure, we'd help Joan climb
a ladder of increasing levels of canine contact. We might start by
having her look at pictures of dogs while using controlled breathing to remain relaxed. Then we'd ask Joan to stand a block away
from a pooch before having the pooch come near, and so on.
Sooner or later, Joan could find herself enjoying, or at least comfortably tolerating, being close to a dog.

Returning to Jamie, I can tell you that I pulled myself together
and said gently, "Wait. Let's hold off on reaching out to your dad.
I think that we can figure this out together." Jamie clearly did not
like the fact that I intended to block her escape, but the thought
of bolting from school had relaxed her enough to make a conversation possible.

"What's the story in chemistry?" I asked. "Are you having a
hard time in that class?"

"Not usually, but I'm really confused about the topics we cov-
ered for this test."

"Did you ask your teacher for help?"

"I did, and she was great. But I'm still not sure I get it."

"I can see why you're scared," I said, "and I can see why you're
here in my office. But I'm worried that you'll end up feeling worse
if you don't meet this head-on." Jamie sighed and indicated that
she was open to suggestions. I asked, "Do you have any free periods between now and the test?"

"Yes, I'm free right after lunch."

"How about this . . . why don't you look for your chemistry
teacher to see if she can offer you some last-minute clarification.

If she can't, I want you to hop online and find a video tutorial on the topics you're worried about. Most important, I want you to take the test, even if you feel that you won't do as well as you want."

Jamie agreed, unenthusiastically, to my plan. A few days later I ran into her in the hallway and asked how things had come out.

"I couldn't find my teacher to get help before class, and I don't think I did all that well on the test. But right before the test a lot of girls were asking the teacher about the stuff I didn't understand, so she said that we could go over it again later and, if needed, make corrections to get some points back."

"That doesn't sound too bad," I said in a way that sounded half like a question.

"No," Jamie agreed, "it's not that bad at all. I think it will end up okay."

When your girl wants you to stand between her and something she fears, resist acting on your gut instinct—the protective impulse to rescue her—and turn your attention toward helping her approach the source of her anxiety. For example, if your daughter tells you she can't possibly go to her piano recital, find out what she thinks she *can* do. Can she play the piece for you while thinking about the recital? Can she invite over a few neighbors and practice playing for them? Can she check in with her piano teacher to see what happens if she attends the recital but then changes her mind about performing? Can she get up on the stage and see how much of her piece she can play? Failing these options, see what you can learn from your daughter's teacher about where she's hitting a snag. In short, organize yourself around helping her move *toward* the threat, even in baby steps, rather than running away from it. Your daughter may not love this approach, but the immediate relief she'll feel when she avoids the threat is not worth the guaranteed exacerbation of her anxiety in the long term.

How to Manage Meltdowns

You may want nothing more than to encourage your daughter to face her fears. And you may have already tried to share your wonderful suggestions on how she could approach a situation that has her wringing her hands. If you've gone down this path, you have likely discovered what most parents find when they try to help their daughter at the height of her discomfort: she considers every single one of your excellent ideas to be useless and rejects them all. There are many fun moments in parenting, but this is not one of them. In fact, it can be especially miserable to try to support a young person who lays her violent distress before us and then becomes even more upset when we try to be helpful.

What the heck is going on here?

She's letting you know how helpless she feels by making you feel every bit as helpless, too. There are many ways to share a feeling. At our best, we can put our emotions into words and express them to the caring, supportive people in our lives, knowing that they will respond with warmth and compassion. At our not-so-best, we become overwhelmed by our emotions and communicate them by inducing them in others. This is what happens when we feel angry and decide to pick a fight. And this is what happens when a girl who is at the end of her rope engages loving adults in a way that quickly brings them to the end of their ropes, too.

Attempting to help, cajole, or advise anyone who is overtaken by distress rarely works (just as telling someone to calm down almost always seems to have the opposite effect). If we want to get to the place where we really can be useful to our daughters, we need to find a way to bear with them when they feel powerless in the face of emotions that have spun out of control.

There's an ingenious strategy for responding to girls who feel frenzied, which I learned, almost in spite of myself, on a trip to

Texas. I was spending time with some colleagues at an excellent girls' school in Dallas when we got to talking about how forceful and overwhelming girls' emotions can be. "That," said one of the counselors, "is when we get out a glitter jar."

Before continuing with this story, I need to acknowledge that I am not always a nice person. I can be sharply critical of anything that I view as pop psychology, and I'm equally tough on anything I deem to be excessively girly. You can imagine that the term *glitter jar* put me on high alert on both counts. The counselor left and quickly returned with said glitter jar—it was a clear jar, about four inches tall, filled with water and a sedimentary layer of sparkling purple glitter. The lid was secured with glue, and when she put the jar on the table between us, the glitter that had been stirred up in transport soon settled to the bottom. We were looking at a jar that we could see right through. Skeptically, I listened to what the counselor shared next.

"When the girls come to my office in a panic," she continued in her Dallas drawl, "and I can tell that they're just a wreck, I get out my glitter jar and I do this." She picked up the jar and shook it fiercely the way one shakes a snow globe. The placid water immediately became a sparkling purple tempest. "And then I say to the girl, 'Right now, this is what it's like in your brain. So first, let's settle your glitter.'" The counselor set the jar down on the table between us and I stared at it, completely mesmerized. As the swirling slowed and the glitter storm abated, I realized that these counselors had created a terrific model of how emotions act on the adolescent brain.

You see, somewhere between the ages of twelve and fourteen, the teenage brain undertakes a spectacular renovation project. It trims those neurons that are dead weight and matures into a nimble thinking machine that can poke new holes in old arguments, spin ideas around to view them from multiple perspectives, and simultaneously entertain competing viewpoints, such as happily following the antics of the Kardashian family while articulating a detailed and devastating critique of their lifestyle choices.

For better or worse, this neurological overhaul unfolds in the same order in which the brain developed in utero; it begins in the primal region that sits near the spinal cord and proceeds to the sophisticated area located behind the forehead. In practical terms, this means that the brain's emotional centers, which are housed in the primitive limbic system, are fully upgraded before the brain's perspective-maintaining systems, which are located in the highly evolved prefrontal cortex. When a teenager feels calm, her capacity for logical reasoning can equal or outstrip any adult's. When a teenager becomes upset, her supercharged emotions can hijack the whole neurological system, unleashing a blinding glitter storm and turning your otherwise rational daughter into a sobbing puddle on your kitchen floor.

My personal hang-ups about glitter have kept me from purchasing the supplies I would need to make glitter jars for my private practice or my office at Laurel. This, however, has not stopped me from enthusiastically encouraging friends and colleagues who also care for adolescents to make glitter jars for themselves. But my encounter in Texas has changed how I respond, both at home and at work, to girls who are spinning in a cyclone of distress. In my head, I actually hear the words of that counselor saying, "First, let's settle your glitter." I now start by asking if a drink of water would be helpful or, should I have access to it, perhaps a snack. I force myself to be patient and to hold myself steady while wondering aloud, and without any urgency, if it might feel good to stretch our legs with a short walk, or to work on some coloring pages I keep handy.

It is not easy to restrain my urges to jump in with reassurance, suggestions, or questions about how the girl got herself into such a bad spot in the first place. But when I hold off, and focus on making space for the turbulence in her brain to subside, two critical events occur.

First, the girl can see that I am not frightened by her feelings. This may not seem like much, but we need to remember that her prefrontal cortex is hobbled by emotion and cannot possibly, at least for the moment, take an objective view of whatever happened to trigger her frenzy. When adults respond calmly and without being dismissive, girls can see that we are taking the situation in stride. This is a lot more reassuring to adolescents than a frenetic, all-hands-on-deck reaction, which signals that their crisis scares us as much as it scares them. Plus, as most parents have learned the hard way, pressing advice on a girl who already feels overwhelmed, or asking her what she did to land herself in the crisis, usually seems to be the equivalent of shaking her mental glitter jar.

Second, once the glitter storm subsides, a girl's rational cortex comes back online. Now clearheaded, she can think about how to tackle the source of her overwhelming anxiety or conclude that the problem isn't so bad after all. This explains the bizarre, yet common, sequence of events that occurs in any home with a teenager. First, the adolescent falls to pieces. Next, she rebuffs any help or suggestions her parents offer before retreating, in an agitated fit, to her room. Her parents—who are now in pieces themselves—frantically consider packing their daughter off to the psychiatric emergency room, asking the family minister or rabbi to stop by for an emergency consultation, or relocating to a new community where their daughter can start from scratch.

Eventually, the girl reappears in a completely reasonable state of mind. She shares her thoughtful response to her predicament with her utterly befuddled, yet sincerely relieved, parents. Or she seeks their advice. Or she is in good spirits and acts as though nothing has occurred at all. It's a good rule of parenting to remember that making time and space for a girl's neurological glitter to settle almost always either solves the problem or at least makes solving the problem possible.

That said, weathering a teenager's glitter storm may be one of the most taxing events in all of parenting. It does not matter that a girl's feelings are, at these times, overblown or irrational; they are very real to her and to any loving parent in her presence. When your daughter loses perspective, it's easy for you to lose perspective, too. Accordingly, it often helps to have an advance plan for these moments. A friend of mine keeps a large stash of tea in the pantry for when her daughter becomes overwrought. To keep herself calm while her daughter's glitter settles, my friend pulls out the tea collection and studiously lays out the choices before her daughter. Might herbal tea be best, or would some caffeine help? What flavor sounds good? Might milk or honey make the tea even better?

As parents we want to respond, but not react, to our daughters' meltdowns. Weighing tea options allows my friend to offer her full presence and support without becoming caught up in her daughter's swirling yet fleeting emotions. Other parents accomplish this delicate balance by listening quietly to their girl before discreetly turning to their partner, a trusted friend, or a seasoned parent for support or guidance. Still others hold themselves to a twenty-four-hour rule: they refrain from taking any action in response to their daughter's torrential distress until at least a day has passed. All parents need strategies for riding out their daughter's glitter storms; give yourself time to find an approach that works well for you and your girl.

How to React to Overreactions

Even when they're not in a full-blown swivet, girls of all ages sometimes express worrisome and irrational fears. They say,

"I won't have anyone to sit with at lunch tomorrow," or "I'll never get a role in a school play," or "I'm not going to get into college." I have heard all of these claims and more from girls who are well liked, talented actors, or on the cusp of being admitted to several colleges. Our natural instinct, in these moments, is to offer reassurance. We say, "Of course you will!" and hope to leave it at that.

Our daughters would not be as stressed and anxious as they are if responding this way typically worked. Occasionally, of course, our tender words do succeed in vanquishing an anxiety for good. More often, however, offering reassurance can feel like playing that old arcade game, Whac-A-Mole. Up pops the plight of the moment and down comes our padded mallet of optimism. We bang that worry back into its hole and a fresh concern pops up elsewhere. We bonk that one on the head only to discover that the original worry has since reappeared.

Why doesn't reassurance work, especially in response to irrational concerns? Because it doesn't take the problem, however silly it may seem, seriously and thus strikes girls as dismissive. If we want to get rid of a worry for good, we must earnestly engage it.

To do so, we have some options. Your knowledge of your daughter and the context of her concerns will help you decide how you want to proceed. Sometimes I ask girls playfully, "Are you up for a game of 'Worst-Case Scenario'?" If the girl is agreeable, I'll begin with, "Okay, let's say that you're right—that there won't be anyone to sit with at lunch tomorrow." I offer this in a tone that falls somewhere between neutral and upbeat in order to convey my total acceptance of this unpleasant possibility. "If that happens," I ask, "what will you do then?"

Modeling the ability to tolerate a bad situation helps our daughters to do the same. From there, we can figure out a way forward. Taking time to strategize seriously with girls, even about concerns that we view as overblown, helps them to feel calmer and more in control.

"I don't know," one girl told me, "maybe I'll ask someone early in the day if she wants to eat lunch together."

"Good idea. And what if that doesn't work? What else could you try?"

"We have the option of taking our lunches to a quiet study area if we want to."

"Do you want to?"

"Not really, but I like some kids who usually go to the quiet study area. I could see if they want to eat lunch together in the cafeteria the next day."

And so on.

When I suspect that offering to play a round of "Worst-Case Scenario" might come across as a bit glib, I often turn to a closely related approach that can work just as well. For this approach, I start by reminding myself that the stuff of life can be divided into three categories: things we like, things we can handle, and things that constitute a crisis. Anyone who spends time with young people knows that when children and teenagers become upset, they can forget about that middle category. They sometimes believe that when things don't go the way they want, they are facing a crisis. It falls to adults to help them see the situation otherwise.

One evening in late October, a high school junior named Molly reminded me how very stressful it can be to feel that there is no margin between a desired outcome and a disaster. Because basketball season had just started, Molly's appointment at my office had moved from our regular 3:30 P.M. time to 6:00 P.M., so that we could meet after practice. When I went to retrieve her from my waiting room, Molly looked absolutely spent. Her slumping shoulders and the stony look on her face told me that her troubles—whatever they were—went beyond the fact that we were meeting late in the day after a hard workout.

We greeted each other and Molly followed me to my office. Unlike my den under the stairs at Laurel School, my space at my private practice has large windows on two of the four walls. I almost never turn on any lights during the day. But by early evening in late October the sun had nearly set. For the first time in the five months we had been working together, Molly and I met in the glow of the overhead fixtures and table lamps I use when the natural light fades.

"What's up?" I asked, making it clear that I was happy to let her set our agenda for the appointment.

"Basketball is killing me," Molly replied in a tone of utter defeat. "I'm not even kidding about this: I think that I may end up being the only junior on JV."

"Oof, that doesn't sound so good," I said sympathetically. "Why?"

"I almost made varsity last year and I had a good season, so it shouldn't even be an issue. But an ankle sprain that was bugging me over the summer has started to hurt again. My coach knows that I'm doing as much as I can"—Molly paused as discouragement clouded her face—"but I have to sit out a lot."

"What does the athletic trainer say about your sprain?"

"He seems optimistic about it. He thinks that if I go easy on it now, I may be okay pretty soon. But I can tell that my coach is already trying to prepare me for being on JV." Molly's voice tightened. "She's been talking about how many good seniors there are—and of course they'll all be on varsity—and telling me that I can still be a leader regardless of how they sort out the teams."

"I'm so sorry," I said, "and that really stinks about your ankle."

"Right?" said Molly. "It's making me nuts. I'm so stressed about it that I'm not even paying attention in class. Instead I'm thinking about when I can get it iced and wrapped again. Instead of doing my work, I'm looking online for information on how to heal ankle sprains."

"Look, I know that being on JV this year is the last thing you want to have happen."

"Yep," she said before adding with some unexpected levity, "I might as well be babysitting since I'll be the old lady of the team."

"But even if it's not something you want, I think it's something you can handle."

There are two words I find myself using a lot with kids and teenagers who are stuck in stressful situations: *stinks* and *handle*. When they first share their bad news, I find that responding with a heartfelt, "Oh, that stinks," lets young people know that I won't try to talk them into feeling better. Though it doesn't seem like much, this gesture alone provides a surprising amount of support. Indeed, I'm reminded of the near-magical healing powers of simple and straight-up empathy every time I use it.

When still more help is needed, I turn my attention to addressing how the girl would like to play the cards she's been dealt. To me, asking a girl how she wants to handle something feels like a vote of confidence. It gives her some say in her misery and moves her out of the position of simply hoping the problem will go away. If it turns out that there actually is something she can do about the situation, all the better. If she's stuck, we can fall back on what we have learned from the research on managing intractable stress: first she must find a way to accept the situation, then she must find a happy distraction.

"I can handle the idea of playing JV," said Molly. "I just don't want to."

"Understandably," I said, "but it sounds like being on JV may be a done deal." Molly tilted her head in response and made a face that communicated her reluctant acceptance of this likelihood. "What if you don't fight it?" I asked. "What if you lean into the idea that you won't be having the basketball season you hoped for?"

Molly suddenly looked sad and also more relaxed.

After a pause she replied, "I can live with playing JV, I guess. And I can make sure that my ankle is in really good shape before next year."

"Is there any part of being on JV that might be okay? Is there a way to make it more bearable?"

"There are some fun tenth graders on the team—I actually like them better than some of the varsity girls. Since I'll probably be stuck with the sophomores, I might as well enjoy them."

Getting anyone to accept an unwanted situation isn't easy. But when we can tolerate our daughters' emotional discomfort, we help them to withstand painful circumstances. Despite its instinctive appeal, offering rapid reassurance—"I'm sure JV will be great!"—can sound a lot like, "Your distress makes me uneasy." In contrast, acknowledging that a situation *stinks* and will need to be *handled* sends a powerful, stress-reducing message: "I'm truly sorry about what you are facing. The good news is that this is not a crisis and that I'm here to help you manage it."

Our reassurance reflex never kicks in harder than when girls express totally absurd concerns. I have practically pulled self-restraint muscles when met with statements such as "Midterms might actually kill me!" or "I'll spend weekends alone the rest of my life!" In these moments, we need a handy reply that neither dismisses nor indulges their fears. Lucky for you (and my over-worked self-restraint), I've stumbled upon a reliable solution: empathize with how wretched it must be to feel that way.

The next time your daughter hits you with, "All of my teachers hate me!" try offering a heartfelt response such as, "Oh honey . . . it must feel awful to even think that." For, "I'm going to fail algebra!" try, "Well, I don't think that will happen, but in the meantime, it sounds like today was rotten." If you find yourself trapped in an exchange that leaves you feeling utterly helpless (as in, "There's nothing *anyone* can do to help me through algebra!"), pull out of that conversational death spiral by letting your daughter know that she has effectively communicated her emotional state. Tenderly offer, "I know you're feeling helpless, and I can only guess how miserable that must be."

Actively empathizing with our daughters' distress is not only effective, it's also far superior to the alternative of offering reassurance. Think about it this way. A girl who insists that all of her teachers hate her knows, at some level, that this cannot be true. What she is really trying to communicate is that she feels very, very upset. If we quibble about the facts or respond with cheery optimism, we're missing the point. Your daughter will let you know that you are off the mark by becoming increasingly dismayed. But when we make it clear that we get it—that we can accept the reality that she feels just awful—our daughter can take comfort in our compassion. From there, she can decide to move toward a solution or simply let go of the problem altogether.

Snit Happens

If you are parenting a normally developing girl, she will sometimes have meltdowns. Nothing you do can prevent this. The good news is that her emotional eruptions, in and of themselves, say very little about her overall psychological health.

All the same, it's not easy to be standing there when a girl unleashes a raging storm of frustration, becomes so stressed that she snaps back rudely when you ask what she wants for dinner, or doubles over in distress while sobbing. These moments ask a lot of parents and often require a great deal of patience to handle well. While you cannot control the fact that your daughter will sometimes become undone, you have a lot of say about how you react.

Decades of research tell us that our daughters read our reactions—right down to our most fleeting facial expressions—

for cues that will contain, or increase, their own discomfort. Fret-fully rushing to rescue girls from manageable threats, trying to reason away their glitter storms, attempting to vanquish their concerns with hollow reassurances, or responding with anger can, unwittingly, fuel our daughters' fears. In contrast, offering a measured and calm response can have a powerful, positive effect on girls' immediate and long-term distress.

But just as one drowning person cannot rescue another, so it is impossible to respond to meltdowns calmly when our own nerves are frayed. If you are feeling overwhelmed by stress or if you often experience high levels of anxiety, make sure that you are getting the support you deserve, both for your own sake and for your daughter's. Again, research shows parents who are very nervous themselves are more likely to have children who become easily afraid and struggle to manage stress.

To be clear, we need not—and certainly should not—parent as though we are placid Zen masters who greet emotional chaos with detached profundity. And when we do react to our daughters in ways we later regret (such as losing our cool with a girl whose stress comes out as snarkiness), we can remember that our daughters are plenty resilient and do not need for us to be per-fect.

All the same, we should reflect seriously on our baseline levels of emotional strain and take steps where we can to reduce the tension in our own lives. Our girls are deeply attuned to our psy-chological states and the emotional atmospheres we create in our homes. So, let's turn our attention to the concrete things parents can do to first secure their own oxygen masks so that they can react helpfully when their daughters seem to be suffo-cating from stress.

When the News Frays Our Nerves

While employing psychological defenses sounds like a bad thing, this is not always the case. It's never a compliment to say that someone is "being defensive," but none of us could get through the day without our automatic psychological shields. We call on our defenses to withstand distressing emotional experiences often without even being aware of it. For example, if we miss the bus and say, "Oh, well. It's always good to get a little extra exercise by walking," we are using the defense of rationalization to make the best of a bad situation. And when we are mad at our boss and take our anger out by going on a long, hard run, we are relying on sublimation to channel a dark feeling in a productive direction.

Defenses can be harmful if we deploy the same one all the time or if they distort reality, such as when people refuse to acknowledge events that have actually occurred (denial), or persistently ascribe their own unwanted feelings—such as lust, hate, or envy—to others (projection). But so long as we use a variety of defenses and avoid the ones that warp the truth or damage relationships, these mental shields make it possible for us to withstand the psychological slings and arrows of everyday life.

Compartmentalization is a relatively unheralded, but valuable, psychological defense. It can best be described as the "I'm just not going to think about that right now" defense, and we use it regularly in daily life. For instance, drivers know that at any intersection a person coming the other way could run the red light and cause a serious accident. But we would not be able to get behind the wheel if we actually *thought* about this possibility all the time. So we just don't think about it as we hop into our cars to get to where we need to go.

Being in touch with the bad news of the world takes an emotional toll. Modern life—specifically the omnipresence of digital devices that can keep us updated on happenings from around the globe—makes it harder than ever to "just not think about" upsetting events that occur outside of our daily sphere. There has always been bad news in the world, but it was so much easier to compartmentalize it back when we were limited to reading the newspaper in the morning and watching television news in the evening. There is, of course, a lot to be said for having a broader, deeper, and at times up-to-the-minute awareness of what is going on in the world. Undoubtedly, there's value in being an informed person. Even more, knowledge of current events and empathy for the suffering of others can spur us toward valuable action and remind us not to take our own good fortune for granted.

All the same, we must recognize that having constant access to the news can come at a cost, especially when the news is stressful. A steady stream of upsetting updates can scrape our nerves raw and leave us compulsively checking our devices for the latest developments.

We should also remember that the media, by nature, highlight unfortunate events that *are* happening, not unfortunate events that *aren't* happening. This lopsided picture can unnecessarily amplify our fears. While the world may seem to be more war-ridden now than in decades past, objective evidence suggests that conflict-related deaths were much more common in the 1960s, 1970s, and 1980s than they are today. In a similar vein, surveys conducted by the American Psychological Association tell us that more adults feel highly stressed by concerns about personal safety now than at any time in the past decade. Whether or not these concerns reflect reality almost certainly depends on the individual in question, but the overall spike in worries doesn't align with data demonstrating that rates of violent crime and homicides in the United States have fallen sharply from where they were ten years ago.

Closer to home, the media's infatuation with clickbait means that when we hear about teenagers, we usually hear alarming news. This can leave parents feeling unduly worried, especially given that we are now raising the best-behaved generation of teenagers on record. Compared with teens of past generations, our adolescents are less likely to have ever tried marijuana, cocaine, or hallucinogens, or to have tried or abused alcohol, or to have smoked cigarettes. They are more likely to wear bike helmets and seatbelts and to refuse to ride with drunk drivers and less likely to have had sex. When they do have sex, today's teenagers have fewer partners and are more likely to use condoms. Our teens do face emerging perils, such as e-cigarettes and opioid abuse (which, incidentally, is much more common among adults than teens). The bottom line is clear. Today's kids, as a group, manage themselves better than we ever did.

Needless to say, that doesn't mean we should stop worrying about our teenagers—that is what parents do. Nor should we dismiss or ignore the real human and environmental catastrophes that unfold around us on a daily basis. But we should recognize that the media and the digital platforms that bring us the news share the single aim of grabbing our attention. Obviously, it has never been easier for our attention to be grabbed now that most of us carry a news delivery device around with us during every waking hour.

Choosing how much to know about world events is a highly personal decision. But it is a decision that modern technology now requires us to reflect upon and make, especially when the cost to our mental health starts to outweigh the benefits of staying current. It is all too easy to assume that if having information is good, having more information is better. While this may be true for some people, it's not true for everyone. If knowing too much about the news of the day turns us into an overreactive bundle of nerves, our own anxiety will inevitably spill over onto our children. And if the media's preoccupation with the latest bad news about teenagers causes us to treat our own sturdy and steady daughters as if they are fragile and reckless, we owe it to our girls to reconsider our relationship with the news cycle and, perhaps, to decide to engage in some conscious compartmental-ization.

Collecting Emotional Trash

Just as we now have more anxiety-provoking information about the world at large than ever before, so also do we, thanks again to digital technology, know more than any generation of parents before us about the details of our own children's lives. Here, too, we should not assume that having a steady stream of informa-tion, especially about the moments when our children are feeling upset or anxious, is always a good thing.

Psychologists have long understood that teenagers sometimes deal with painful feelings by handing their unwanted emotions off to their parents. Before the dawn of the cellphone, adoles-cents did this by casually dropping bombs at the dinner table—as in, "Oh, by the way, the car needs a new windshield"—then pro-testing that their parents were overreacting in becoming upset. In truth, the teenager likely spent all day feeling horrible about the events that caused the cracked windshield but eventually came to the limit of her ability to tolerate her discomfort. So she dumped her distress on her parents in the same way one gets rid of a piece of trash; she tossed it off and wanted nothing further to do with it. This timeworn approach works well for the girl who feels relieved of her emotional rubbish, but not so well for the parents who are now stuck holding it.

Cellphones, it turns out, are the world's handiest trash chutes. Indeed, the following scenario should be familiar to almost any parent of a teen who is lucky enough to have a phone at her disposal. It starts when an adolescent sends a preposterous, yet still worrisome, midday text, perhaps something along the lines of, "Just an FYI, I'm dropping out of school." In response, her loving parent sends a curious reply along with a concerned emoji-face—"Oh, no! What's up?"—which the teen refuses to acknowledge. From there, the parent carries on with the day, dogged by concerns about what could possibly have triggered the alarming text, maybe even reaching out again and still finding him- or herself unable to get any more information from the daughter. Why? Because the girl simply wants to be rid of the emotional trash, not discuss it with the parent who is now carrying the horrible feeling that used to belong to her.

When the parent and daughter see each other at day's end, the reunion could go any number of ways. But the most likely outcome is that the daughter felt better the moment she digitally dumped her emotional junk. In short, it usually turns out that the parent worried all day about a problem that the girl hardly remembers, or at least has no interest in addressing, by the time she gets home.

A friend of mine came up with a brilliant way to improve upon this interaction after enduring several nail-biting weekdays fielding texts sent by her fourteen-year-old. My friend bought a beautiful notebook and gave it to her daughter, saying, "Let's try this. Anything you want to text me during the day, write it down in here. Then, at the end of the day, you can show me what you want me to know." Her daughter did, indeed, use the notebook as a repository for the uncomfortable thoughts and feelings that popped up at school. By the time the evening rolled around, she rarely had any interest in sharing any of her notes about events that were, by then, barely visible in her rearview mirror. From time to time, however, she did come home eager to tell her mother about some wrinkle in the day.

The notebook solution effectively accomplished three things

at once. First, it halted the teenager's barrage of worrisome texts without being the least bit dismissive of her concerns. Second, without even saying as much, my friend communicated to her daughter that nothing could possibly happen during the school day that would require her mother's immediate intervention and that, if it did, she trusted that she'd hear about it from an adult at school—in other words, the notebook served to remind the teenager of that massive "stuff I can handle" category that teenagers sometimes lose sight of when they become upset. Finally, on the occasions when the girl did have a concern to share, she was now discussing it with a mother who, thanks to that blessed notebook, had not *already* spent the entire day fretting about her daughter. Without question, this made it a lot easier for my friend to respond to her girl's concerns in the calm, measured way we know to be most helpful.

Parents Can Know Too Much

Parenting in the digital age means that we have access to a stunning amount of information about our children's lives beyond what they elect to share with us. If we choose, we can read their conversations with friends, see how they participate in the milieu of social media, know what they searched for online, and even track their physical location.

I have found that I cannot come up with a one-size-fits-all answer to the question of how much parents should monitor their kids' technology use, or use technology to monitor their kids. There are too many variables at play, such as the child's age, impulsivity level, track record, and so on. But if we approach our children's digital lives from the perspective of managing our own parental anxiety, I think that we should acknowledge that it is now possible to know too much about our kids. This became clear to me one afternoon in my practice when a friendly and thoughtful seventeen-year-old named Hailey described a blow-out she'd had with her father.

Clearly irritated, she said, "My dad lost it with me this weekend. It was awful."

"What happened?" I asked without hiding my surprise. She was as well-behaved as any girl I knew, so I was curious what had caused the eruption in her father, a kind man whom I knew to be a quite anxious and doting parent.

"Homecoming was on Saturday night and the big after-party was over at Trina's. She's not a close friend of mine, but we hang out with a lot of the same people and all of my friends were headed there after the dance. My parents didn't want me to go because they had heard stories about how it's always crazy at Trina's house."

I nodded to indicate that she did not need to explain further. I am well aware that most high schools have at least a few students whose homes are known to be notoriously light on adult supervision.

"I agreed not to go, which kinda bugged me," she said, sounding at once frustrated and resigned. "But everyone else in my group was going and I was one of the drivers. So I dropped my date off at Trina's house and hung out on the front porch for about five minutes with Trina's older sister who was back from college.

"When I walked in the door at home, my dad went ballistic. He had been tracking my location on my phone and was super pissed that I had gone to Trina's. It didn't matter that I hadn't stayed, and he didn't care that I hadn't even gone in."

"Oh," I said somewhat feebly, while trying to figure out how to respond without taking sides.

"He calmed down a little bit once he let me explain that there weren't enough cars to get my group from the dance to the party." Crestfallen, Hailey then added, "He thinks I should have called to let him know I'd be stopping by Trina's—and he said that now he doesn't feel he can trust me."

"Oh," I said again before asking, "Does he usually track you on your phone?"

"Honestly, I don't know—and I don't think that he was trying to catch me or anything. I think he just gets worried when I'm out at night and wants to know that I'm safe."

As I listened to her story, I found myself feeling awful for Hailey, who truly had done nothing wrong. I also felt terrible for her father who, because he had more information than was helpful, was now looking back on a rough weekend and ahead at a strained relationship with his daughter. Sitting with Hailey and other teenagers who have gotten into trouble with their parents over activity our own parents never would have had a way of knowing about has left me thinking about a parallel situation in medicine: the availability of whole-body computerized tomography.

CT screening, as it is often called, provides a highly detailed X-ray of the body and has been touted as a way to catch the early signs of grave diseases in apparently healthy individuals. Yet most physicians feel that scanning people who have no signs of disease does more harm than good. The Food and Drug Administration actually forbids the makers of CT systems from promoting their machines for the symptom-free, because normal results can be misleading, and "false positives" (hints of illness that turn out to be inaccurate) can trigger further unnecessary and risky tests. For parenting, cellphones aren't altogether different. Like CT scans, they can provide a ton of information that stands to be both anxiety-provoking and difficult to interpret.

While there are plenty of good reasons to monitor a kid's technology use, I think that we should proceed with caution when we detect what seems to be alarming information. For example, it often happens that parents who scan their child's text messages or social media banter are surprised to discover that their daughter and several of her friends speak fluent profanity. This news can be received in a few different ways. Parents might worry that their daughter's swearing represents the tip of a naughty iceberg, wonder where they failed in her moral upbringing, and start to regard her with relationship-straining suspicion. Alternately, they might remember that irreverence and boundary-pushing are actually signs of normal and healthy development in teenagers and that, when we were teens, most of us tried out colorful language in locker rooms, in the back of the bus, and in the notes we passed in class.

While it can be tempting to whitewash our memory of our own teenage years, it's probably more accurate and useful to recognize that the biggest difference between our generation and our kids' is that our parents simply had no way of knowing what we were up to when we weren't home, how we spoke with our friends, or even where we were. And they probably slept better for it.

With this perspective in mind, another possible response to discovering a trove of online obscenity would be for the parents to separate *what* they found from *where* they found it. They might say, "We get it that you and your friends swear when you're not around adults—no problem there. But you're breaking the 'don't post anything you wouldn't want Grandma to see' rule you agreed to when you got your phone. If you need to tell your friends that the online cursing ban comes from us, feel free."

Obviously, this approach presumes that the parents have been transparent about monitoring their daughter's technology use. I'm not usually a very prescriptive psychologist, but if you are checking up on your girl's digital activity, I think it's best to let her know. For one thing, telling your daughter that you've reserved the right to check her phone or computer inserts a speed bump that might slow her down when she's tempted to make a bad choice online. For another, it means that you can readily talk with your daughter about any concerning information you find. In practical terms, if a CT scan were to discover a spot on your liver, you'd want to find out quickly how worried, or not, you should be about it. If something in your daughter's digital profile makes you nervous, talking with her about it will almost always be the best way to address your own discomfort.

With the CT scan metaphor in mind, the question certainly arises about whether it makes sense to monitor a well-behaved teenager's technology at all. That decision is as individual as the choice we make about how closely to follow the news. But the critical issue is the same: it's not always better to know more.

If I had a simple solution to the challenge of supervising digital denizens I'd offer it. Until then, I can tell you that decades of being a practicing clinician have convinced me that the most powerful force for good in a young person's life is having a caring, working relationship with at least one loving adult. As modern parents, we need to ensure that the time we spend monitoring our girl's technology doesn't get in the way of or threaten to take the place of that connection.

To safeguard our relationship, we should remember that supervising our daughter's digital activity cannot keep her safe if we don't also have a clear and direct line of communication with her. When parents do find themselves relying heavily on digital surveillance to feel that they have a link with their daughter, I always recommend that they work to reboot their relationship with their girl, recruiting the help of a counselor if necessary. Furthermore, we should stay alert to the possibility that what we learn online might, without any benefit, add to the worries we feel as parents and contribute to tense, unhelpful interactions at home.

Putting Slack in the System

Every day I get to walk my younger daughter to our neighbor-hood elementary school, and once I've dropped her off, I usually spend the ten-minute walk back to my home catching up with other parents who follow the same routine. One spring, I found myself in a series of morning conversations with a dad who lives near me and who also has two daughters. His older girl attends our neighborhood school and, at the time, his younger daughter went to a preschool about fifteen minutes away by car. My friend and his wife were trying to decide if they should move their younger girl to our neighborhood school for kindergarten in the coming fall or if they should have her stay one more year at her current school, before moving her to the neighborhood school for first grade.

Ten minutes at a time, we weighed their family's dilemma. There were pros and cons to both decisions, and the more we talked about it, the more apparent it became that one choice was not clearly better than the other for their daughter. Finally I asked, "Is there a choice that would make life easier for your family—that would put more slack in the system?"

"Oh, yeah," said my neighbor, "it would be easier to have them both at the same school. They'd have the same vacations and snow days, and we wouldn't have to drive to pick up our little one."

"If it's otherwise a wash," I replied, "and moving her for kin-dergarten makes life easier for you and your wife, then I think that's the best choice for your whole family."

This, I can say, is a lesson I've learned the hard way. Personally, I happen to enjoy being very busy. Unfortunately, my preferred volume of activity rides very close to an amount that overwhelms me. In my early days as a mother, I would see just how many plans I could pack into each week. I could always find a way to wedge in an extra art class for one of my girls, or I'd rustle up a babysitter so that I could give a talk on a night when my husband also had to be out. When it was time to send birthday treats to school, I'd get it in my head that they needed to be healthy, delicious, and homemade. I would spin ten plates in my own slightly manic fashion and it would all seem to be going reasonably well.

Until someone barfed.

Or my car refused to start.

Or a babysitter had to cancel.

Then the plates would come crashing down and my activity dial would jump from bustling to toxic. In half a panic, I'd try to reconcile my tightly packed schedule with the needs of a sick child, to figure out how our family could do its hectic hustle with only one car, or to find a last-minute babysitter.

I was about three years into this mothering mania when I first encountered the research on daily hassles, thanks to the fact that I was coauthoring a textbook with a colleague. I'm constantly reading studies in my field, but I can point to only a handful that have inspired me to make real changes in my own life. The news that the stress of minor hassles can be as significant—if not more significant—as the stress of true calamities fit with my experience. When one of my daughters came down with the flu, the problem was not that she was sick. The problem was that everyone's calendar was so jammed that her illness created an avalanche of scheduling problems. In hindsight this seems obvious enough, but once I learned to build slack into our system (a luxury, I'm aware, that not all families have), it turned out to be a really effective antidote to the unexpected and unavoidable stresses of daily life. Whenever possible, I've tried to stop asking myself, "*Can* I squeeze this fill-in-the-blank into the week?" and to wonder instead, "*Should* I?"

Of course we can't know ahead of time if our scheduling calculations will be correct, and I am constantly falling back into my old overbooking habits. Every time this happens life finds a way to remind me, again, that it's best to try to set our family's baseline activity levels at about 75 percent of what we can actually accomplish.

When we're not operating at maximum capacity, everyone in the family feels less stressed and anxious. Chronic frenzy is replaced by relative calm, and, when things go wrong, we're dealing with a frustration, not a crisis. There are now times when I sheepishly deliver store-bought doughnut holes to school knowing that I had plenty of time to make something healthier (not that that would have been the kids' preference). But now there are also times when a sick day isn't a disaster, just a call for me to shuffle my duties into the openings in my calendar so that I can stay home and watch movies with the barfer of the moment.

When things are going well, having time on hand also creates room for spontaneous delights. One day, during a downpour, my younger daughter thought it would be great to put on all of our rain gear and walk to school instead of driving as we would normally do when the weather is bad. I went along with her plan only because I happened to have time to come back home and change into work clothes after I dropped her off. Our puddle-pocked walk was actually so much fun that we continue to reminisce about it three years later.

Our time with our children is short, and every caring parent feels pressed to make the most of it. This can lead us to think that we make the most of time by *filling* it, especially with structured activities with clear goals such as pursuing sports, or taking lessons, or making adorable homemade cupcakes. I have to work against my own nature to appreciate that, often, we make the most of time just by *having* it. Deliberately underscheduling my family—always against my own instincts—continues to prove itself a reliable strategy for reducing the strain in our lives, and on many days increasing the joy.

Money Can Buy Stress

Just as we might choose to be less tightly scheduled so that we can better absorb the inevitable calamities that come with family life, new research suggests that kids actually feel less pressure when their parents elect to live more modestly than they can afford. We have long known that growing up in poverty causes unrelenting stress. But in the last decade, studies have clearly established that affluence may not always be as good for children and teenagers as one might think. In fact, psychologist Suniya Luthar and her colleagues have done an excellent job of documenting the elevated rates of emotional problems among young people with prosperous parents.

Surprisingly, Dr. Luthar's work has found that teenagers from wealthy families are more likely to suffer from depression, anxiety, and substance abuse than young people being raised in lower tax brackets. To explain these unexpected but well-established findings, experts have noted that growing up in a context of abundance can create intense achievement pressures for children. Furthermore, research suggests that wealth can create physical and psychological distance between parents and children, as high-earning parents often work long hours and may turn their children's care over to nannies, tutors, or after-school programs.

Recently, however, psychologists Terese Lund and Eric Dearing approached the bad news on affluence and adolescent well-being from a new perspective. They wondered whether simply coming from money created problems for young people or, instead, if their mental health was compromised by choices that wealthy parents alone are empowered to make. To address this question, they teased apart two variables that had been lumped together in previous research, namely, how much the parents earned and where the families chose to live.

By studying an economically and geographically diverse sample, Lund and Dearing found that prosperity, in and of itself, posed no risk to healthy psychological development. The affluence of a family's neighborhood, however, *did* matter, and it mattered a lot. Remarkably, girls raised in the wealthiest neighborhoods were two to three times more likely to report symptoms of anxiety and depression than girls living in middle-income areas. In parallel, boys in the most upscale communities were two to three times more likely to get themselves into trouble than their peers living in middle-class neighborhoods.

There's another cardinal rule in psychology: under stress, girls collapse in on themselves and boys act out. In other words, while the girls and boys living in wealthy neighborhoods had different problems, the nature of their troubles (girls caving in, boys misbehaving) suggests that both groups were suffering from the pressures related to where their parents had chosen to live. Who, you might be wondering, were the least stressed kids in the study? Those residing with wealthy parents in middle-class neighborhoods.

These remarkable findings encourage us to consider two important issues. One is that the affluent adults living in middle-class communities were electing to put financial slack in their systems by living below their means. Their homes may have been smaller and less opulent than what they could afford, but they also had cash on hand to absorb large and unexpected expenses, such as needing a new roof. There are certainly wealthy families living in upper-class communities who can easily afford to replace their roofs if they have to. But there are also plenty of families who stretch themselves to their limit to live in the most upscale communities they can afford. When their roof needs replacing they, and their children, will feel the strain of a financial crunch.

The other issue is that children whose parents live below their means may also feel less stressed about their own futures. Almost everyone aims to live at least as comfortably in adulthood as they did in childhood. This means that young people raised in the lap of luxury can feel pressed to figure out how they will independently maintain their costly lifestyles.

In my work, I have been surprised to discover that ambitious adolescents from wealthy families can seem preoccupied with their own future professional success, focus on only a few careers (such as those in business or finance), and consider only a few major American cities where they might want to live. In contrast, I often find that teenagers from middle-class backgrounds are more likely to talk about a wide range of jobs they might do and places they might land. Over the years, there have been several moments in my practice when I've been struck by the irony that teenagers from wealthy families often seem more strained and constrained when thinking about their futures than teenagers coming from more modest circumstances.

Looking at it this way, we can see why kids from affluent families living in middle-class neighborhoods would find themselves in the low-stress sweet spot. They may worry less about their futures because, for them, adult success is not a narrowly defined target. Alongside this, they likely enjoy the stress-reducing benefits of affluence: the atmospheric ease that comes with having a financial cushion, living with parents who don't have to work over-the-top hours just to make ends meet, and being able to graduate from college without debt.

As parents, if we are fortunate enough to have financial choices, we can't learn about this research without reflecting on the ones we make. Our decisions about where we live, how we vacation, what we drive, and all of the other ways that we spend money on or around our children are, to be sure, highly personal. This is also true of how much we choose to know about the news of the world and how thoroughly we decide to monitor our own children's technology. These are not choices we make once, but at many points along the way.

We can take steps to contain our own anxiety and our daughters' by taking a fresh look at these decisions. It's too easy to fall into the assumption that when it comes to having information, scheduling activities, or enjoying personal luxuries, more is always better. Surprisingly, it is sometimes true that we can ease the stress that we, and our daughters, feel by deciding to know, do, and spend less.

As parents, we should work to manage the strain that we feel in our own lives, both for the sake of ourselves and because our own emotional tension can contribute to an anxious climate at home. And a tense atmosphere at home makes it harder for our daughters to feel at ease on their good days, and likewise harder for us to be the calm presence they need on their bad days. Next, let's turn to a topic that is often a source of distress. At some point along the way, every one of our daughters will feel uneasy about her relationships with other girls her age.

CHAPTER THREE

· · · · · · · · · · ·

Girls Among Girls

MORE OFTEN THAN NOT, GIRLS' FRIENDSHIPS MAKE THEIR LIVES BET-
ter, not worse. From early childhood on, our daughters have fun
with their girlfriends when all is well and look to them for company and support when the road gets rough. *Most* of the time,
our daughters' social lives help to ease their stress and anxiety.
This chapter will focus on the *rest* of the time. At some point
along the way, your daughter will almost certainly find herself
feeling troubled by her interactions with one or more of her female peers.

We'll start by addressing some of the age-old tensions that
arise in girls' relationships with one another. From there, we'll
turn to the game-changing impact of social media and what parents can do to ensure that their daughter's online activity doesn't
leave her feeling constantly on edge. Finally, we'll address the taxing and treacherous world of competition among girls.

Anxious Is the New Shy

On an overcast day in April, a couple in their thirties visited my
practice to discuss their daughter's upcoming transition to the
fifth grade. When making the appointment over the phone, Toni

explained that her daughter, Alina, had always felt uneasy in social settings. While Alina had two steady buddies at her cozy elementary school, her parents were already worrying about how she would manage in the coming fall. In our town of Shaker Heights, all of the neighborhood early elementary schools merge into Woodbury School, a large building that houses every fifth and sixth grader in the district. With ten fifth-grade classrooms, Alina couldn't count on being grouped with one of her close friends.

At our first meeting, Adam and Toni sat together on my couch and took turns describing their nine-year-old girl to me.

"Alina was one of those babies who had a hard time feeling settled," Toni explained tenderly. "She was fussy and tense—we didn't realize just how true this was until her little brother, who was really easygoing, was born two years later."

"Her social anxiety started very early," Adam added urgently. "As a baby she cried when strangers approached, and even as a toddler she hid behind my legs when my folks came to visit from out of town. Her brother, by comparison, can't seem to get enough of other people." Amused, Adam added, "He loves going to birthday parties and would have three playdates a weekend if we'd let him."

Toni continued, "When we try to nudge her to be outgoing, she only gets more tense. At that point, we don't know what to do, since she's clearly too uncomfortable to have fun with anyone."

"When we spoke on the phone," I said to Toni, "you mentioned that Alina has a couple of good friends. What are those relationships like?"

"Yes, she's got Zoe and Erin at school—and they do so well together. Alina's known them since she was in preschool, but when we ask if she wants to have them over on the weekend, she always says no."

Clearly concerned, Adam added, "We've tried to work on her anxiety, but it hasn't seemed to help. In fact, it only seems to get worse."

Curious, I asked, "What have you tried?"

Shaking his head in a way that expressed both worry and despair, he said, "We've worked on building her confidence and talked with her about being brave. But it doesn't seem to do anything."

Toni jumped in. "I know what it's like to feel nervous around new people. I get that way sometimes, too. But we're scared that her social anxiety is getting worse. At this rate, we can't even picture what middle school will look like. We're hoping that you can help her get her nerves under control."

"I do think that we can move things in the right direction," I responded. "But first, I think we might start by framing the problem a little bit differently. Instead of saying that she's got social anxiety—which I'm not convinced is the case—let's start with the assumption that she was just born shy."

Any parent with more than one child knows that babies have personalities from the day they are born. Some are mellow, some are tetchy, some are sunny, and some are highly active and wiggle all of the time. Long-established research tells us that newborns come preprogrammed with dispositions and that most babies can be assigned to one of three categories: easy children, who are generally cheerful and adapt quickly to novelty; difficult children, who have irregular routines, dislike change, and can be pretty cranky; and slow-to-warm-up children who are pretty low-key and need a long time to adjust to new experiences.

Here's the most important thing to know about these categories: all three are normal, and children from all three categories mature into well-adjusted adults.

"Ten years ago," I offered, "we probably would not have used the term *anxiety* to characterize what you're seeing in Alina. We'd likely say that she's 'slow to warm up,' which is one of the ways we describe totally normal, if cautious, children."

From there, I told them about the landmark research conducted with infants as young as four months showing that some babies have a strong negative reaction to unfamiliar people and situations while other babies love anything new. Remarkably, we can even predict which young children will be shy based on brain wave patterns measured during infancy. In babies who go on to be wary toddlers, the right frontal lobe—which is associated with a negative emotional response—lights up in response to a changing display of colored Ping-Pong balls; babies who become outgoing toddlers show the opposite neurological pattern.

"Based on what you're telling me," I said, "Alina has probably been wired from day one to be hesitant in new situations." Toni and Adam nodded to indicate that this fit with what they knew about their daughter. "The great news is that she clearly knows how to make, enjoy, and keep friendships."

"Yes." Toni smiled. "She really loves Zoe and Erin—and they love her back."

"The next step will be to help Alina learn how to manage when she finds herself in new places or has to meet new people. There's no question in my mind that she can become more comfortable with unfamiliarity. But to get her there, we need to work with, not against, her wiring."

"We're in," said Adam gamely. "So, what do we do?"

"Starting today, you can help Alina observe and accept her reactions to new situations. If you notice that she tenses up when you suggest that she might go to a classmate's birthday party, try saying, 'I see that you're feeling cautious about the party, and that's your first reaction.'" Still modeling an easygoing, compassionate tone, I continued. "'Soon, let's see if you have a second reaction. Let's hang out with this birthday party invitation for a little while and find out what that second reaction might be.' You don't want to help her avoid the situations that make her uncomfortable—doing so will make it that much harder for her to try new things—but you do want to let her come to new things on her terms whenever you can."

I have spent more time than I care to admit trying to help people change unwanted first reactions. In retrospect, I count those efforts as almost entirely wasted. Individuals who are uneasy with change tend to have a first reaction that amounts to an automatic instinct to withdraw. And that instinct activates very quickly and cannot necessarily be stopped. When we think about first reactions this way, it leaves us with two options: fight the reflex, or accept and allow the withdrawal reflex and then see what happens next.

I now believe that opposing a person's innate first response can be more than just useless. It can actually be harmful. This is a lesson I learned while caring for a teenager named Tya who had convinced herself that she would only be "cured" of her anxiety once her chest no longer tightened in response to awkward or difficult situations. Every time she felt her familiar—and probably hardwired—clenching feeling, she took it as a sign that her anxiety remained out of control. Unfortunately for Tya, her chest tightened, often fleetingly, several times a day. Having set herself an impossible goal, she spent a lot of time feeling both helpless and hopeless about what she saw as a failure to master her nerves.

When weeks of effort to help Tya maintain a steady state of calm were clearly going nowhere, I decided to take a different tack. One day I said, "What if we just accept that the feeling you get in your chest might not go away? And what if, instead of worrying too much about it, we simply take it as a normal warning sign that something's up?"

Tya was amenable to this idea and willing to step back and learn more about what the tightness in her chest actually signaled. Interestingly, we soon discovered that her gripped feeling sometimes happened in response to an outside threat—such as a pop quiz at school—but that it was just as likely to be alerting her to an uneasy internal experience, such as feeling annoyed or frustrated with someone else.

Once Tya and I learned to take an impassive yet curious stance toward her first reaction, it stopped giving way to a cascade of distress. Instead, her physical discomfort simply let us know that something around her, or inside her, had triggered her internal alert signal. Our next step was to learn more about what had set off her hair-trigger response in the first place. Once we knew what was bothering her, she could reflect on what her second reaction might be. In the time that we worked together, the anxious feeling in Tya's chest never went away. But she was much better able to manage whatever set off her anxiety when she no longer felt frightened of her automatic first reaction.

Wanting to share this perspective with Toni and Adam, I added, "In the longer term, I think you might want to help Alina *appreciate* her tentative style. There's no reason for her to feel bad about it and no reason for you to worry that she's unduly anxious." Though our culture rewards extroverts who jump into new situations with both feet, there's a lot to be said for those who watch and wait before deciding how to move forward.

"When you talk with Alina about the transition to fifth grade, I think that you can be very reassuring while pointing out that she—unlike her brother—doesn't go charging into new situations. She likes to take her time and size things up before she joins in. You can let Alina know that there's nothing wrong with her approach and that you're there to support her while she gets comfortable, especially with the start at Woodbury next year."

Toni asked, "Is there any possibility that telling her that it's okay to hang back will only make her more shy?"

"Actually, it's probably the opposite," I explained. "If you push her, she's likely to dig in her heels. If you tell her that she can take her time before moving forward, that will probably help her to relax. You can also let Alina know that, over time, it probably won't take so long for her cautious first reaction to give way to a second reaction once her visceral response dies down. And that second reaction might be a sense of curiosity, of wanting to engage, or of not wanting to miss out."

"This does feel like the right way to go," Adam agreed, "but how do we know for sure that she doesn't have a problem with anxiety? At the end of the day, we'd like for her to make lots of friends."

"For now," I replied, "everything you are describing about Alina is well within the normal range. I know that there's a lot of concern these days about anxiety, but we don't want to risk the possibility of creating a self-fulfilling prophecy. If we treat Alina as though she's broken, she might start to feel anxious about *that*. She will probably never be a party animal like your son, but she will almost certainly learn to become more comfortable in new situations."

I wrapped up our first meeting by reassuring Toni and Adam that decades of studies tell us that children's personalities do, indeed, become more flexible over time. And from that research we've identified the critical factor that helps children to adapt and thrive: having parents who will work with, not against, their inborn traits.

Numbers Bring Drama

I bit my tongue when Adam, in the most loving and well-meaning way, expressed his sincere wish for his Alina to have "lots of friends." While I know this is what many parents want for their daughters, experience has taught me—and research confirms—that the happiest girls are those with one or two solid friendships. Having a couple of reliable buddies reduces stress by lending predictability to girls' social lives. Girls with true best friends or tiny friendship groups know whom they'll see on the weekends, and whom they'll turn to for support when life throws a curveball.

If your daughter exists in a small but contented social cocoon, don't expend any of your energy urging her to become a social butterfly. In fact, go out of your way to let her know that she's doing it right. Girls who move in small circles can sometimes worry that they are uncool or marginal. They may envy their classmates who belong to larger groups and wish that they, too, were "popular." Indeed, popularity really can sound like a good thing, especially in middle school when girls seek a sense of belonging and spend a lot of time fretting about whether and where they fit in.

But here's the problem: numbers bring drama.

Social turmoil almost always comes with the territory for groups of four or five girls or more. The reason behind this has nothing to do with girls being catty or mean or exclusionary (though they can, at times, act in all of these ways). It is simply the case that one cannot possibly assemble a group of five or more human beings *of any age* who like one another equally. Yet tweens, with their wobbly social skills, attempt this.

Girls who belong to large friendship groups run into all sorts of predictable stressors. While small groups are usually composed of girls who have handpicked one another, compromises are invariably made when girls coalesce in large numbers. And these compromises usually cause a great deal of social stress. Perhaps two or three girls in the group really enjoy being together and don't always want to include the whole crew in their plans. When they decide to invite everyone, they feel unhappy about it. When they don't include everyone, they're stuck dealing with the aftermath of having left certain girls out. Or perhaps two girls in the group have an oil-and-water relationship. This happens all the time, and it means that the other girls in the clique are invariably pressed to serve as mediators or confidantes, or to pick a side in the conflict.

To make matters both better and worse, research consistently shows that girls are especially plugged in when it comes to thinking about other people's feelings. Studies find that girls are more empathic than boys, a difference that is explained by how we socialize our daughters and sons, not by some innate biological factor. Girls, more than boys, are raised on a steady diet of encouragement to "think about how the other person would feel," which means that if your daughter's friend finds herself on the sharp end of a social stick, your daughter will feel some pain, too.

This is all to say that even under the best conditions, a surprising degree of stress and anxiety attends our daughters' garden-variety social interactions. Girls in small groups sometimes worry that they'll end up friendless if they find themselves at odds with their few buddies. Girls in larger groups often surf from one wave of drama to the next. And even when your daughter is having a good day, she can be knocked off balance by a friend who isn't.

Regardless of the size of her social group, you can help your daughter manage the inevitable ups and downs that come with her peer relationships. Girls who are good at dealing with social friction spend more time enjoying their friends and less time ruminating about the latest social kerfuffle. As we know, our daughters look to us for cues about how troubled they should be when things go badly, so in order to be most helpful, we need to accept that it's normal for girls to have difficulty getting along. If we are alarmed by the mere presence of social discord, our girls will feel alarmed by it, too. When we recognize interpersonal discord as a fact of life, we can take a pragmatic stance toward helping our daughters learn how to navigate it effectively.

Healthy Conflict 101

Girls, as a group, are bad at dealing with conflict because people, as a group, are bad at dealing with it. And we cannot teach our daughters what we don't know. Though in the past I have declared my certainty that we will never find a cure for the seventh grade, and I have sometimes felt pessimistic about helping girls (and adults) improve their ability to manage disagreements effectively, I have lately changed my tune.

While conflict is inevitable, handling it poorly is not. Once we accept that putting more than one conscious person in the same room guarantees that, eventually, there will be friction, we can turn our energy toward understanding the ins and outs of interpersonal discord. Some approaches to engaging in conflict are preferable to others, and this complex and murky topic becomes a great deal simpler when we recognize that there are three common unhealthy forms of conflict management and only a single common healthy one.

The three forms of unhealthy conflict are instantly recognizable: acting as a bulldozer, acting as a doormat, or acting as a doormat with spikes. A bulldozer deals with disagreements by running people over, while doormats allow themselves to be run over. The doormat with spikes employs passive-aggressive tactics, such as using guilt as a weapon, playing the part of the victim, or involving third parties in what should be a one-on-one disagreement. Girls often have elaborate doormat-with-spikes repertoires, because we don't always help our daughters learn to recognize, accept, and directly express their angry feelings. Given this, it's really no surprise that their darker impulses are often expressed indirectly.

For healthy conflict, the guiding metaphor is a pillar. It stands up for itself without stepping on anyone else. But when conflict comes, to be a pillar is really hard; for most of us it's certainly not our first reaction. Fortunately, if we can recognize and observe our first reaction—to be a bulldozer, doormat, or doormat with spikes—without allowing ourselves to act on it, we can usually find our way to reflecting on how we might become a pillar as our second reaction.

One Monday morning at Laurel School, Liz, an eighth grader, caught me in the hallway to ask if I had any time available to meet later that day. We determined that she had a study hall when I had an opening, so we made a plan to meet in my office early that afternoon.

"What's up?" I asked as Liz settled into the chair across from mine. Though Laurel has a uniform, each girl finds a way to put her personal stamp on it. That day, Liz was wearing a sweatshirt, athletic socks, and running shoes—a look common among the students who are athletes.

Liz picked up one of the fidget toys I keep in my Harry Potter office and said, "I just want to get your advice on this weird thing that happened with one of the girls who plays on my club volleyball team."

"Sure," I said.

"I've known her forever and we're friends—not *great* friends—but good enough. She doesn't go to Laurel but she knows a lot of the girls here and we hang out with some of the same people on the weekends."

She continued, "I went to her birthday party last year, and a few weeks ago she came up to me at volleyball to tell me that her mom said she couldn't have a party this year because they had too much other family stuff going on. That was fine and I didn't even really think about it until Saturday night when she posted all these pictures of what was *clearly* her birthday party." Now sounding really bothered, Liz added, "She didn't have to invite me . . . I get that . . . I just don't see why she had to go out of her way to tell me that she *wasn't* having a party."

"Right," I offered. "I can see why you're upset."

"So I'm not sure what I'm supposed to do, because I'm going to see her at practice tonight . . . it's so uncomfortable."

I empathized with Liz's discomfort and told her that I was sorry she'd been put in this position. Given her tricky social situation, I walked her through the ways—three bad, one good—that people usually deal with conflict.

"Obviously," I said, "you and I are going to try to figure out a pillar response, but sometimes it helps to get some of the other options out of your system." Lightheartedly, I asked, "If you were going to bulldoze her, what would that look like?"

"I actually thought about that. There's a part of me that just wants to go up to her at practice and say something nasty to her face."

"Sure. You're hurt and mad—it makes sense that you'd want to just let her have it. And if you decided to doormat this, what would that look like?"

Now picking up the playful mood, Liz replied, "I suppose that I'd just walk around feeling sad about it and cry myself to sleep or something."

"Right. And how would you doormat-with-spikes this one?" I asked, enjoying this exchange.

"There are so many ways," she said, now fully into our game. "I don't even know where to start!"

"Go for it."

"Well, I suppose that I could talk bad about her to my friends on the volleyball team or here at Laurel, or I could invite a bunch of girls over and post pictures of us having a great time and tag her so that she sees them. Or I could subtweet about it."

"What's that?"

"It's talking bad about someone on Twitter without using her name—but everyone knows who you're talking about. I could tweet something like, 'Doesn't it suck when you realize that someone you thought was an honest friend actually isn't?'"

"Ouch!" After pausing for a moment I added, "You have to admit, social media can be a doormat-with-spikes *bonanza*."

Liz gave a quick nod that expressed her total agreement while saying, "Oh, yeah," slowly and keenly.

"There's probably no easier way to involve a whole lot of other people in a conflict, and it also offers a million ways to go after someone indirectly."

"For sure," agreed Liz, now leaning forward in her chair.

"Okay, now that we've gotten our ugly impulses out of the way, how might you pillar this? How could you stick up for yourself while also being respectful of her?"

Liz started, "I suppose that I might say something to her at practice like 'I saw that you had a party.'" She continued in a level tone, "'And that's fine, but you didn't need to tell me that you weren't having one.'"

"That's pretty good! What if you wanted to say even less? Sometimes being a pillar involves starting a conversation, not trying to end one."

"I guess I could just say, 'I saw the pictures of your party, and my feelings were kinda hurt.'"

"Yes . . . I think that something like that might be a good place to start. Because what if something random happened? Maybe her mom decided to throw her a surprise party and didn't really know who to invite. Letting her know how you feel might also give her the chance to offer you an apology if she owes you one."

"That's true," said Liz sensibly. "I don't really know the whole story."

"Asking a question can also be a good way to be a pillar. Perhaps you could say something like, 'I saw that you did have a party after all. Did I do something that made things hard between us?'"

"Yeah, I could do that. That's good."

It was time to wrap up. Before Liz left, I made a point of telling her that I did not expect that she would, from now on, be able to come up with pillar responses quickly and easily whenever she felt hurt or upset. Indeed, I shared with her that I still find that when I'm miffed, my first impulse is to be a doormat with spikes. I'm resigned to this unpleasant truth about myself and will sometimes even indulge in daydreaming about the passive-aggressive things I'd *like* to do when I'm mad. In my actions, however, I do try to be a pillar.

Given that girls' interpersonal worlds come with unavoidable stress, we need to do our part to help ease some of the social strain our daughters feel. We can start by accepting that strife comes with human contact and help girls appreciate that they will inevitably have conflicts with their agemates. Further, we can recognize that, being human, our daughters (and other people's daughters) will sometimes feel compelled to act like bulldozers, doormats, or doormats with spikes. Then, when peer conflicts do arise, we can have matter-of-fact conversations with our girls about the better and worse ways to handle them.

To the degree that our girls let us in on social turmoil that is taking place online, as it often does, we should talk with them about how it is basically impossible to be a pillar online because pillar communications rely heavily on tone. Indeed, if you think about it, the same exact phrase—"Can we talk about why I wasn't invited to your party?"—could come across as aggressive (bulldozer), woeful (doormat), sneering (doormat with spikes), or respectful (pillar), depending on the tone in which it is delivered. All the emojis in the world cannot communicate the subtleties of the human voice. When it's time for your daughter to act as a pillar, help her appreciate that doing so will, almost certainly, require a face-to-face interaction.

As we help our daughters handle peer conflict, we can remind them that nobody always gets it right the first time and nobody gets it right every day. But with practice, they can learn to deal with interpersonal discord in ways they can feel good about and to use strategies that should calm, rather than stir up, their social dramas.

Freedom to Pick Her Battles

A week later, Liz was back in my office. I felt surprised to see her again so soon, given how quickly and completely she had latched on to my advice about how to have a healthy conflict.

"So . . . what happened?"

"Honestly," she said, "it wasn't good. I saw the girl at practice and I could tell that something was wrong. She avoided me during warm-ups and wouldn't really look at me during drills."

"What do you think the deal was?"

"I think that she felt bad about leaving me out of the party, but she wasn't going to apologize about it, either."

"Did you say anything to her about it?"

"No, it just didn't seem right. But now I feel like I've been a total doormat about the whole thing, and that doesn't feel right, either."

I could see Liz's point and could see how she had landed there given our conversation. Still, I had an idea.

"You know," I offered, "you've got another option for handling this problem." Liz's face took on an expression that was simultaneously curious and skeptical. "You could try some emotional aikido."

Her look shifted to fully skeptical.

"I know that adults encourage girls to stand up for themselves— and that's an important thing to be able to do. I can also see how our conversation from last week gave you the impression that *not* responding to your teammate makes you a doormat." Liz raised her eyebrows and nodded. "But there's also the option of strategic sidestepping."

Liz said nothing but looked at me expectantly. I took this as permission to continue.

"Here's what I mean. In some forms of combat, like boxing or wrestling, people fight by punching or pushing against the other person. In other forms of conflict, like aikido, if someone is coming at you, the first thing you do is step out of that person's path. This pulls you out of harm's way, and it can leave your opponent off balance."

Liz was still listening but, to her credit, doing nothing to hide the fact that she found my metaphor to be ridiculous.

"Bear with me," I said. "I know that this sounds strange, but here's how I want you to think about it: making the decision that it is *not worth your time* to engage in some dumb drama actually gives you the upper hand."

Liz's skepticism lightened by a shade.

From there we talked about the fact that she alone could determine how much she cared about being left out of the party and how much energy she wanted to expend on trying to repair or improve the relationship with her teammate, who had, after all, never been a close friend in the first place. I told Liz that she certainly had my support to decide against taking an open stand on the matter.

Liz seemed relieved by the idea of not having to confront her teammate. Going forward, we agreed that she'd be cautious, yet civil, at practice and that she'd resist her temptation to be a doormat with spikes by trashing her teammate to others. I invited Liz to come back my way if she continued to have a hard time with the girl. At that point, she could decide what, if anything, she wanted to do about it. In the meantime, she could conserve her energy by electing to sidestep what appeared to be a fruitless showdown. While agreeing to this plan, Liz was still leery.

"Are you sure I'm not just letting her walk all over me?"

"You'd be letting her walk all over you if you were crying in the corner about not being invited to her party or if you were sucking up to her to try to be included in the next one."

Liz agreed.

"In this situation," I added, "you are making a considered choice about how much of your attention this situation deserves. You are not ignoring or forgetting how she acted—that information is yours to keep—but you are deciding, for now, not to let this girl take up any more of your time. Just because she threw a problem at you doesn't mean you have to catch it."

In my work with girls I have tended, in the past, to automatically encourage them to stick up for themselves when slighted and to push back against any degree of mistreatment. This guidance fits with my conscious commitment to helping other people's daughters, and my own, mature into empowered young women who take guff from no one. Yet I've come to realize that the advice we give girls doesn't mirror how competent adult women often handle interpersonal conflicts. We pick our battles. We decide when, and with whom, a confrontation is worthwhile. And we often dispatch trivial or pointless disputes with nods and fake smiles because we have better things to do with our time.

In truth, confrontation, even when done well, is psychologically taxing. It is also true that some social problems suffocate for lack of attentional oxygen. Of course, there will be times when it makes sense for our daughters to take someone on. That's when we want to help our girls act as pillars who effectively assert their own rights while respecting the rights of others, which offers the best possible chance of resolving the conflict successfully. All the same, our daughters should know that overtly standing up for themselves can be optional. Indeed, we unwittingly add to girls' stress when we suggest that they *must* address themselves to every injustice or snub. Holding one's fire is not the same as surrendering. Adults know that discretion can be the better part of valor, and we should let our daughters know this, too.

Round-the-Clock Peer Stress

Thanks to digital technology, our daughters now conduct their social lives on multiple planes and, as we know, run into conflicts both in person and in cyberspace. But even when girls are getting along online, they can find that their social media activity takes an emotional toll.

Growing up in the digital age almost certainly plays a role in the spiking levels of stress and anxiety we see in today's teenagers. While the available evidence does not support exaggerated claims that smartphones are turning our kids into psychologically stunted screen-zombies, omnipresent technology has, beyond question, changed how we live. Not all of those changes are for the better, and adults are still coming to terms with what it means to raise children in a fully wired world.

The more that we, as parents, understand how the digital environment shapes our daughters' interpersonal lives, the better equipped we'll be to help them ease some of the tension that comes with being plugged in. Experts note that adolescents aren't enthralled by technology—they're enthralled by the peers on the other end of the technology they happen to be using. Indeed, teenagers have always been obsessed with their friends. Decades ago, we wanted to connect with our peers just as desperately as our kids now want to connect with theirs.

At this point, you might be thinking, "Okay, fine. But not like *today's* teenagers. With their surgically attached phones and their mortal fear of missing out on even the most frivolous peer communication? We were never addicted to each other like *that*."

Actually, we were. To plug into our own peer-obsessed pasts, we need to remember how we employed the connective technologies of our time. I, for one, can easily summon the memory of that hot, damp, and even slightly painful ear sensation that would set in after spending hours with the family phone pressed to the side of my head. I even recall that, most evenings, a point would arrive at which my ear became so uncomfortable that I finally had to interrupt my friend at the other end of the line to say, "Wait . . . hold on a minute . . . I have to switch sides." To which she would reply, "Yeah. Me, too."

And do you remember when call waiting came out? That changed *everything*. Before call waiting, there would come a time each evening when my mother would interrupt me mid-call to say, "You have to get off the phone. Someone might be trying to reach us." I'd stall, hang up eventually, and—now completely disconnected from my friends—sullenly resign myself to doing my homework. With the arrival of call waiting, I became the self-appointed family receptionist who commandeered the phone for the entire evening on the promise that I would hand over the line if (and only if) my parents happened to receive a call or wanted to make one.

We really were no different from our own children. We just had lame technology.

Once we recognize that there's nothing new or strange about young people's intense desire to be connected to one another at all times, we can remember something else: being connected to one's peers can be very stressful. As much as I loved being on the phone with my friends, there was often a lot of drama going on.

Even with our limited technology, we found ways to simulta-

neously script and follow the latest episode of our own adolescent soap opera. We'd get together to listen in on each other's
conversations, maintain a frenzy of connections by ending one
call to take another before calling the first (or second or third)
person back, or use call waiting to toggle back and forth between
two conversations at once. When my mother eventually kicked
me off the phone for the night (even, sensibly, *after* we had call
waiting), I'm sure that my outward resentment was secretly lined
with a modicum of relief.

Girls' relationships with one another have always been
charged. Today's unprecedented capacity for connection only
makes these interactions more complex, consuming, and flat-out
stressful than they ever were before. In the old days, we took
much-needed breaks from interacting with our friends, simply
because we had no choice. Now we need to help our daughters
push the pause button on their social lives—to engage in some
conscious compartmentalization—so that they can get their
much-needed breaks, too.

Accomplishing this can be fairly straightforward, but you
should not measure the success of your approach by how enthusiastically your daughter embraces it. Limiting a young person's
access to technology is rarely a popular decision, but making un-
popular decisions is, to be sure, an important part of being a
parent.

You can reduce the resistance to any rules you make by holding the whole family to them. Many parents (myself included) are
as absorbed in their technology as their teenagers are and can
benefit from placing some limits on their own use. It can also be
easier to draw lines around the time we spend on digital media
when we make it clear that we're not so much *against* technology
as we are *for* other things. Here are some aspects of your daughter's life that you might actively look to protect from the intru-
sion of technology: enjoying face-to-face conversations with

family members, having uninterrupted time to concentrate on homework, being physically active, pursuing hobbies, playing outdoors, and being able to fall asleep quickly and stay asleep through the night. Needless to say, digitally mediated social interactions pose a threat to each of these.

Involve your daughter in deciding how she wants to implement any rules you lay down. Some will be relatively straightforward, such as setting the expectations that phones are never guests at your dinner table, that her technology shuts down by a certain time each night, and that she engages in meaningful activities that require her to take breaks from social media. Other rules will be trickier to make and enforce. It is often the case that teenagers use digital technology to do their homework together, each from her own home. Accordingly, you'll need to talk with your daughter about how she'll know when being connected to her friends while doing homework lowers her stress by helping her get her homework done or when it only adds to it.

Don't underestimate your teenager's capacity to come up with smart solutions. Plenty of girls figure out that they complete homework more efficiently when they use "do not disturb" settings to turn off pinging text notifications and site-blocking software to silence the siren song of their favorite social media sites. A colleague who works at a girls' school discovered a particularly inventive way that several high school juniors barred themselves from social media for the duration of finals. They handed over their passwords to one another and authorized their friends to change them, setting them back again once the exams were over.

That said, girls cannot always be counted on to taper their own social media use when it is causing them more stress than joy, or when it gives rise to poor decision making. I especially admire parents who notice when social media is taking a particularly heavy toll on their daughter and, at least for a little while, reduce her access to technology or adjust her smartphone to turn it into a dumb phone for a few days. Every parent I know who has done this has told me the same story. At first, they encountered fierce resistance from their daughter, who had no interest in scaling back her social media use. Soon thereafter, she seemed more relaxed than she had been in a long time and became her happy old self again.

Just as digital connection can hijack our daughters' waking hours, it can also derail their nights. Protecting a girl's ability to get as much sleep as she needs often means that she'll have to renegotiate her evening relationship with social media.

Sleep vs. Social Media

Few of our daughters get enough sleep, and this is likely one of the simplest, yet most powerful, explanations for girls' high levels of anxiety. Sleep is the glue that holds humans together, and by adolescence girls tend to get less sleep than boys. With the onset of puberty, all teenagers experience a natural phenomenon known as sleep phase delay, which makes it easier for them to stay up later at night and sleep longer in the morning. This biological curveball accounts for why your seven-year-old awakens hours before school starts while your thirteen-year-old might struggle to get up in time to catch the school bus. Girls on average enter puberty around age twelve (versus age fourteen for boys). Unfortunately, this means that by early middle school, our daughters often struggle to fall asleep before ten or eleven at night. With early school start times, it becomes impossible for girls to get the nine hours of sleep—you read that right, *nine* hours—that teenagers actually need.

There's no rocket science behind the connection between sleep loss and anxiety. When we get enough sleep, we can handle most of what life hands us; when we don't, we become frazzled and brittle. An event that would have been merely bothersome to a well-rested high school sophomore, such as leaving a needed textbook at school, can set off a full-blown panic attack in a teenager who is exhausted.

It can be easy for girls to assume that they can swap sleep for caffeine and willpower. But any clinician used to working with teenagers will start by asking one question of a girl who arrives at her office complaining of anxiety: How much sleep are you getting each night? If the answer is that the girl routinely sleeps fewer than seven or eight hours, her anxiety cannot be evaluated, much less treated, until her sleep deprivation is addressed. It's no different than if a person wearing three parkas indoors were to complain of being hot—trying to solve the problem by offering a cool glass of water would be a senseless place to start. When a girl who is bone-tired says that she feels fragile, breathing techniques aren't the answer.

Plenty of things keep girls up at night. Many of our daughters have busy lives after school and may not even dig into their schoolwork until late in the evening. But it is often the case that even when a girl finally puts herself to bed, she's unable to fall asleep. At these times, social media is usually to blame.

Girls' online social activities keep them up in more ways than one. As most of us now know, light emitted by backlit screens suppresses melatonin, a naturally produced sleep hormone that rises at day's end. For this reason, it is incredibly difficult for anyone to fall asleep immediately after interacting with technology for any length of time. Helpfully, many girls use digital applications that adjust the light radiating from their screens to blunt its melatonin-curbing effects. But the light is only part of the problem.

Often I hear from girls that it's the *content* they encounter on their social media sites that keeps them up at night. Picture a girl who successfully stays away from socializing online while she diligently completes her homework. We can easily imagine that she might want to relax at the end of the night by checking in with her online crew. Just as discovering a worrisome, late-night email from one's boss would have any adult staring at the ceiling all night, a girl can be kept up for hours if her quick peek at social media reveals that the *one* classmate she cannot stand is now dating the *one* boy she's crazy about.

All of us, and especially adolescents contending with the realities of sleep phase delay, need to protect our ability to fall and stay asleep. This usually requires that we equate falling asleep with finally coming to the end of a ramp that eases us toward dozing off and not think of it as a switch that we can flip at will. Humans really do need time to unwind—both physically and psychologically—in order to fall asleep. To this end, our daughters should find ways to relax that do not involve social media, such as reading or watching a show they like, for an absolute minimum of thirty minutes before they want to sack out. Furthermore, good things rarely come from having technology in an adolescent's bedroom, especially overnight. Studies show that, even after a teenager falls asleep, it is not unusual for her to be awakened throughout the night by incoming text messages from friends.

Separating your daughter from social media during the pre-bedtime stretch has a double benefit. It forces her to take a break from the taxing constant engagement with her peers, and it will also help her get more of the anxiety-buffering sleep she needs. Indeed, a recent research study that followed teenagers over time found that having nighttime access to a phone undermined the ability to sleep, which, in turn, led to a decline in both self-esteem and the ability to cope with everyday challenges. In sum, sleep loss leads to emotional fragility and increases the likelihood that our daughters will feel on edge throughout the day.

The High Cost of Social Comparison

To be a teenager is to compare oneself to others. We ourselves did it when we were young, and now our kids do it as well. But with ever-present social media, our tweens and teens can now measure themselves against meticulously curated versions of their peers, and carry on with this all day and all night. There is almost no way for this to go well for your daughter. Why? Because she is weighing what she knows about herself—that she is whole and complex and imperfect—against her peers' crafted, polished, and depthless online posts. This is like comparing a lived-in home to a furniture showroom. If outward appearance is the yardstick, the furniture showroom will win every time. And social media, by design, is all about outward appearance.

When girls (and, as they can at times, adults) forget this, they spend a lot of time feeling inadequate as they scrutinize other people's posts. Not surprisingly, research confirms that viewing the social media images of peers who come off as happier, prettier, or better connected takes its toll on a girl's self-esteem. Studies also tell us that girls, more than boys, suffer as a result of their online social comparisons, perhaps because they have been taught by our culture to prioritize their physical appearance. We can't always stand between our daughters and their normal inclination to evaluate themselves against one another, but we can help them gain some stress-relieving perspective about their online worlds.

On a recent caffeine run, I was reminded of just how complex adolescent social comparison becomes when it plays out over social media. As I stood at the end of a long line at my local coffee shop, Shauna, a good friend of mine, slipped out of her place toward the front of the line and took the spot behind me. After we greeted each other warmly, she said, "It's funny that I'm seeing you—I almost picked up the phone to run something by you last night, but it didn't seem like a big enough deal to call about. Is now okay?"

"Of course," I replied. And I meant it. I don't usually wear my professional hat when I'm with my friends, but if they ask for my input, I'm happy to try to help.

"Danielle," she began, dropping her voice and referring to her thirteen-year-old daughter whom I knew well, "was a wreck last night." She paused to collect her thoughts, then continued, "She's got a good group of friends at school but wants to be in with the more popular crowd. So last night we hear her crying up in her room. At first, she refused to talk about what happened. Then it all poured out. Danielle showed me a picture she'd posted—a selfie she took in her room. She actually looked really cute in the picture. But one of the girls in the popular group took a screen shot of the post and shared it in a group text to several classmates. She said in the text that Danielle was 'So fake.' One of Danielle's friends—in what I think was a genuine show of kindness—forwarded the text to Danielle, who, of course, was devastated."

Shauna explained further. "In trying to help me understand what was going on, Danielle showed me that her selfie had gotten more likes and comments than some of the selfies posted by girls in the popular group. The whole thing was so weird that I didn't even know what to say." I shook my head sympathetically and told Shauna that I'd heard similar stories before.

"Last night," added Shauna, "Danielle said that she was too upset to go to school today. She was in better shape this morning, so she went without too much grumbling. I sent her off with a hug, but I wasn't sure what else to do."

"I'm sorry that happened," I said, "and in the short term I think you could point out that what the popular girl did was really mean and that Danielle is probably better off with her real friends in the lower social ranks."

"I did that, and it seemed to help a little."

"Longer term, I think that you might want to have a bigger conversation with her about the fact that there's really no such thing as being 'genuine' on social media."

We headed outside to take advantage of a Cleveland rarity—a mild, sunny day in February. While we leaned against my car in the parking lot sipping our coffees I continued, "Girls get so anxious about what they put up on online and how it will be received. It's a teenager's job to worry about how everyone sees her, but it's our job to help teenagers take a few steps back from the whole thing."

"True," said Shauna, "but I would so love to just do away with social media altogether—I hate how much energy it sucks from Danielle."

"I know, but think of it as giving you an opening to have a conversation we should probably be having with our daughters anyway."

Shauna nodded for me to go on.

"We need to help girls get past judging one another on how 'real' or 'authentic' they are and help them appreciate how we all—both teenagers and adults—craft our online presence to try to present a particular picture of ourselves."

"Yes, that's true," said Shauna. "I know that I use Facebook as a place to try to be funny and interesting—I certainly don't share everything that's on my mind, and I sometimes go back and edit my posts if the tone seems off."

"Yep," I said, "everyone does—and that's not a problem. It's only a problem when teenagers run with the crazy idea that a two-dimensional pixelated space could accurately represent the whole of a real person."

"Right. But how do I bring this up with Danielle?"

"I think that you could tell her what you just told me: that there's an agenda, and for you a totally reasonable one, behind what you choose to share online. And that this is true for everyone."

Girls really do feel better when we remind them that social media is just one big furniture showroom. In the words of Jill Walsh, a sociologist who studies how teenagers engage with social media, young people (and most adults, to be sure) use their posts to show the "highlights reel." They take hundreds of pictures and put up only the best one. They stage and curate their online presence to garner likes and comments, not to let people in on what's really happening.

It can be tempting to be critical of how teens operate online, but it's probably more accurate to assume that if social media had existed back when we were teenagers, we would have used it just as our girls do. In lieu of judgment, we should offer support. This means having conversations designed to reduce some of the stressful inadequacy teens feel as they scrutinize their peers' highlights reels and as they anxiously contrive their own.

Dr. Walsh notes that teenagers use social media to tell a story about themselves and that we can help our daughters engage in some literary criticism about those narratives. "We might ask our teenage girls," she says, " 'What do you think of that picture?' or 'Why was it taken?' or 'Who is it for?' and start a discussion about the agenda behind the image." It's unlikely that raising these questions will inspire your daughter to forsake social media or to stop comparing herself to others. But those aren't realistic goals. Our objective is actually a simple one: to remind our daughters that what they see online does not, and cannot, represent the wonderful, messy complexity of her peers any more than what she posts online tells the whole story about herself.

Finding Comfort with Competition

Our daughters compete with one another both online—as Danielle did when assessing how many likes her selfie received—and offline. Regardless of the arena, peer competition among girls quickly becomes fraught as they struggle to square their wishes to get along with their girlfriends with their wishes to outdo them. It's hardly a surprise that this seemingly no-win situation often becomes a potent source of stress.

One Monday afternoon a couple of years ago, a local pediatrician and longtime colleague left me a voicemail saying, "I've just sent an eleventh grader named Katie your way. She's been complaining of stomach pains for a couple of weeks, but we've ruled out everything we can and are pretty sure that it's just stress. You'll hear from her dad in a day or two about setting up an appointment. By the way, you'll love Katie. She's terrific."

Katie's dad soon called, and I hurried his daughter into my practice because her stomach troubles were so bad that she was leaving school early some days. When I met Katie in my waiting room, I saw immediately what my pediatrician colleague was talking about. Katie announced with her clothing that she was creative and self-assured. Instead of the skintight jeans and extremely fitted tops that are the unofficial uniform of most girls in our community, she wore patterned leggings under a vintage A-line dress that was almost certainly a thrift shop treasure.

We quickly got down to business.

"Your dad told me over the phone that you're doing well in every way he can name—but that your stomach is really bothering you."

Katie answered as if we'd already known each other a long time. "I don't know what's going on. Things seem fine, but about two weeks ago, these stomach pains just showed up out of nowhere, and my doctor can't find a medical explanation."

"Did anything stressful happen around the time the pains started?" I asked. "Our bodies sometimes break down when we're taxed, but everyone's body breaks down in a different way. I get eye infections when I'm on overload but don't always realize that I'm maxed out until one of my eyes starts acting up."

Katie reflected briefly before saying, "Well, a couple of weeks ago, our adviser for the school newspaper announced the application deadline for next year's editors . . . and the application process isn't going well." She paused. "Yeah, to be honest, I think that's been bugging me more than I've wanted to admit."

Katie told me that she had worked for the school newspaper since she was in ninth grade and had decided to pursue a career in journalism. At the end of the school year, juniors were invited to apply for the upcoming year's editorial positions, and Katie was eager to be the paper's editor in chief. Though she went to a coed school, the newspaper staff was dominated by girls, many of whom were Katie's close friends.

She explained, "We don't like to compete against one another, so we decided to pick for ourselves who would apply to each role—chief, sports editor, opinions editor, and features editor. I wanted to apply for chief, but somehow my friends tapped Maddie for it. I love her, and she'd be great at it, but I really wanted a shot. Now I'm stuck. I want the job, but if I apply and get it, my friends will be pissed at me. Even if I didn't care about my friendships, which I do, I'd be setting up a terrible year as chief."

"Sounds like you're damned if you do, damned if you don't."

"Damn right," she joked. "No wonder I'm sick to my stomach."

Our daughters have taken up our encouragement to be wildly ambitious, yet they struggle to compete with their peers in ways that feel socially acceptable. Rigorous competition always involves a dose of healthy aggression, a drive to outperform others. But girls don't always know how to reconcile their competitive feelings with the lifetime of instruction to be nice. As we could predict, this leaves girls, far more than boys, worrying that competing against their friends will damage their friendships. They often find themselves trying to figure out how to make a splash without making any waves.

It's both impressive and alarming to catalog the many ways that ambitious girls twist themselves into pretzels to avoid the appearance of being cutthroat. When they do well, they cloak or misrepresent how hard they actually worked. Or they feign disappointment with a test result when they have, in fact, gotten a very high score. Or they ask forgiveness for their success; one tennis coach told me that he spent an entire season beseeching a talented player to stop apologizing every time she hit a winning shot. Or, like Katie and her friends, they come up with elaborate schemes to try to avoid the problem altogether.

We can help our daughters feel less stressed when competing by illuminating the difference between being an aggressive competitor and being an aggressive person. When they are young, we can model this distinction as we play games against our daughters. Though it can be tempting to let our daughter win, doing so unhelpfully suggests that beating her is somehow unkind. Instead of going easy on girls (or taking gleeful delight in defeating them), we can play to win while simultaneously encouraging and celebrating our girl every time she makes a smart move or scores. If our daughters feel discouraged about losing to us, we can say with compassion, "It's not easy to play against an adult. But when you win, which you will, you'll know that you beat me for real. You'll feel great about it, and I'll be excited for you, too."

We can also point to the many excellent examples of professional female athletes who are fierce competitors *while competing* and incredibly gracious people once the match has ended. When watching Olympic swimming (my favorite) with my own daughters, I'll often say, "Just look at these women. In the water, they are sharks. On land, they do nothing but cheer for one another." We can tell our daughters that they should go all out when they are in the proverbial pool, such as on tests, at auditions, when performing, and during competitions. Then we can remind them that, once back on land, we expect them to celebrate and support their peers, regardless of how things went in the water.

Envy's Inevitable

It's easy enough for a girl to celebrate her competitors when she's winning, but it's much harder when things are not going well. Given how devoted our daughters are to their friends, it can be exquisitely painful for them to resent the success of someone they really like and care about. My work with Katie drove this point home.

As we talked through the problem that had brought her my way, Katie realized that she could alert the newspaper adviser, who happened to be a teacher she really admired and trusted, to what was going on.

"She's solid—and I know that she'd want us to have a fair competition. Of course she's expecting to get more than one application for each spot so I could let her know that that will only happen if she requires us to apply for at least two jobs each. Then she decides who gets the spots. And we don't." Looking visibly relieved, Katie added, "That would be much better."

Her idea was a great one. I gave Katie my number and let her know that she should feel free to update me on how things unfolded and to come back for another appointment if her stomach pains didn't go away.

Two weeks later, we were meeting again at Katie's request and with her parents' support. Her plan to talk with the newspaper adviser had worked, and she'd applied for the jobs of editor in

chief and opinions editor. To her disappointment, Katie was ap-
pointed the opinions editor.

"My friend Trish will be the editor in chief, and she'll do the
job well," she said with her eyes cast down. "But I really wanted
it . . . I feel like it's what I've been working toward since ninth
grade."

Now teary, Katie added, "I can live with being opinions editor.
But honestly . . . the hardest part is that I'm really jealous of
Trish. We hang out all the time, and it's just hard to be comfort-
able around her because I feel like I should be okay with it. But
I'm not."

"Listen," I said, wanting to ease Katie's conscience, "competitive feelings aren't always rational. There's no need to feel guilty
about them. They just come with the territory of being an ambitious person."

Katie studied me as I explained, "It's okay to be jealous of your
friend or to be angry that she got the job you wanted. Those feelings don't cancel out the fact that you like her, respect her, and
may even feel happy for her, too."

"Yeah. I actually *am* happy for her—and I know that she's really
psyched about it."

"It's strange, but your envy of Trish and your happiness for
her can actually live side by side. The only thing you should feel
bad about is if you *act* on your jealousy in some unkind way."

"Oh. No. That's not something I'd do," Katie said hastily.

I nodded vigorously to let her know that I didn't think she
would.

"We're cool in person, but I've just been mad at myself for feeling mad at her."

"Well," I said, "I'm hoping you can let yourself off that hook.
Judge yourself for what you do, not what you think or feel.
Because if you're going to be someone who really goes for it"—
I smiled warmly to indicate that I loved her determination—

"you're going to feel crummy, and perhaps a little bitter, when things don't go your way. Don't beat yourself up about it or get weighed down by it. Acknowledge it to yourself, then just keep going."

While it can be agonizing for our daughters to envy their close friends, it's also painful for girls to covet the trendy clothes, cool summer plans, or lax rules of other teenagers they know. As parents, we are often caught up in the stress our daughters feel as they compare themselves to their peers because we either cannot, or will not, help them keep up with the Joneses at school.

Even when we refuse to stretch our values or family budgets, we can ease our daughter's discomfort by acknowledging how helpless her envy makes her feel. We might say, for example, "It's natural to want the nice things that other people have. I sometimes feel that way when I see an expensive car. But, as an adult, it's easier for me to stand my envy because I've made decisions about my priorities along the way. For now, you're stuck with the choices we make for you and I know that's not always so great. Before long, though, you'll have more say."

Girls' relationships with their female friends can be both wonderful and fraught. The same can be said for their relationships with boys. What we teach girls about how to have healthy conflicts extends to all of their relationships; and if they ever feel pitted against one another for a boy's attention, the guidance we provide on weathering competition with other girls will come in handy. But these aren't the only ways that guys add to girls' stress and anxiety. So let's turn our attention to how we can help our daughters navigate the sometimes challenging waters of connecting with boys.

CHAPTER FOUR

Girls Among Boys

IN ADDITION TO MEETING WITH GIRLS AT LAUREL SCHOOL FOR ONE-on-one conversations, I also have the privilege of talking with them in groups about the common challenges they face. When the students are in the ninth grade, we convene weekly to address the social, emotional, and intellectual demands that come with the transition to high school. Our regular sessions allow me to get to know the girls in each class and to lay the groundwork for our ongoing future meetings that happen once every couple of months from their sophomore year until they graduate.

In the fall of 2017, my first visit with a group of the older high school girls fell in November. Not having seen them since the year before, I was excited to check in. With the ninth graders, I usually have an agenda, so that we can be sure to cover key health and safety topics ranging from sleep to substance abuse. But when I get together with the tenth, eleventh, or twelfth grades, my plans are less structured. I come to our sessions with a few ideas about what we might discuss and always ask if there's something particular on their minds.

On that late November morning, sixty-five girls assembled in one of Laurel's larger classrooms. There weren't enough chairs and desks for everyone, but as usual, plenty of students welcomed the chance to sit on the floor, with their legs crossed or stretched out. They didn't have a collective, pressing concern to address, so I floated a topic that was front and center for many adults at that time. The #metoo movement was dominating the headlines and had triggered a massive and unprecedented public examination of the sexualized abuse of power. I thought it might be helpful to chat with the Laurel girls about the nature of sexual harassment and how they could advocate for themselves should they come across it.

I asked, "Do you guys want to talk about the #metoo stuff?"

"Yes," they replied almost in unison. They then proceeded to spend the next fifty minutes pouring out alarming and detailed accounts of the sexually aggressive behavior to which they were *already* subjected by the boys in their social circles and strangers out in public. I was floored. For as much as I think I know about teenage girls, and as close as my professional life brings me to their day-to-day experiences, I truly had no idea what many of the girls were encountering on a regular basis.

I should note that I did not, on that day, talk with the girls about their enriching friendships and romances with boys. And the girls did not bring up their positive connections to guys their age because they don't need my help with those relationships. Although I know that many girls at Laurel do have boys in their lives who are dedicated and delightful friends or devoted and car-ing boyfriends, our discussion centered on their interactions with boys that left them feeling uneasy or afraid. This chapter, like my conversation with the Laurel girls, will focus on the ways in which boys sometimes add to girls' stress and anxiety.

There is no question that guys often make girls' lives better as well. In fact, appreciating just how great boys can be helpfully illustrates—for ourselves and our daughters—that being out of line is a choice some guys make, not a form of treatment girls somehow provoke.

Daily Disrespect

The stories came out slowly in the beginning but gained speed as the girls built on one another's experiences. First, one girl volunteered that the guys she knew outside of school casually threw around slurs such as *ho* and *slut*.

"They even do it," another girl jumped in, "about the most random stuff. Like if you trip while walking, they'll say," deepening her voice and adopting a mocking tone, "'You tripped—you're such a whore!'"

"And if you push back, they're so immature about it," a third girl added in exasperation. "They'll say that you're being ridiculous—that they were only kidding. I know that we joke around with them sometimes . . ."

"They grab our butts, too," said a girl who was sitting cross-legged on the floor and fidgeting with a ring she was wearing. Several classmates nodded to confirm her point.

"What?!" I replied, making no attempt to hide my surprise and disapproval.

"Yeah," a girl with long, dark hair chimed in matter-of-factly, "if you're taking a group photo, they think it's totally okay to put their hands on your butt."

"Really?" I said. "Can't you tell them to knock it off?"

"You can try," she replied, "but they'll usually just be jerks about it or say that you're overreacting."

A student in the back of the room raised her hand to share that she had, indeed, made an issue of it with a guy she knew from her old school. "I was hanging out with a bunch of my friends and one of the guys in the group thought it was really funny to come up behind me and snap my bra strap through my shirt. I told him to stop it and he got all mad." She paused before adding, "He cut me off on social media and doesn't talk to me anymore."

"Wow . . ." I said slowly before shifting from shock to sympathy to ask, "are you okay with losing that friendship?"

"Yes. I am. Especially if that's how he's going to act." Then she added with a tinge of sadness, "But honestly, I did not expect him to take his reaction that far."

The stories kept coming. They talked about boys they knew who wanted every greeting to include a hug, and guys they didn't know following them around the mall with a persistence that felt not only unwelcome but menacing. Over and over they described how guys crossed lines with them *and* how they were made to feel as though they had no right to react to these boundary violations.

"Once, when I was doing community service downtown with my youth group," offered a girl who was swinging her legs back and forth while sitting on a desk, "I was catcalled by some road workers. It really freaked me out, so the next time we were leaving the place where we do the service project, I asked the boys who were with me if we could walk a different way." She continued, "They asked what my problem was, so I told them. And they said that I was being dumb about it."

I really shouldn't have been as surprised as I was by what the Laurel girls had to share. Though they spend their days in an all-girls' environment, the descriptions of the harassment they receive from boys and men outside of school have been confirmed by research from around the country. A report from the American Association of University Women found that nearly half of all eighth- through eleventh-grade girls had been touched, grabbed, pinched, or intentionally brushed up against in a sexual way *while at school*. In the same survey, girls also reported that boys at school drew penises in their notebooks, commented on their breasts, stared down their shirts, and started rumors about their sexual lives.

The girls at Laurel and the survey data bring two problems to

light: that sexual harassment is commonplace among adolescents, and that girls are routinely made to feel that they should
not complain about it. Indeed, the survey found that girls who
shared their sexual harassment experiences with others were
often told that the harassment was just a joke, that it wasn't a big
deal, or that the girl should forget it or at least stop worrying
about it.

Our meeting also brought a third, and perhaps even more
troubling, concern to the surface: many of the girls seemed to
feel ashamed of the harassment they'd endured and uncertain of
their culpability. As much as the girls clearly wanted to talk about
what they were experiencing, there was a strange undercurrent to
our conversation. The girls weren't just telling me about what
they'd endured; it was as though they were *confessing* their experiences of sexual harassment. These empowered young women
seemed, at some level, to be wondering what *they* had done wrong
to bring about their mistreatment.

We were nearing the end of the class period, and I had done
little but listen. It was clearly useful for the girls to talk openly
with one another about what they'd been through, but I didn't
want class to end before I could say something about the un-
named, yet palpable, sense of shame that some of the girls were
harboring. Thankfully, a student sitting near the front of the
room put the question of blame right before us.

"But," she said sheepishly, "we *do* wear leggings as pants sometimes."

"True," I said, feeling grateful for the opening she'd created,
"but let's get something totally clear: you are *never* at fault when
boys or men degrade you. The fact that guys sometimes make
inappropriate comments or advances has absolutely nothing to
do with what you are wearing, how you look, whether you're at a
party or a dance, or anywhere else. Harassment is about, and *only*

about, someone trying to feel big by making someone else feel small. It's that simple, and I can prove it to you."

From there, I went on to tell them about an encounter I'd had only a few months prior. I was at a business event and wearing a professional outfit when I found myself talking with a group of men whom I'd just met. Shortly into the conversation, one of the guys in the exchange learned that I had written the book about adolescent girls that was, at the time, resting on his wife's bedside table. Without skipping a beat, he said to me provocatively, "I bet you're in *lots* of bedrooms."

"Whoa!" said the girls in response to my story. "What did you do?"

"I froze. That's the problem when someone crosses a line. The interaction swerves so quickly that you're knocked off balance."

"So nothing happened? You just dropped it?" they asked, clearly disappointed with where the story seemed to be headed.

"Actually," I replied, "the other men in the conversation called him out right away. I was so appreciative. The guy who said it soon clearly wished he hadn't, and I wasn't the one who had to push back." Sharing my story gave me an idea for how we could end our session on a helpful note. "Before you go," I said, "let's talk about whom you can tell if you run into sexual harassment, and how you can stick up for one another if you're around boys who are being inappropriate."

Helping Girls Handle Harassment

When I walked out of my meeting with the Laurel students, it was clear to me that adults have not done nearly enough to acknowledge, much less address, the harassment teenage girls face on a regular basis. Furthermore, it was obvious that our girls needed effective strategies for dealing with tawdry, humiliating slurs and unwanted advances. Girls are stressed by harassment, and they feel threatened by the boundary crossings they encounter. If we are going to help girls manage the tension and anxiety that sexually aggressive behavior inspires, we'll need to create the conditions that allow them to talk openly about it.

It's easy for parents to underestimate how much indecency girls endure because our daughters are often reluctant to tell us about it. The more I reflected on the undercurrent of shame that ran through my meeting with the Laurel girls, the more I came to appreciate just how diabolical sexual harassment really is. How we are viewed by others can shape how we view ourselves. This can happen in good ways. When a respected friend or colleague calls to ask our advice, we rise to the occasion, feeling smarter or more capable than we did before the phone rang. It can also happen in bad ways. If a friend is cagey about some personal news, we can question whether we're as trustworthy as we once thought.

When an adolescent girl (or adult woman, for that matter) is addressed in a degrading way, she might be reduced by the knowledge that she is viewed, at least by one person, as somehow deserving of such treatment. A teenage girl might keep a demeaning experience to herself because she believes that it reflects poorly on her that she was subjected to harassment at all.

Our daughters may also be reluctant to tell us about their runins with boys because they worry about how we'll react. They're probably right to assume that we won't be happy to hear the news. From there, a girl may fear that if she tells us about any sexually aggressive behavior she's endured, she'll actually land *herself* in the hot seat (as in, "What were you doing hanging out with that kid in the first place?" or "Are you sure you weren't flirting with him?" or "What were you wearing?"). Alternately, she may fear that our protective instincts will prompt us to intervene in ways that, as far as she's concerned, will only make matters worse. With this perspective in mind, we shouldn't wait for our daughters to bring up the topic of sexual harassment.

By seventh grade or sooner, consider asking your daughter how the boys at her school are acting and whether they are being consistently respectful of the girls. If she has stories to share about what she's already managing or witnessing, tell your daughter how glad you are that she let you know and that you stand ready to help her take steps to resolve any problem she's having with a boy's behavior. If she seems surprised by the question or clams up, let her know that you have heard about guys crossing lines with girls, assuring her that you'll never make her feel sorry if she seeks your help on this topic. To this you might add, "Harassment doesn't say anything about the victim, but it says a lot about the person who does it." The more we pull sexually aggressive behavior out of the shadows, the more we minimize the needless shame girls feel about being mistreated.

As you introduce these conversations, make it clear to your daughter that you're ready to talk with her about situations that may feel murky to her. What if she flirts with somebody who then takes the interaction down an offensive road? What if she goes to the mall wearing leggings and then hears from guys who comment on the shape of her butt?

Sometimes the guidance we offer as part of these conversations will be clear-cut. For example, we can remind our daughter that it is never okay for someone to be rude or sleazy toward anyone else. At other times, we may find ourselves wrestling with tough questions. When his daughter was thirteen, one of my friends said to me, "I can't stand the idea of guys catcalling her, yet I worry that telling her how to dress makes it sound as if she's at fault if it happens. What should I do?"

"I'm not sure," I said, "but a good first step might be to say to your daughter what you just said to me and see what she thinks you—and she—should do."

Do not assume that your daughter is insulated from being harassed by boys if she identifies as lesbian or bisexual. Studies document that high school girls who are not heterosexual are subjected to at least as much sexual harassment as their straight classmates. Research also shows that being sexually harassed is linked to higher levels of psychological stress and lower levels of self-esteem in all girls, and that these outcomes are intensified for girls who are gay, bisexual, or in flux about their sexual orientation. It's challenging enough to be a sexual minority in middle school or high school; having to cope with harassment about one's sexual identity almost certainly makes an already stressful situation even harder. To make matters worse, lesbian, bisexual, or questioning students may not feel they can seek help from their peers or parents when they are on the receiving end of sexualized slurs, teasing, rumor spreading, or worse.

There are two key takeaways from the research on the high levels of sexual harassment endured by girls who aren't straight. One is that we need to go out of our way to address hostile behavior targeted at students who are sexual minorities. Fortunately, research establishes that a protective school climate and strong support at home buffer the harmful effects of harassment directed at nonheterosexual adolescents. The other is a reminder to check any impulse to blame the victim when we hear that girls and young women are being sexually harassed. Should girls complain about guys' behavior, they often run into questions about the signals they're giving off. The fact that girls who aren't straight are routinely harassed underscores that indecent behavior on the part of boys has nothing to do with how girls are conducting themselves in the heterosexual marketplace and everything to do with guys making a decision to act out.

Once we're openly discussing sexual harassment, we can talk with our daughters about how frightening it can be. Catcalling, leering, and sexual comments aren't harmless. Girls get nervous with good reason when boys are out of bounds, and the *last* thing we want to do is tell girls that these situations are not a big deal. The anxiety girls feel when boys and men cross lines with them is the healthy kind—the brand of discomfort that alerts us to threats and tells us to get up our guard.

To your daughter you might say, "It's actually scary when a guy says or does something inappropriate. Even if it's not something big, at some level, every girl or woman thinks, 'If he'll try that, what else will he try?'" Males usually hold more cultural sway and almost always have more physical strength than females. Accordingly, most girls and women have a primitive fear reaction that kicks in when a guy advertises that he's willing to try to abuse his power. "Even if a guy is just giving you the creeps," we might add, "I want you to take that feeling seriously and get some distance from him or get some help."

Having established that our daughters shouldn't feel ashamed if they are harassed—and that they should pay attention to the discomfort they feel when treated in degrading ways—we can talk with them about the fact that harassment is actually a sexualized form of bullying. Bullies use social or physical power to intimidate and demean others. Harassers put a sleazy spin on the same dynamic, simply deploying vulgar language and unwanted advances to accomplish the same end.

Girls usually know a lot more than adults think they do about being bullied by boys. The cultural preoccupation with mean girls has drawn our attention away from the well-established research finding that girls are more likely to be bullied by boys than by other girls, in part because boys go after both male and female peers while girls rarely target guys. Boys not only outpace girls in their use of physical and verbal bullying tactics (such as name-calling), but they have also been found by some studies to engage in more relational bullying (e.g., rumor spreading, exclusion) and cyberbullying, two forms of aggression for which girls are disproportionately blamed. Research on girls comparing the psycho-logical costs of being bullied versus being sexually harassed shows that both forms of mistreatment cause harm, but that sexual harassment is even more likely than bullying to under-mine their academic performance and leave them feeling both unsupported by their teachers and alienated from their school communities.

Years of research on bullying and harassment have taught us a few things about what to do. First, as already noted, we need to make sure that shame doesn't keep young people who are being mistreated from speaking up and seeking help. Second, we need to empower bystanders—any witnesses who are present when bullying or harassment occurs—to stick up for the victim. To both our daughters and our sons we should say, "If you're stand-ing there when someone's being mean or sexually inappropriate, you've got an obligation to do something. You need to protect the person who is being attacked, tell an adult what's happening, or both."

Above all, our daughters should not feel helpless in the face of cruelty, and they should not be expected to deal with guys' inap-propriate behavior without support, and perhaps intervention, from grown-ups. Most adult women feel confounded by sexual harassment when it occurs, so we should not expect that our daughters will be able to manage it on their own.

The Harmful Offense-Defense Paradigm

Some girls are sexually aggressive with boys. While guys are more likely to harass girls than the other way around, mistreatment is not a one-way street. Research reveals that girls harass boys some-times in person, but more frequently in digital environments. By their own admission, 6 percent of girls had badgered a boy to send nude photos, 9 percent had sent an unsolicited risqué photo, and 5 percent had, in online environments, pressured boys to engage in sexual activity (for boys, the comparable numbers were 22, 8, and 19 percent, respectively).

These findings match some of the stories I hear in my practice. On more than one occasion, parents of sons have asked me what they should do about girls who seem to be downright predacious. To state the obvious, I don't think that we should welcome it as a positive step toward sexual equity. There's no reason to celebrate girls when they join the boys who are rolling in the mud of beastly behavior. That said, we should pause for a moment to recognize that, even when girls do mistreat boys, research tells us that it doesn't usually have the same negative impact as the reverse. The differentials in social power and physical strength between males and females probably explain why girls who are harassed by boys consistently report feeling more threatened than boys who are harassed by girls.

For example, a close colleague recently called me to consult about a twelve-year-old girl she was seeing in her practice. The girl's parents had engaged my friend for help after a routine check of their daughter's cellphone revealed that she'd been pestering a boy in her class to send her a photo of his genitals. In return, she offered to send along a picture of her breasts. When the boy finally gave in to the girl's repeated requests, the girl made good on her promise. "I'm not sure where to begin," said my colleague, "because this poor kiddo now has two problems. We started working together because her parents wanted to get to the bottom of why she thought it was okay to bug the boy for nude pictures. Yet in the meantime, the photo *she* sent has started a social firestorm at school. None of the kids at her school cares that *he* texted *her* a picture of his penis, but several of them are putting up posts calling my client a whore. She's now refusing to go to school, and I can understand why."

Obviously, being coercive or degrading toward others is out of bounds for everyone. And though I don't have a watertight explanation for what's going on with the girls who are crossing lines with boys, I do have an idea for how we might understand this unwelcome turning of the tables. Without being consciously aware of doing so, adults give young people the impression that, in the romantic sphere, one person plays offense and the other plays defense. We advance this misguided idea in more ways than we realize, and when we do, we suggest that boys are usually the ones trying to score and that it falls to girls to hold them off.

When I hear about sexually aggressive behavior in girls, I see it as a by-product of this toxic premise. Girls who are uneasy with this arrangement but know of no other might decide that if the only choices are to be the one who presses or the one who succumbs, they'll take a turn at pressing. None of this is good for our daughters or our sons, but the situation won't improve until we dismantle the problematic framework itself. Let's address how we arrived at this troublesome place so that we can guide young people down a healthier path.

Gendered Sex Ed

Both in our homes and in our schools, a strange pattern reveals itself when we talk with young people about their emerging romantic lives. It turns out that adults tend to give two different versions of "the talk," one to girls and one to boys. To girls, we usually say something along these lines: "As you think about your love life, there are a few key things to consider. First, you don't want to put yourself in a bad position where things can go further than you wished. Second, you don't want to get a sexually transmitted infection. And third, you don't want to get pregnant." Some adults also add, "Oh, and watch out for your reputation. You don't want to be known for being loose or easy." Research tells us that boys usually get a different and much shorter message, which transmits roughly as, "Dude, when you have sex, be sure to wear a condom and be sure to get the girl's consent."

Teenagers aren't dumb. They pick up the clear, if unspoken, meanings behind these gender-specific spiels. Boys hear adults saying that all guys possess a strong desire to have sex, and while giving guys full license to act on this drive, we caution them against exposing themselves to infections, the possibility of an unwanted pregnancy, or accusations of misconduct. And girls only hear a list of *don't*s. After several years of giving the don't-centric talk to girls at Laurel School as part of our sexual education program, it dawned on me, quite uncomfortably, that my underlying message was really "Ladies, the adults would prefer it if you weren't sexually active." Reflecting further on the matter (and becoming even *more* uncomfortable), I realized that underneath the "please don't have sex" message was another one: "Also, ladies, we're going to ask you to be in charge of regulating adolescent sexuality. Because we're not going to ask the boys."

As an advocate for girls, it was hard to stomach the fact that I'd been actively participating in advancing a double standard around young people's love lives. As a psychologist, it became clear to me that the stock sex talk for girls probably caused them a significant amount of psychological stress. When we fail to acknowledge that girls come equipped with sexual desire, we essentially say to them, "The adults are not okay with the fact that you have erotic leanings. So we're going to ignore those impulses entirely and focus instead on telling you to ride the romantic brakes while the boys step on the gas."

This messaging essentially communicates that there's something beyond the pale with girls who take an interest in sex. So what's a young woman to do when her mind and body are telling her one thing and the adults are telling her another? Often, girls are left feeling anxious and ashamed about their normal and expectable feelings.

You may have already bucked this unfortunate cultural trend in your own home by greeting the dawn of your daughter's love life as a happy and healthy development. But even if your messaging about her emerging sexuality is positive and equitable, your daughter will hear something different from the rest of the world, so we need to address that, too. I'm sure that I don't have to tell you that the cultural bias against female desire is firmly encoded in our language. We have a noxious glossary of terms that describe girls and young women who are seen as sexually permissive, such as *slut, thot* (a newish term that's short for "that ho over there"), *tramp, floozy, bimbo,* and so on.

Player is one of the very few terms that we have to describe guys with busy love lives. However, unlike the comparable words we have for girls, many boys would wear *player* with pride because they have been raised in a culture that prizes virile men. The most derogatory sexualized term now available for males seems to be *fuckboy,* which applies to guys who are known to toy with girls, to pursue several flings at once, and to want only fleeting, physical encounters. Yet when I ask girls if it's as damaging for a guy to be called a fuckboy as it is for a girl to be called a slut, they respond with a resounding and unqualified "no."

Sexual double standards come at a high cost to our daughters' psychological health. A research report aptly titled "Damned If You Do, Damned If You Don't . . . If You're a Girl" examined the dynamics that unfold around sexting between teenagers. This study, like others, found that both boys and girls send nude digital photos but that boys are far more likely to pressure girls to do so. Moreover, the girls in this study reported that they were disparaged by boys no matter what they did. Those who refused to send nude photos were dubbed prudes, while those who gave in to the pressure to sext were called sluts. And as my colleague found with her young client who harassed a boy in her class for a nude photo, the guys in the study were "virtually immune from criticism," whether they sexted or not.

Of course, it's a bad idea for any minor to send along a nude photo. To this end, we have made a widespread practice of telling girls not to send sexts, but we almost never tell boys not to *ask* for them. And ask for them they do. One study found that more than two-thirds of girls between the ages of twelve and eighteen had been asked, and sometimes harassed or threatened, by boys to share nude photos. That we fail to make an issue of boys badgering girls for sexts highlights how much adults, without even meaning to, accept and perpetuate the problematic boys-on-offense-girls-on-defense framework. We charge girls, and only girls, with responsibility for policing adolescent sexual behavior. All of this leaves our daughters in a psychologically taxing position: where in the end they are, as the study says, damned if they do and damned if they don't.

Bringing Equity to "The Talk"

To do right by our daughters and our sons, we should toss out our gender-specific sex talks and move toward a single approach for advising young people on their emerging love lives. While we're at it, we should follow the guidance of Dr. Mary Ott, a pediatrician specializing in adolescent sexual health, who notes, "We want our teenagers to develop meaningful relationships and we want them to experience intimacy." To this end, she recommends that we "move our conversations about sex away from sex as a risk factor category and toward sex as part of healthy development."

In practice, this means that we should say to our tweens and teenagers, "As you're thinking about the physical side of your romantic life, you should start by reflecting on what you *want*. You should tune into what you would like to have happen, what would be fun for you, what would feel good." I appreciate that these are not always comfortable discussions to have with our children and that parents who utter these two sentences might tempt their teenager to contemplate throwing herself from a moving car to bring the conversation to an end. But say these words, or something like them anyway. If we want to help relieve our daughters of the tremendous stress created by our prevailing sexual culture, we need to not only acknowledge but also warmly approve of their healthy desire.

When you feel your daughter can stand to continue on this topic, you should add, "After you get a sense of what you'd like to have happen, the next thing to consider is what your *partner* would like to have happen. This will require some communication—you'll need to know each other well enough to learn this." In other words, we want to underscore the value of having an honest and trusting relationship with one's romantic companion.

When I talk with girls about their romantic lives, I always say *partner* and almost never say *boy*, unless I happen to be talking about a distinctly heterosexual phenomenon, such as unintended pregnancy. My one-size-fits-all spiel outlines the rules of engagement for both those who are straight and those who are not and, actually, for people of all ages. Too often, adults unwittingly (or, perhaps, wittingly) sideline young people who are gay, lesbian, bisexual, or questioning by framing romance only in heterosexual terms. *Everyone* benefits when we drop our troublesome vanquisher-vanquished heterosexual framework and remember that physical intimacy should be a joyful, collaborative endeavor in any form it takes.

Though I am offering a compact guide here, the reality is that talking about physical romance is something we should do repeatedly with our children. There are two good reasons for this. First, as already noted, girls are not always eager to discuss their love lives with their folks (plenty of adults find this topic to be intensely awkward, too!). Accordingly, it can be helpful for parents to make their points efficiently, dip in and out of these conversations, and expect little in the way of a response. If your daughter happens to be eager to talk about her romantic life, feel free to follow her lead into a deeper discussion. But if your efforts to broach the subject—perhaps by saying, "This is probably obvious, but it still feels worth mentioning: you should really enjoy your love life and only share it with partners who care that you do"—are met with a chilly reception, don't despair. It's still valuable for your daughter to know where you stand.

Second, the nature and focus of these conversations will change as our daughters grow. With younger girls (such as those in late elementary or early middle school), we can adopt a decidedly G-rated approach to introducing the idea of girls attending to what *they* want. Should your daughter mention that a boy in her class had already announced his intention to slow dance with one of her friends at an upcoming sixth-grade social, you can ask lightheartedly, "That's sweet . . . do you think that's also what she wants?" As our girls get older, the plots of their favorite shows, the lyrics in the music they listen to, or even the comments they make about their classmates can provide parents with openings to underscore their daughters' right to an enjoyable and equitable romantic life.

At times, girls may take the lead in these conversations. But if they don't, we should. When my older daughter was in seventh grade, I found myself standing behind the mother of one of her classmates, a girl named Lexi, when I was checking out at the grocery store. I like this mom a lot and often run into her at school functions and around town. When she saw me on that day she said enthusiastically, "Oh, you'll love this! A few nights ago Lexi asked me out of the blue, 'Why are there words for girls like *ho* and *slut,* but nothing similar for boys?'" While loading her groceries onto the conveyer belt Lexi's mom continued, "I said, 'Good question!' and then pointed out that our words say a lot about what we believe as a culture and that, unfortunately, we don't really have positive words for girls with active love lives."

"I'm glad Lexi asked that question, and I'm glad you took the opportunity to highlight how sexism gets built into our language." To that I added, "Let's hope that our daughters find the right words to describe healthy female sexuality, because *we* certainly didn't grow up with them."

We want our daughters to cultivate a strong sense of personal agency in their romantic lives: they should enjoy themselves and never be exploited or mistreated. So let's turn our attention to how we have *that* conversation.

Consent Doesn't Cut It

Taking a positive view of our daughters' emerging love lives when the topic first crops up—usually in middle school—lays the groundwork for addressing the next element of any healthy romance: coming to agreement. "Once you know what you want and what your partner wants," you might say, "then you can figure out where you enthusiastically agree." I recognize that this is the part of the conversation where we usually talk about consent—often in high school—but I think that we need to seriously reconsider our widespread use of that word when we're offering guidance to young people about sexual intimacy. Put simply, to require mere consent sets an incredibly low bar for entering into what should be the shared pleasure of physical romance.

With both our daughters and our sons, we can point out that even though adults often emphasize the critical importance of consent, the word itself is a legal term that articulates a minimum standard of one person granting permission to another. We can say, "Something's wrong if you're granting someone *permission* to take you on a date, to hold your hand, or to do anything else. Your love life should be a whole lot more fun than that!" We should also add that we would never want our child to take a response of "Okay . . . fine" from a romantic partner as a green light for sexual activity. A healthy love life centers on finding areas of joyful agreement. As we're welcoming young people into the world of romance, we should hold them to the highest possible standards—not the lowest.

We can continue to talk in terms of granting consent when describing interactions such as authorizing an endodontist to perform a root canal. And we can confirm for our children what they will hear elsewhere, that if they don't gain clear consent from their romantic partners, they risk committing a crime. But we should not stop there when talking with young people about what their love lives should look like. Accepting bare permission as an adequate standard reinforces precisely the anxiety-provoking offense-defense framework we are trying to move beyond.

And from a slightly different angle, although consent is a two-way street, when we use the term, we often have in mind the fact that boys can physically overpower girls, and therefore they should be sure to acquire consent before proceeding. So when we talk about sexual activity largely in terms of consent, girls hear the stressful message that boys are going to press them to do things and that they must act as the gatekeepers who determine what boys can and cannot do. When we instead talk in terms of coming to enthusiastic agreement with one's partner, we replace a stressful model with a happy one.

Sexual Empowerment Protects Sexual Health

Once we have clarified for our daughter that she and her romantic partner should be in enthusiastic agreement about their plans, what comes next? Our daughter should ask herself if the agreed-upon activity comes with any hazards that need to be managed. We might say, "When you and your partner decide together what you want to do, next you should consider what risks you might face. Could feelings get hurt if your plans mean one thing to you and another thing to your partner? Could you get a sexually transmitted infection? Could you get pregnant?"

Some adults may worry that talking about risk management *after* we talk about the delights of physical romance might keep girls from prioritizing their sexual health. Research, however, suggests the opposite. Girls who aren't well acquainted with their own sexual wishes are the ones who are most likely to make compromises in their physical relationships, to go along with sexual activity they don't actually want, and to put their health at risk. Studies have also found that young women who subscribe to conventional gender roles—such as embracing the idea that, in the bedroom, boys lead and girls follow—are less likely to use contraception or take steps to prevent a sexually transmitted infection than girls who question gendered conventions.

In the Netherlands, adolescent sexuality has long been seen as healthy and natural, for both boys and girls, and is discussed openly at home and at school. Experts point to these cultural factors, as well as the Dutch health system that provides easy access to contraception, when explaining the fact that the Netherlands has the lowest rates of teen pregnancies, births, and abortions among industrialized countries, while America has the highest. Indeed, researchers who interviewed American and Dutch college women about their sexual educations and attitudes found a stark divide between women from the two countries. For example, a Dutch college woman explained that she and her partner "made a plan together about how far we wanted to go and what protection we would use," while an American college woman declared that taking steps to prepare for the possibility of having sex, such as purchasing condoms, "means a girl is a slut."

Here's the bottom line: girls who feel that they *don't* have a right to enjoy physical sexuality lead romantic lives marked by stress and anxiety. During make-out sessions they fret about their reputations instead of enjoying themselves. They let boys dictate the terms of engagement instead of advocating for what they do and don't want. And they fail to take the necessary steps to protect their sexual health, turning physical intimacy into a high-risk, worrisome event. When we encourage our girls to become comfortable with their developing sexuality, they are more likely to go on to have the safe and enjoyable love lives they deserve.

Many Ways to Say No to Sex

We should not, of course, address our daughters as if they, but not boys, are responsible for regulating what happens in their heterosexual love lives. But there *will* be times when your daughter wants to do less than her partner does. Unfortunately, that same treacherous offense-defense framework informs the guidance we currently give girls and young women about how to handle these moments. We routinely teach girls that the only way to turn down sexual activity is with a clear, direct, unmodulated, and unvarnished "no."

This guidance partly comes, like our focus on consent, from the courtroom. It is certainly well-meaning, as questions about whether or not a date rape occurred often pivot on how *clearly* the young woman stated that she did not wish to have sex. It also partly comes, I believe, from our all-important wish to teach our daughters that they are equals of men, entitled—especially in matters pertaining to their own bodies—to use their veto power without embarrassment or apology. There are, however, *many* ways for our daughters to unambiguously articulate what they do and don't want. Prioritizing a bald "no" over all other options may not always be practical in real life.

I was recently reminded of this when I got together for lunch with an astute colleague who works at a university counseling center. We met up at a fast-food Asian restaurant, placing our orders up front and carrying our trays to a quiet corner. After we checked in on each other's families and upcoming summer plans, she shifted gears abruptly and said with some urgency, "There's something I feel like I'm seeing all the time now, and I want to know if you're seeing it, too." The level of concern in her voice put me on edge. She went on. "Over the past few years, I'm hearing from more and more young women who come in for help because they're upset with themselves for having sex with someone when they didn't want to." I nodded for her to continue. "They knew at the time that they didn't want to go through with it, so they come to my office for two reasons. They feel violated, and they're bothered and confused about why they never said 'no' or did anything else to express their refusal."

My colleague described the typical scenario. Usually, one of her clients began her evening at a party, either at a fraternity or elsewhere, where she found herself talking and flirting with a guy. From there events advanced to the point where the young woman, still doing as she wished, agreed to go to his room or hers to hook up. As the make-out session progressed, the young woman became aware of two things: that she did not want to go as far as having intercourse, and that she was receiving powerful, nonverbal signals that her partner fully assumed that that's where the night was headed.

My colleague explained that her clients were telling her "that they found themselves deciding to 'just go through with it' because they couldn't bring themselves to turn the guy down. It's as though they feel that by agreeing to get in bed with the guy and start hooking up, they've signed on to a social contract that they didn't feel they could break."

I confirmed to my friend that I knew exactly what she was talking about, because a smart, self-possessed college sophomore had recently brought a nearly identical incident to my practice. "I was struck," I told my colleague, "that she was almost as upset with herself for being a 'failed feminist' as she was about the unwanted sex she'd had." My colleague nodded eagerly. "Yes, these are strong women—they're not timid. And they come to my office angry with themselves because they know that they should have spoken up. But they are worried they'll hurt the guys' feelings or be trashed around campus for being a 'tease' if they just say 'no,' so they go along with something that they know they don't want."

Of course the young men in these situations should not take the absence of an explicit "no" to mean "yes," and the young women should not have to worry that the guy would respond badly to her honesty. Thankfully, many high schools and colleges are actively engaged in efforts to help their students embrace sexual ethics and learn how to communicate openly and effectively with their sexual partners. But our daughters shouldn't be rendered speechless if they don't happen to be hooking up with someone who attentively secures agreement every step of the way.

We should continue to advise our daughters of their right to decline sex with a pure and simple "no," if they feel that approach fits the situation. But this good advice doesn't go far enough. There are, in fact, many ways to express an unambiguous "no," and we don't want young women to feel that there is only one way to turn down sex. Here's why: my colleague described two common scenarios in which young women were unwilling to say a flat "no." The first was when they were worried about hurting a guy's feelings, and the second was when they were fearful that doing so could provoke a hostile response.

Indeed, every culture has elaborate norms for refusals because it's a big deal to contradict someone's expectations (and let's just assume that this is especially true when that someone, who may or may not be sober, thinks he's about to have intercourse). In everyday interactions, flat-out refusals are rare because they are usually humiliating. Instead, most people decline requests through a combination of saying something nice, expressing regret, and offering an explanation or excuse. In other words, when an acquaintance invites you to a dinner party you don't want to attend, you almost certainly won't respond, "No. I don't want to go to your party." You're much more likely to say, "Oh, thank you for asking. I'm bummed that I can't make it, but I've already got plans that night."

Serving up unvarnished "no"s makes a lot of sense when our daughters are not worried about the recipient's feelings or their own safety (for instance, when creepily propositioned at a party). From there, we should expand on our basic "just say no" advice by talking with girls about how to unambiguously turn someone down while protecting their relationship with that person, if that is what they want to do. We can let our daughters know that there might be times when they should feel free to say, at any point in the interaction, "Hey, this is really fun. I'm not sure what you had in mind, but I don't want to have sex tonight."

We worry, of course, that a courteous refusal could be taken as an ambiguous "no." Or as the start of a negotiation. Or even as a "yes." In truth, all three of these possibilities would require a deliberate misreading of the situation. That said, we can tell our daughter that she is free to set aside her worries about her partner's feelings if her refusal needs to be repeated. At that point, she should be encouraged to read the moment and decide if she wants to default to a flat-out "no" or if she'd prefer to use another interpersonal strategy, such as offering an excuse.

Indeed, researchers who surveyed young women about their strategies for avoiding sex found that excuse-making (e.g., not feeling well, fear of pregnancy) was a widely used tactic. The women in the study felt it was important to "soften the blow" to prevent the possibility that their partner might become "really upset." This brings us to our second scenario: the one in which a young woman might worry that a blunt refusal could trigger an angry response. Language scholars note that direct refusals, especially those provided without explanation, are often taken to be rude or hostile given our society's clearly established and overwhelmingly indirect conventions for saying "no." Deborah Cameron, a feminist linguist, points out that the available evidence calls into question our standard "unadorned no" advice, which, in essence, tells young women to "aggravate the offense of rejecting a man's advances by verbalizing their refusals in a highly confrontational way." If a young woman is afraid that a guy won't take her refusal well, why would we coach her to turn him down in a way that's likely to sound insulting?

My colleague and I lingered over lunch, reluctant to leave before coming up with a way to help the young women in our practices. She had spoken with her clients about their plans for future sexual interactions, and they had volunteered that they could, like the women in the research study, get behind the idea of going in with a preplanned excuse, a rhetorical trapdoor, such as suddenly "remembering" that they had to leave because they had promised to meet up with a friend by a certain time, or saying that they did not want to have sex because they weren't feeling well. As my friend and I sat together, now drinking the last of our melted ice through straws, I could tell that we both were slightly uneasy about the solution her clients proposed. On the one hand, we were desperate to help these young women avoid sexual activity they didn't want, and on the other hand, we were hesitant to suggest that they should use excuses to avoid sex.

For several weeks afterward, I kept turning that lunch conversation over in my mind. Thinking about it further, I realized that I have long encouraged teenagers to feel free to make up excuses to get out of doing things, such as smoking marijuana at a party. And I have done this because offering an excuse—as in "I would, but my dad says he'll test my hair for drugs"—allows teenagers to turn down their peers without generating social blowback. To put it another way, expecting total transparency in tricky social situations is unrealistic for most people. I'd rather have teenagers tell a white lie than do something dangerous, or something they don't want to do, for lack of a handy way of saying "no."

None of this excuses our daughters' romantic partners from the responsibility to recognize any form of a "no" for what it is. But a girl won't always know at the outset how well she and her partner will communicate. Accordingly, we need to prepare our daughters for both the love lives we hope they will have and the love lives they might, at times, unexpectedly have.

Ultimately, I have come to feel that the guidance we give girls is only as good as its results. If our daughters won't always feel willing to issue a straightforward "no" when they find themselves in a highly charged intimate situation, it's time to get creative and expand our advice to include the options of a gently couched "no" or offering an excuse. As we do so, we should emphasize that girls might use different approaches in different contexts, but they should all be unequivocal: "I'm not really in the mood for sex" isn't adequate, but "I don't want to have sex tonight, but

I'd like to get together again" is, just as "I think I'm supposed to meet up with my friend" doesn't cut it, but "I just remembered that I told my friend I'd take her home. I have to leave now" does. Our daughters can enjoy their romantic lives only if they're comfortable expressing what they *do* want and have practical ways to steer clear of doing things that they don't.

The Truth About Hookup Culture

Stories like the ones my colleague shared suggest that the romantic landscape has shifted quite dramatically in recent years, especially among college students. We now hear about a "hookup culture," in which romance, courtship, and commitment have been replaced with drive-by sexual encounters. Popular films and television shows have certainly done their part to suggest that one-night stands, no-strings-attached sex, and booty calls (having regular sex with a partner to whom one has no emotional attachment) are now the norm among young people. And research does find that, compared to young people from the late '80s and early '90s, today's generation is more likely to report having sex in the context of a close friendship or a casual date as opposed to a clearly defined couples relationship. But for the most part, the reality of the hookup culture doesn't match the hype.

The results of large-scale surveys tell us that, relative to eighteen- to twenty-five-year-olds from two to three decades ago, the most recent generation does not report having had more sexual partners since age eighteen, more partners in the last year, or more frequent sex. In fact, today's young people seem to be having *less* sex than their predecessors. For twenty- to twenty-four-year-olds born in the 1980s and '90s, 15 percent had had *no* sex since they were eighteen, compared to only 6 percent of those born in the

1960s. Similarly, surveys show that the number of high school students who reported being virgins rose from 46 percent in 1991 to 60 percent in 2017. We don't entirely know why today's teenagers and young adults are more sexually conservative than previous generations, but we do know this: the statistics don't match the perception that we are raising a highly promiscuous bunch.

Unfortunately, however, research also tells us that our daughters (like almost everyone else) believe the headlines. When asked to estimate the number of eighteen- and nineteen-year-olds nationwide who had had more than one sexual partner in the last year, eighteen- to twenty-five-year-olds guessed well over half, though the real number was only 27 percent. Likewise, when asked to estimate how many students had engaged in casual sexual activity ranging from kissing to intercourse with more than ten people during their college years, young people again guessed well over half, with the reality being only 20 percent.

For the romantics out there, I've got good news. A recent survey of college students found that 63 percent of men and 83 percent of women said they would prefer a traditional romantic relationship to an uncommitted sexual one. And another study found that only 16 percent of eighteen- to twenty-five-year-olds said that their ideal Friday night would involve having casual sex, while the remaining 84 percent said that they'd prefer to have sex in the context of a serious relationship or do something else altogether.

It's not good for our daughters to adopt the widely held belief that having sex with virtual strangers is just what college students do. Accordingly, we owe it to our girls to let them know that only a fairly small minority of students hook up with more than one partner each year and that most young people, both men and women, would prefer a meaningful relationship to a one-night stand.

Believing the hype about the hookup culture can create real

discomfort for our daughters. Those who don't want to take part in emotionally detached physical intimacy may worry that there's something wrong with them for not wanting to go along with the (actually nonexistent) trend. Alternately, some young women who feel ill at ease about having casual sex may decide to agree to it anyway because they believe it's the norm. And how do those who feel uncomfortable about casual sex get themselves to go through with it? Often, with the help of alcohol.

Liquid Courage

Engaging in physical intimacy with a virtual stranger would make most people anxious, and getting drunk is one of the easiest ways to reduce anxiety. So it comes as no surprise that most of the time hookups involve drinking. Research consistently finds that casual sexual encounters among college students happen after a few drinks and that the more a college woman drinks, the more likely she is to have a drive-by physical encounter, and the further things are likely to go.

Interestingly, drinking is more closely involved with hooking up for women than it is for men. While some young women may drink to quiet their misgivings about having casual sex, there are other anxiety-driven explanations as well. Experts note that some women who would like to be sexually active feel less inhibited by our culture's double standards when they have been drinking. In a similar vein, young women may feel that they can avoid being judged for their sexual pursuits if they can blame their behavior on being drunk.

Alcohol use and casual sexual activity can be so intertwined that young people may not even question the relationship between the two. Accordingly, it may fall to adults to help girls reflect on why drinking and hooking up seem to go hand in hand.

A prime opportunity presented itself to me a couple of years ago when I was meeting with a group of ninth-grade girls. We were talking about the free-flowing alcohol sometimes available at parties and the many reasons they'd want to be cautious about drinking. In the midst of this discussion, one of the girls astutely observed (in the sophisticated language that many fourteen-year-olds have already mastered), "Also, when people have been drinking, it can complicate questions of consent."

"Well, yes," I said, "but let's back up a step. If you're going to make out with someone, why would you want to be drunk?" From there I continued, "There's not a whole lot in life that we do just for fun. On my short list, there's watching television, there's eating ice cream, and there's making out!"

The girls could see where I was headed and kindly indulged me.

"If you're going to be physical with someone, I want you to fully *enjoy* it. Really, there's no other point. Think of it this way. If I offered you some Ben & Jerry's, you'd never say, 'Okay, I'll have some, but first let me get a little bit drunk.' Right? You wouldn't want to blunt the sensory experience of it. It's the same thing with making out. If you feel like you need to drink before you hook up with someone, I want you to ask yourself what's going on."

Even though we were being playful, the girls got my point, and in making it, I was really trying to do two things at once. First, I did want to encourage the girls to spend more time questioning the link between drinking and hooking up. Second, I try never to miss an opportunity to talk with young women about the fact that their love lives should be full of pleasure. When we succeed in getting that message across, we help girls to embrace, as opposed to feel ashamed of, their romantic interests. And when girls feel self-possessed in the romantic sphere, they don't need liquid courage to be physically intimate.

The Downstream Effects of Mainstream Porn

While the sexual landscape for young people seems, in many ways, more conservative than in recent years, there is one notable exception. Widespread broadband service has made hard-core pornography available to anyone with Internet access. Research now finds that by age seventeen, 93 percent of boys and 62 percent of girls will have been exposed to pornography, and what they are looking at is not soft-focus erotica. In the words of researchers who study the effects of porn on sexual relations, "mainstream commercial pornography has coalesced around a relatively homogenous script involving violence and female degradation."

Statistics tell us that pornography consumption is changing what happens in intimate settings. It is tied to decreased enjoyment of real-life sexual encounters and to an increase in practices that are common in X-rated scripts, such as anal intercourse. A study tracking the sexual behavior of college women over many years found that the frequency of anal sex jumped from 26 percent in 1999 to 46 percent in 2014. In interviews, the women in the study drew a direct link between the pornography their partners were consuming and what they wanted to do in bed. As one research participant explained, "Men want to . . . have anal sex, which is common in pornography and it is easy to think that anal sex is standard, but it is not." While some women report enjoying anal sex, studies usually find that the majority of women who try it find it to be a negative or painful experience.

Pornography's problematic impact on young women was laid out for me by a college freshman whom I had known since she was in the seventh grade. I first met Kim when her parents were splitting up and she, precociously, asked them if she could talk with a psychologist about their divorce. We met regularly for several months until her family life found a comfortable new rhythm. After that she checked in with me periodically—always at her own initiative—until she graduated from high school. Late one fall, I picked up a voicemail from Kim asking if she could have an appointment when she came home for Thanksgiving break. Having known her so long, I was eager to hear about how she was doing.

We settled into my office and caught up quickly. Kim, a young woman who usually took good care of herself, looked a bit ragged. But she said that she was generally happy at college and things with her family were going okay.

"What brings you in?" I wondered.

Kim's face clouded over. She suddenly seemed despairing and ashamed. "I think I have a drinking problem."

"Okay," I said gently, hoping to sound supportive and non-judgmental. After a pause I added, "Can you tell me what's got you worried?"

"When school started, I didn't drink much. Sometimes I'd have a couple of beers or smoke weed at parties, but nothing crazy. In October I met a guy I liked, so I started spending time with him and his friends. They party hard," she said, "and I started drinking more with them. I was really into Chris—that's the guy—but I didn't want to be thirsty about it, so mostly I'd spend weekend nights playing drinking games with him and his friends." Noting my quizzical look, Kim backtracked. "Thirsty is what we call slutty girls who throw themselves at guys."

I nodded but didn't interject. Kim was clearly eager to keep going.

"After a couple of weeks of hanging out with Chris and his friends, I ended up staying over at Chris's place. We had sex. It just kinda happened. I don't remember a lot of it. I was really hammered, which made me start to wonder about my drinking.

But I'm not sorry we hooked up. I like him, and we've kept hanging out."

Kim picked up on the slightly worried look on my face.

"I've been on the pill for acne since I was in high school, so I won't get pregnant. Anyway, I'm not sure where things stand with Chris—I wish we had more of a relationship, but I don't want to make a big deal about it. I'm now drinking most nights while I wait to see if he texts me about coming over. I'm definitely trying to take the edge off while I wait."

I finally chimed in. "Your situation with Chris sounds as if it often leaves you feeling as though you're on shaky ground. Is that a fair description?"

"Yeah. That's fair. He's a good guy, and I'd like to do more with him than hook up. But I don't want to get the reputation of being a girl who tries to pin guys down."

"Are you and Chris in touch over the Thanksgiving break? Do you stay connected when there's nothing physical happening?"

"Um, I haven't heard from him since break started. The way we left things was kinda weird. We've had sex a few times, but the night before break, he wanted to try anal. I know that lots of guys are into that, but I was pretty scared." Then, as if it were a totally normal thing to say, Kim added, "So I got wasted really fast, and we did it. I think he liked it, but I can tell you there's no way I would have gotten through it sober." She paused. "I called you the next morning. That round of drinking really scared me."

I felt grateful for my long connection to Kim, because the moment sitting before us was a delicate one. I didn't want to blow her away with the full strength of my reaction to what she shared, but I also didn't want to underreact and seem to tacitly endorse the destructive, hookup-centered, porn-informed, and not clearly consensual relationship she was describing.

Aiming for a middle ground, I began carefully. "I'm not sure if you have a drinking problem, but I do think that you're facing another problem that you're not naming." I took the open look on her face as permission to proceed. "I know that what you're describing with Chris isn't an altogether unusual arrangement"—Kim nodded—"but to me, it sounds really lopsided and anxiety-provoking."

"Thank you," she replied in a relieved whisper.

"From what you're telling me, you feel uncomfortable asking for what you want or telling Chris what you don't want. My sense is that you're getting drunk to manage your nerves in this relationship."

"I think that's true."

"There's also another problem," I added. "You and I both know that it's not okay for Chris to take your drunkenness as a go-ahead for sex."

Kim agreed, then asked abruptly, "So, should I stop drinking for a while?"

"Well, that certainly won't hurt. And it will give us a way to test two things. First, if you can stop drinking easily, you may not have a drinking problem to worry about. Second, if hanging out with Chris doesn't work when you're sober, then you'll want to renegotiate the terms of the relationship. Or move on."

She sat quietly before saying, "I know that you're right, but I don't know what to say about Chris. I don't know how I'll shift gears with him, and I'm not ready to drop it."

"Look," I said, "you're being put in a terrible position, and your situation with Chris isn't a healthy one. I know you know this, but it's sometimes hard to remember that your romantic life should be built around what *you* want. I think we can find a way for you to move in that direction."

Kim and I met twice before she returned to school and then made an appointment for when she returned at the semester break. When she arrived for our meeting in mid-December, she looked like her old self again. She got right down to business.

"So," Kim began, "I kept my promise to myself to stop drinking for a while . . . the timing was good anyway, given that we just had finals . . . and it really changed things with Chris."

"How so?"

"Well"—she paused—"it seems like our relationship, or whatever you would call it, just sort of ended. I never heard from him over Thanksgiving break, and when I got back to campus, I decided to wait to see if he'd reach out. I was pretty anxious while I waited to see if he'd text me . . . and I finally did hear from him"—she tucked her hair behind her ear—"but it was basically a booty call."

I nodded to let her know that I was still following.

"He asked me to come over, so I did. Chris was friendly when I got there, but then he hardly even talked to me, and it was incredibly boring to hang out with him and his friends while they were drunk and I was sober. So after a while, I just left. I haven't heard from him, and I'm not going to reach out."

"What I think I hear you saying is that you know you can do better."

"*Way* better," she said with a sheepish smile.

"Yeah," I said, "I think so, too. Here's the deal: your friendships and romances should help you feel good—not leave you feeling unhappy and anxious."

When it comes to helping our daughters conduct their relationships with boys, we know what we need to do. We must teach them to stand up for themselves if they are ever bullied or harassed, encourage them to pay attention to what they want from their love lives, and to seek out the guys, as friends and perhaps as lovers, who treat them with the warmth and kindness they deserve.

From here, let's turn our attention to another common source of stress and anxiety for girls: school. Not only is school the place where our daughters often run into many of the social strains that we've already considered, it's also where they meet the substantial pressures that come with their academic lives.

CHAPTER FIVE

. . . .

Girls at School

THERE HAS NEVER BEEN A MORE ACADEMICALLY IMPRESSIVE GENERA-tion of girls than the young women we are raising today. Beginning in elementary school and continuing through college, statistics show that girls get better grades than boys in every subject. As high school students, girls take more Advanced Placement classes than boys, and they are more likely to be valedictorians and to enroll in college immediately after high school. Once in college, women outnumber men, and they graduate and earn advanced academic degrees at higher rates.

Given the fantastic gains that girls have made in the academic arena in recent years, it should come as no surprise that our daughters, more than our sons, report feeling stressed by school. No one wants to roll back the advances young women have made, but we do need to find ways to reduce how much pressure and tension they're feeling as a result. This chapter will take a systematic look at the forces that bear down on our daughters in academic settings and suggest ways that we can keep them from feeling overwhelmed by worries about school.

School Is Supposed to Be Stressful

Let's start with a look at a fundamental cause of school-related distress for girls: their misunderstanding about the very nature of stress. Stress, as we know, is often constructive, but adults in our culture sometimes wrongly believe that it's invariably harmful and hand this view down to their daughters. In truth, being pushed beyond one's comfort zone is often a *good* thing, and the stress that students encounter at school for the most part happens to be the healthy kind. All growth comes with some discomfort, and we send our children to school precisely so that they will be stretched and improved.

There's really no better metaphor for the healthy stress of school than the strength-training model of progressive overload. The most effective way to build strength is by gradually lifting heavier and heavier weights. The term *progressive overload* describes the familiar training program of adding repetitions or lifting bigger dumbbells over time to trigger muscle growth.

School, ideally, is one long program of academic progressive overload. From the day a child first steps foot in a school building until the day she graduates, her teachers should steadily increase the difficulty of her work. As soon as she masters new material, they should give her something more challenging. This is all obvious, of course. But many adults and students have collectively lost sight of the reality that getting smarter—like getting stronger—is often an uncomfortable process.

Girls who believe that stress can never be good find school to be doubly trying. They feel stressed by their academic demands (as, mostly, they should), but they also feel worried about the fact that they are stressed. That second dose of psychological strain is unnecessary and unhelpful. Here's the good news: research demonstrates that we can change how girls think about the demands of school. In order to study people's mindsets about stress, researchers randomly assigned people to one of two groups. The first group was shown videos that explained how stress can benefit the body (naturally using muscle building as an example), enhance creativity, build relationships, and help people succeed in clutch moments. The second group watched videos detailing how stress can harm physical health, mood, and self-esteem, and lead people to freeze up when the stakes are high.

When the experimenters surveyed the members of the two groups several days later, they found that those in the stress-is-helpful group reported improvements in their mood and in the quality of the work they were doing. The stress-is-harmful group, though, did *not* report such changes. From this the researchers surmised that the bad news they learned about stress only reinforced what most people already believe, so nothing had changed for them. In a similar vein, a different study found that teenagers with a stress-builds-strength mindset were much less upset by difficult life events, such as having a close friend move away or having their parents separate, than those with a stress-does-harm mindset.

Our view of stress can even alter how our mind and body react to it. In other research, one group of participants was taught that the bodily response to stress, such as a racing heart, actually improves performance. A second group was told that the best way to manage a worrisome situation was to try to ignore the source of the stress. After that, participants in both groups were hooked up to heart monitors and asked to do something that almost anyone would find nerve-wracking. They gave a five-minute speech to a hostile audience made up of research team members who frowned, crossed their arms, and furrowed their brows while listening.

This study, like the one before it, found that it's *helpful* to embrace the benefits of stress. The participants who were taught to welcome the physiological arousal that comes with tense situations found the speech task less demanding and even had a more adaptive cardiovascular response than those who had been told to try to ignore whatever got them worked up.

We can bring these research findings home to our daughters through our own responses to their complaints about school. When our girls are young and grouse about disliking a particular teacher, being annoyed by certain classmates, or dreading a given subject, we can say, "Yep. I get it. There will always be aspects of school you don't like. But figuring out how to succeed under imperfect conditions is a big part of what you learn how to do at school."

As our daughters age, we can talk in more direct terms about the progressive overload model of education. I often point out to high school girls that their demanding programs are designed to help them build the mental brawn and endurance they'll need to take on life after graduation. I'll note that, for many students, ninth grade is like an orientation to the weight room. It can be a relatively gentle introduction to the brain building that's ahead. In tenth grade, however, we basically lock girls in the weight room for a steep intellectual training program. Indeed, the sophomore year is much harder than we tend to acknowledge. Tenth graders often take chemistry, a subject that requires them to apply their math skills to a brand-new field that comes with a totally unfamiliar set of principles. And ambitious high school students often take their first AP class—with its college-level workload—during sophomore year.

The intensive mental workout of tenth grade makes it possible for girls to meet the high demands of their junior year, when their workloads increase further still (often through the addition of more AP classes), and many tack on the challenge of preparing for and taking college placement exams. For the college-bound, senior year takes the training program up one notch more by throwing the demands of the college application process on top of everything else. When we think about school this way, we gain a fresh appreciation for how our daughters transform from capable eighth-grade colts into the racehorses we see at high school graduation.

It's important to frame the demands of education in positive, capacity-building terms, because doing so actually changes how our daughters experience school. Girls go from feeling hammered to feeling fortified (if often exhausted) by it. Happily, there's more than one way to make this point. Sometimes, we can celebrate the awesome gains girls are making thanks to their intellectual workouts. And at other times, we can talk with our daughters about how their downtime, just as in weight lifting, is a *critical component* of their ongoing growth.

When visiting schools around the country, I often ask groups of high school students how they recover from having a very bad day. I always receive a wide range of answers. Some students take naps; others have a good cry in the shower. Some play with the family dog; others clean up their rooms, watch a favorite episode of a show for the umpteenth time, go for a run, or listen to their happy, angry, or sad music playlists.

I have found that students love to reflect on their preferred strategies for putting themselves back together, and once we've come up with lots of examples, I always end our meetings by making two points. First, recovery strategies are highly personal. What works for one person won't necessarily work for another, and everyone needs to figure out what works best for them. Second, having a good recovery strategy is vital because, as with muscle building, intellectual growth depends on both doing hard work *and* replenishing one's reserves.

In short, how girls view the mental strain that comes with learning makes a big difference. Students with the stress-is-harmful mindset approach school as a demoralizing merry-go-round where the routine burdens of school interfere with the goal of feeling relaxed. The stress-is-helpful view can turn school into a beneficial, progressive program that builds capabilities by alternating periods of demand with interludes of recovery. In the plainest terms, Monday morning feels far better for the girl with the stress-is-helpful viewpoint than it does for her stress-is-harmful counterpart.

Girls, Especially, Worry About School

We need to do everything we can to shape how our daughters perceive academic challenges, because girls, more than boys, worry about school. Research consistently finds that girls spend more time fretting about how they are doing academically, even though they are getting better grades than boys. To explain this paradox, experts have noted that our daughters, more than our sons, take to heart the feedback they get from teachers. Girls tend to view their grades as a telling measure of what they can and cannot achieve. Boys, in contrast, often approach school with more confidence. Even when things go poorly, they don't always take negative feedback personally, or they chalk it up to something they believe they can easily fix. For example, boys may be more likely than girls to tell themselves that they "weren't really trying" when they took that test they bombed.

We can help our daughters take their school performance less personally—and simultaneously help those who actually need to be taking their work *more* seriously—by reminding them that their grades on assignments and tests only reflect their grasp of the material on the day their mastery was measured. If they want to build their mastery, they can do so by putting in more effort. Years of research confirm that students who understand that they can build their skills by working harder or more effectively worry less about how they are doing in school than students who believe that their grades provide a scorecard of abilities they cannot change.

There's another reason why girls, more than boys, feel stressed about school: they care more about pleasing grown-ups. In other words, our daughters often worry that we will be disappointed in them if they don't excel academically. As the mother of two girls, I've spent a lot of time thinking about what we, as adults, should make of this well-established research finding. To be honest, my reflections on this topic have forced me to admit the fact that I sometimes make my "disappointed face" (as my daughters call it) to push my girls along in school.

Here's how this plays out. Both of my daughters happen to be strong spellers who, during elementary school, routinely brought home 100 percent on their spelling quizzes. I would usually discover these quizzes when I went to clean out their backpacks, and typically I'd pull out the perfect quiz and say, "Wow! Great job! I'm so impressed!" But every once in a while I'd come across a quiz with errors. Then (and it makes me cringe to admit this) I'm sure that the quiz taker would see me put on my disappointed face. While looking over the sheet of paper in my hand, my lips would purse and vertical lines would appear between my eyebrows. To make matters worse, there were also days when I would say in an ever-so-slightly crestfallen tone, "Oh! What happened here?"

There's nothing horrible about this interaction, but it's still not okay. Because here's another thing about girls: they are *highly* attuned to our moods. We don't have to show anger, or even say that we are disappointed, for them to get the message. Whether we mean for it to happen or not, it's easy for them to sense that they are letting us down.

A similar dynamic can unfold at school where even the most caring teachers may unwittingly signal disappointment in their students. Imagine an interaction between a busy teacher and a diligent girl who asks for an extension on a paper because she has spent the last three afternoons at the hospital visiting her very sick grandmother. Even while granting the extension, the teacher only has to hesitate before saying, with just a hint of tightness in his voice, "Well, yes . . . okay . . . how much more time do you need?" for the girl to wish she hadn't made the request in the first place.

Why do we adults do this? I truly doubt that any one of us is consciously aiming to deploy the passive-aggressive tactic of using guilt as a weapon. At the same time, I often feel spread thinner than I'd like, and I know that this is true for many teachers as well. A girl's imperfect quiz or her request to hand a paper in late can feel as though it makes extra work for the adult on hand or requires an adjustment to the teacher's grading schedule. At some level, most parents and teachers know that we can use the subtlest of signals—a facial expression or a slight hesitation in response to a request—to get girls to fall in line and stop adding to our already overfull plates.

Though these interactions are small, their impact is not. They risk creating the all-too-common dynamic in which a girl is motivated to perform well in school because she is fearful of disappointing adults. I'm all for helping girls find ways to feel inspired academically. But this isn't one of them.

To be sure, not all girls are anxious about school because of feedback they've received from their parents or teachers. Some have parents who are nothing but supportive, and yet these girls still hold themselves to sky-high academic expectations. And even those schools that wait to give marks until late middle school sometimes discover that several of their third-grade girls fretfully convert every smiley face or star on their assignments into what they think would be the equivalent letter grade.

Regardless of the source of their anxiety, girls' approach to school should not be driven by fear. Angst-driven learning creates the obvious emotional problem of making school a source of chronic stress. It also creates a huge practical problem as well. When anxiety calls the shots, girls often become highly ineffi-cient students. Why? Because girls who worry too much about how they are doing academically often find that studying actu-ally soothes their nerves. The more nervous a girl feels, the harder she'll work. In sixth grade this may mean that she makes fifty flash cards to prepare for a quiz when twenty would do. In eighth grade she may institute a compulsive evening ritual of allaying her academic fears by using a color-coded system to rewrite her notes from every single class. In the extreme, some girls decide that they can relax only when their work is "perfect."

And the worst thing about the hyper-conscientious approach some girls develop to contain their academic anxiety is that it almost always works. Thanks to their "slavish overpreparation," as some experts call it, these hand-wringing students usually get terrific grades. Ultimately, girls' fear-driven, highly uneconomical studying tactics are reinforced from three sides. Excessive prepa-ration helps girls to quiet their worries about their academic per-formance, it consistently yields excellent outcomes that leave them feeling proud, and it earns them praise from their parents and teachers. For students who are motivated by fear, this system is exceedingly effective. Until it becomes unsustainable.

Natalie, a bright Laurel sophomore and very strong student, emailed me to make an appointment. In her message, she let me know that she wanted to touch base because she was feeling tear-ful all the time but couldn't figure out why. We matched up our schedules and were soon sitting together in my office under the staircase. Right away, I could see that something was wrong. Though Natalie usually seemed to sparkle, her light had gone out.

"What's the story?" I asked, making no attempt to hide my concern.

"I don't know," Natalie said mournfully, "and that's part of the problem." Her eyes welled up with tears. "See? I just cry for no reason."

"It's okay," I reassured her. "We'll figure out what's going on."

Natalie nodded while using the back of her hand to wipe away her tears. I have tissues right where students can reach them but have noticed that girls often avoid taking one. It's as though needing to use a tissue suggests that they have totally lost control of their feelings.

As Natalie crossed her ankles and leaned toward me, I asked about the usual causes of such fragility and found no red flags. Things were good with her friends, at home, and at school. Natalie was looking forward to spending spring break with her cousins who lived in California, and she had summer plans to return to her favorite camp. I checked for signs of depression beyond her tearfulness but learned, again, that I was barking up the wrong tree. Finally, I fell back on a question I had been taught early in my training to go to in situations where I couldn't make heads or tails of a problem that a client was describing. "Can you walk me through a typical day?" I asked.

There were no surprises at first. Natalie described waking at around 6:30 in the morning, getting to school, going through her regular academic day, and taking the bus home. Then she said, "I start my homework by about six at night and finish by around one or one thirty in the morning."

I interrupted with a reflexive, "Wait . . . what?!"

"Yeah," Natalie said, "I mean sometimes I'm done by midnight, but usually not."

Laurel's academic program is demanding, but it didn't make sense to me that Natalie would be staying up so late every single night, so I asked what classes she was taking and how much homework each class assigned. Suddenly, the problem sprang into focus.

"Well, I don't have a lot of work in every class, every night. But I feel that if I spend a certain amount of time on one class, I need to spend about the same amount of time on my other classes, too."

"Hold on," I said incredulously, "you mean that you're spending an hour or two on work for every class—even for the classes when you don't have something due?"

"Yeah," Natalie explained testily, "that's how I've always done it. If I don't have an assignment due in a class or a test to study for, I'll spend time going over my notes or creating a study guide for the next test."

"Right," I said sympathetically, "but you're telling me that you're only getting about five hours of sleep a night. No wonder you're so teary. The schedule you're describing would make anyone feel as if they're falling apart."

"True," she said, now taking a more tender stance toward herself, "but what should I do?"

"We need to reconsider your homework strategy. There's no question in my mind that you can learn everything you need to and get the same grades you're getting now while doing a lot less work."

A cloud of suspicion, and a glimmer of hope, crossed Natalie's face.

Moving from Grind to Tactician

I had met Natalie's parents, and I knew that they were really kind people. Though both were highly successful in their respective fields, no part of me suspected that they had set outrageous expectations for their daughter or ever expressed outright disappointment in her school performance. My hunch was that her folks didn't realize how late she was staying up or know that her study system, which had worked well enough in middle school, had taken on monstrous proportions in high school. Though Natalie's oppressive homework regimen yielded impressive marks, it obviously had to go.

It worried me that Natalie was already well into her sopho-more year, because it's not easy to get successful girls to loosen their grip on study strategies—even really punishing ones—that have earned them the grades they want. Natalie understood she needed more sleep but was reluctant to give up her familiar ap-proach to schoolwork. She was, however, willing to go along with a compromise. Natalie was carrying a very high A in her English class and knew that writing came easily to her, so she agreed to stop spending any extra time on *that* course. When we met a week later, she updated me on how things were going.

"It wasn't a big deal to back off in English," she said, "and I don't even think the teacher could tell that I'd changed how I study."

"That's good," I replied, "and are you getting more sleep?"

"Yeah, some . . . probably still not as much as I need," she said while shifting in her seat. "But it's better than it was."

Despite the fact that Natalie had gone along with my sugges-tion to ease up on her homework, I could tell that she felt am-bivalent about doing so and was worried that I'd encourage her to extend what she was doing in English to her other courses . . . which, of course, was exactly what I intended to do. I suspected, however, that making an aggressive case for my position would only inspire resistance. So I took a gamble.

"You have a brother, don't you?" I asked, recalling that I'd met her family when out to dinner a few years back.

"Yeah, he's a senior at Hawken," she replied, referring to a coed private school in our community.

"Does he study like you do?"

"Oh, GOD, no!" she said, almost cracking up at what struck

her as a preposterous question. "I mean, he gets really good grades, but he's got a lot of other stuff going on, and he likes to play videogames at night."

"So how does he get those good grades?" I asked.

"Honestly, I think that he figures out the absolute minimum amount he has to do to get the score he wants on a test or paper, and he then just does that," she said with an air of mild disdain. "When he was younger," she added, "there were a few times when he really blew it—when he stayed up way too late to finish a project or thought he was ready for a test, but he wasn't. I remember some fights at home about that." She paused and then her tone took on a shade of admiration. "But I guess that hasn't happened for a while."

Conspiratorially, I replied, "Your brother might just be on to something."

Research shows that girls are more disciplined about their schoolwork than boys, which explains why they get better grades. Indeed, many parents raising both girls and boys have observed a dynamic similar to what Natalie described. Their sons coast through school while their daughters floor it in all of their classes. It's noteworthy how little adults actually *question* these trends. We accept that boys will often take a calculated approach to academics; they'll aim to exert the minimum amount of effort required to keep adults off their backs. And we accept that girls will not only do all that we ask of them, but that they'll often exceed our expectations. Both of these patterns are problematic. Boys, as a group, are not doing as well in school as they should, while girls, as a group, are often stressed by their meticulous and inefficient approach to their academic lives.

When it comes to their schoolwork, we need to help our daughters be more like our sons, and vice versa.

. . .

To Natalie I said, "I know that adults often talk in negative terms about students with study habits like your brother's." She nodded to confirm that she knew what I meant. "We say that they're cutting corners or not trying hard enough. In reality, it sounds to me as though your brother has figured out how to be very *tactical* about his academics."

As I suggested earlier, it's not easy to convince girls who are serious students to change how they approach school. For too long, I encouraged girls like Natalie to "let up a bit" or "go easy" or "not be so hard on themselves." Those conversations never went well. In fact, I often sensed that the student I was talking to was offended by my guidance. Most girls are too well behaved to call adults out on their nonsense, but I began to suspect that if I could read the mind of the girl on the receiving end of my advice, I'd hear, "Are you *kidding* me? I'm taking the same disciplined approach to my schoolwork that I always have—and I'm getting good grades—and now you're telling me that I'm doing it wrong?!"

Things improved when I struck upon the word *tactical*. It says what girls need to hear: they can keep their success while becoming more efficient. The utility of the word was borne out in Natalie's nondefensive response.

"Yeah," said Natalie, "my brother doesn't worry about it like I do . . . but he and I basically get the same grades."

"You have such a great foundation at school," I offered admiringly. "You've developed an incredible work ethic, and you're so well respected by your teachers. I think that the next step for you is to become even more streamlined in your approach to getting the grades you want. It's already working for you in English, and I think that it could work in your other classes as well." Natalie didn't respond with wholehearted agreement, but she didn't disagree, either.

Becoming Energy Efficient at School

Experience from years of working with young women like Natalie has influenced my parenting. More than anything, I came to appreciate that I did not want to wait until my girls were in high school to talk with them about being academic tacticians. I have watched too many hard-driving, conscientious students leave middle school thinking that they're supposed to keep the pedal to the metal in all of their classes, all of the time. They may be able to sustain that level of output early on, but if it's the *only* way they know to get through school, they find themselves running on fumes by junior year, if not sooner.

How, in practical terms, do we teach girls to be energy efficient at school? As a first step, we should have open conversations with our middle school daughters about what grades they want. If your girl feels pretty relaxed about her marks, school is unlikely to be a source of intense stress and anxiety for her. In that case, you may find yourself needing to articulate how much energy *you'd* like for her to exert. But if your girl doesn't hesitate to say, "I want to get an A in every class," then you've got some driving lessons to give.

The first thing you should say to your daughter is this: "Well, I'm all for good grades, but here's something you should know. By no means do I expect that you'll *care* equally about all of your classes, even if you're getting good marks across the board." This may seem like a strange thing to spell out, but I have learned from experience that girls can harbor the twin misconceptions that they should always devote their full force to their schoolwork, and that they should feel equally devoted to all of their subjects.

Of course, there are some girls out there who truly love everything about school, but those students are pretty rare. Most young people have classes they prefer and classes they tolerate.

Unfortunately, I've known girls to latch on to the idea that "good students" feel motivated by every subject, and then beat themselves up for not feeling jazzed about all of their work. Having dispelled that unhelpful idea, you can move on to talking with your daughter about the tactical deployment of her academic efforts.

You might say, "For the classes you really like, you'll probably find that it's easy to work hard at the material. And if you're crazy about the subject and have time to give it your all, then go for it! But for the classes that you don't love, or when you don't have enough time to dig into the ones you do, figure out how much work is needed to learn the content or get the grade you want. Then stop there."

Though I routinely proclaim that we need to help girls get comfortable with coasting when they can *before* they get to high school, it hasn't been so easy to put my parenting money where my mouth is. When my older daughter was in eighth grade, she found herself in a demanding math class that took up a disproportionate amount of her homework time. She's a conscientious student, and by March, I could see that her stress level was rising as she tried to maintain her high level of performance in all of her other classes while devoting so much time to math. I knew what I needed to do.

"So," I said, while cleaning up the dinner dishes, "what grade do you have right now in social studies?"

From her spot at our kitchen table, my daughter replied, "I think I've got a ninety-eight percent."

"That's what I thought." I put a plate in the dishwasher and started scrubbing a pot. "At this point in the year, do you think you could get Bs on all of your work in social studies and still end up with an A in the class?"

"Probably."

"Then in social studies," I told her, "I think that you should start phoning it in. Save your energy for math class."

I was scrubbing away and quietly congratulating myself when she asked a question that really put me to the test.

"But what if, at the end of the year, I get an A in social studies, but only a 'satisfactory' instead of an 'excellent' for effort?"

It was a good thing that I was at the sink facing away from her because I had to fight every cell in my own good-girl, teacher's-pet, grade-grubbing body to make myself say with confidence, "That would be just fine if you learned what you needed to."

So she tried me again.

"And what if I'm wrong? What if I ease up in social studies and mess up my grade?"

I now held the pot with a white-knuckle grip and forced myself to adopt a pragmatic tone. "That's what middle school is for. The stakes aren't as high as they will be later, so now's the time to figure out how to coast effectively when you can and how to floor it when you need to. Why not treat this as an experiment and see where it goes."

I've also worked to take moments when I might, in the past, have deployed disappointment as opportunities to talk with my girls about how they direct their academic energies. When I discover a less-than-perfect quiz in my younger daughter's backpack, I try to be easygoing as I say, "These are some tricky words! Do you know how to spell them now, or do you want some help from me or Dad?" If she seems at all apologetic about the grade, I hurry to point out that her scores simply tell her where she needs to do more work and where she doesn't. "You take quizzes," I say, "to help you figure out how to point your studying in the right direction."

Ideally, schools and teachers would do their part, too. If we think back to that hypothetical girl asking for an extension on a paper, here's the response I wish her teacher could have given her:

"You're totally on top of things in my course, so I'm flexible. If you *want* to write the paper, I'll take it whenever it's ready. But I know that you read the book and understood it, so if you'd rather just have me count your next paper grade double, you can skip this one. It sounds like now's the time for you to be with your grandmother." That might seem like a pie-in-the-sky response, and not all teachers have that kind of latitude in what they require of each student, but there are plenty of other ways teachers can do their part to protect girls from their tendency to overexert themselves at school.

Consider, for example, this common scenario. A girl will sometimes do extra credit work in a class where she already has a high A. In my ideal world, the instructor would work to find out what the *heck* was going on. Does the girl so love the course content that she wants to engage with it in any way she can? Or (more likely) is she afraid that if she doesn't do every last bit of work offered, the teacher will be disappointed in her? Unless the girl explains that she just can't get enough of the subject, it falls to the teacher to say, "Look, you probably can't *get* a B in my class at this point. So I think that you should take the time you're spending on extra credit and use it to have some fun, pursue other interests, or get more sleep."

Helping Girls Build Competence and Confidence

I appreciate that I am proposing a pretty radical change to how we guide girls to approach academics. But there's a lot at stake. When we allow our daughters to persistently overexert themselves, they develop tons of confidence in their work ethic and none in their talents. Before they graduate, girls should feel reassured that they can draw on both.

Being low on self-assurance may have real and highly negative consequences for girls as they move beyond school and into the working world. In investigating why women don't always get as far as they should professionally, journalists Katty Kay and Claire Shipman found that displaying confidence seems to be at least as important to success as being competent. Their description of workplaces where men hold most of the top positions sounds uncannily like what we know about how boys and girls typically operate at school: "Underqualified and underprepared men don't think twice about leaning in. Overqualified and overprepared, too many women still hold back. Women feel confident only when they are perfect. Or practically perfect."

If we think about it, school can serve as a confidence factory for boys. When guys get poor grades, they often don't take those failures personally; and when they get high marks, they tend to take pride in their accomplishments, whether they were hard-earned or not. Doing well—especially while exerting minimal or moderate effort—reassures boys that they are fundamentally capable and gives them the sense that they can perform when the chips are down.

Hard-driving, perfectionistic girls may have the opposite experience at school. They never find out what they can do if they hardly try because they *never* hardly try! Even as they ring up one success after another, girls may attribute their achievements to the only thing they've ever known, their incredible self-discipline and willingness to overprepare. This taxing approach helps girls succeed in school, but it may hurt them down the line. Indeed, Kay and Shipman explained that when Hewlett-Packard looked into why there were so few women in top management spots, they found that the women at their company would only apply for positions when they felt they had 100 percent of the qualifications listed for the job. The men, in contrast, put themselves forward when they felt they met 60 percent of the requirements.

There are, of course, inept men out there who get surprisingly far on their confidence in their sparse abilities. But they're not the role models we're looking for. Instead, we should train our attention on capable guys like Natalie's brother who use their schooldays to figure out when they need to work hard and when they can fall back on their talents. By the time they enter the professional world, they feel self-assured, because they have literally spent years testing the limits of their native abilities, constantly calibrating their sense of how much work they have to do to be successful. Our daughters should arrive in the professional world having done the same. They should know when they need to recruit the brawn of their work ethic and when they can coast along on their brains. We want our girls to build real skills, to know how to work hard when they need to, *and* to believe that their talents will help them rise to meet challenges.

Battling Test Anxiety

Test anxiety is not a recognized diagnosis like generalized anxiety disorder or panic disorder. Rather, the term refers to the fact that girls often find themselves feeling nervous when faced with assessments, and this can undermine their academic performance. Girls can often manage their test anxiety by adjusting how they prepare for exams. Our daughters may not always have a say over how they get ready for assessments, especially if they are subjected to frequent state-mandated examinations, which can be stressful, time-consuming, and largely out of a student's control. But when our daughters are left to their own devices to prepare for tests, they tend to study by going over their notes, rereading material, and highlighting passages in their texts. For the most part, these methods are a waste of time. Indeed, a massive review of the research on effective learning techniques found that students' preferred study strategies are far and away the least effective.

So what works?

Spaced practice and sample testing. In other words, girls shouldn't cram all of their studying into a single session, and they should find active ways to engage with the test material, such as quizzing themselves, instead of just passively reviewing it. Do not wait until your daughter has developed an unnatural attachment to her highlighter to let her in on this secret. I'll say it again: girls don't like to give up school strategies that seem to be working.

When test time rolls around, encourage your daughter to start her studying several days in advance and to *begin* her preparations by taking a sample test. She might find one in the back of her textbook or online, or she may even be able to write one herself. If she aces it, she'll develop confidence in her abilities; from there, she should turn to her other homework or go relax. If, as is more probable, she can't answer all of the questions, the sample test will help her home in on the material she needs to master. Here's where the spaced practice part comes in. The next day (or a few days later if she has the leeway), she should take another sample test and see what she still needs to learn.

In sum, students learn material best when they engage with it, step away from it, and come back to it. And they feel less anxious when taking the actual test if they have already tried to answer challenging questions on that exact same content. When working with difficult new material, it's quite a leap to go from looking over the content to grappling with hard questions about it, which is why girls often feel anxious at exam time if they've only studied by reviewing. To make this point with the girls at Laurel

School, I sometimes joke that if they are ever tested on their ability to go over their notes or highlight a book, I want them to prepare for the test by doing those things. Until then, however, I hope that they will get ready for their assessments by practicing what they will actually be asked to do at test time.

As you talk with your daughter about the utility of taking practice tests, you might explain that we'd never ask her to jump from learning lines for a play to opening night without first having a dress rehearsal. And we'd never ask her to go from acquiring basic sports skills to playing in an important game without giving her plenty of time to scrimmage. In short, we routinely expect that girls will learn new things, try out what they've learned under practice conditions, and then—and only then—apply their knowledge in situations where something important is at stake.

While inadequate preparation is one cause of test anxiety for girls, suspecting that other people think you can't do the work is another. Given the fact that girls are such powerhouses at school, you might wonder why anyone would think that they would come across academic challenges they couldn't handle. Unfortunately—and appallingly—research shows that there is a strong and persistent bias against girls and young women in math and science classes *to this day*.

Girls make up half of the students in high school calculus, they outnumber boys in AP science courses, and they usually get better grades than the guys do in their math and science courses from elementary school through college. Yet research published within the last few years still finds that some high school teachers believe math to be easier for boys than it is for girls, even when those girls are getting equivalent test scores and grades. In college, 60 percent of the students in biology classes are women, yet the men in those courses wrongly assume that their female classmates aren't doing as well as they themselves are.

In another recent study, researchers asked college science professors to evaluate application materials for a laboratory man-
ager position. The application, which was fabricated by the
research team, allegedly belonged to a science student, and the
professors were asked to rate the applicant's competence, to assess how likely they were to offer the student the job, to select a
starting salary, and to indicate how much career mentoring
they'd be willing to provide. Using a classic research design, half
of the professors looked at application materials submitted by a
student named John, and the other half looked at identical materials from a student named Jennifer.

I hope you're sitting down.

The science professors were more likely to rate "John" as being
competent, to say they would hire him, to start him at a larger
salary than "Jennifer," and to say that they'd mentor him in his
career. Even *biology* professors were biased against "Jennifer," despite the fact that, as we know, women make up the majority of
their students. Perhaps most remarkably, female professors were
as likely as male professors to favor "John." Essentially, it seems
not to matter how well girls and young women are actually performing in traditionally male fields, many of their instructors—
and even the male students in their classes—still continue to
think less of them.

Bear with me for some more bad news. Being discriminated
against at school can actually raise anxiety and suppress exam
scores. Years of research tell us that girls and young women sometimes worry that their test results might actually reinforce the
belief that they aren't as capable as guys when it comes to math
and science. As you might expect, worrying itself uses up intellectual bandwidth and undermines academic performance. Girls
as a group battle chauvinism in traditionally male fields; girls
who are racial minorities must also contend with sweeping negative stereotypes about their overall intelligence, which can erode

their performance in any subject. In short, prejudice in the classroom has real academic consequences.

Here, at last, is some good news. We can shield girls from the impact of discrimination by helping them understand that being the target of discrimination can make them nervous whether they agree with the negative stereotypes or not. It might seem as though talking about the biases girls face would only make matters worse, but doing so actually helps to safeguard test performance. When girls and minorities sense low expectations but don't realize that these can *cause* test anxiety, they look for other ways to explain their nerves. Unfortunately, girls often assume that they're feeling tense because they don't really know the material or because the test is harder than they thought it would be. Once those ideas take hold, girls' scores start to plummet.

If you suspect that your daughter feels responsible for vindicating her gender or race with her test scores, find a time to say, "I know that you really care about doing well, not just for yourself but so that other people won't underestimate you. That's great if it provides motivation, but it can also create extra pressure. If you feel yourself getting nervous, don't let worries about what other people might think get in the way of showing what you know." Finally, if you fear that your daughter might actually *believe* the stereotype that boys outperform girls in math and science, tell her about the mountains of evidence to the contrary. Replacing a false negative stereotype with a true positive one has also been found to reduce test anxiety and protect test performance.

Not All Girls Learn the Way Schools Teach

School is stressful enough for students who can count on their hard work to deliver decent grades. So it should come as no surprise that the academic world often feels downright harrowing for girls whose brains aren't wired to learn in the ways that schools usually teach. Our daughters' lives are almost entirely organized around their academics, and they quickly start to notice if their reading, writing, or mathematic abilities aren't developing at the same pace as that of their classmates.

Girls with undiagnosed learning or attention disorders often floor it at school but find that their efforts don't succeed as they should. As a result, they spend time worrying that they are disappointing their parents and teachers, or that their inadequacies will be "found out." These fears help to explain the elevated rates of anxiety disorders that we see in girls with learning and attention disorders. Again, feeling nervous clouds thinking, which makes a tough academic situation even worse for girls with unconventional learning profiles.

Once a learning or attention disorder is recognized, we can help girls manage the discomfort that comes with feeling out of step at school. Unfortunately, we can overlook or be slow to recognize learning challenges when they occur in girls. A study of second and third graders found that boys and girls are equally likely to have significant reading problems, but the boys are referred by their teachers for evaluation and support *much* more often. When guys feel frustrated at school, they often disrupt the classroom and bring attention their way; girls, in contrast, tend to fret quietly while trying to cover up the gaps in their understanding.

In a similar vein, we often miss the diagnosis of attention deficit hyperactivity disorder in girls partly due to the fact that they are more likely to be inattentive rather than excessively energetic or impulsive. I've seen extremely well-behaved girls get all the way to eleventh grade before being diagnosed with a long-standing attention problem. They don't get the help they deserve until they finally collapse under the strain of working twice as hard as their classmates to make up for all of the information they are missing during class. When a girl spends a lot of time agonizing about her grades, avoiding certain work, or studying way too hard in an effort to try to keep up, we need to rule out the possibility that she has an undiagnosed learning or attention problem before we do anything else. To do this, parents should share their observations with her teachers and possibly pursue a diagnostic assessment in order to figure out what is going on.

Girls with learning or attention disorders should be supported with some combination of tutors, classroom accommodations, and perhaps medications. Not all schools and families, however, have access to these critical resources, and even the ones that do find that these aids don't sweep away the emotional challenges that come with having a learning or attention diagnosis. In order to come to terms with the reality of being different from their peers and needing to advocate for themselves at school on a daily basis, girls will still need support from adults, even in the most accepting and considerate academic environments.

Coping with the Thirty-Hour Day

Some girls are spread thin at school because they work inefficiently. Others may be square intellectual pegs who wear themselves out trying to fit into the round hole of traditional schooling. Still others become completely overwhelmed because they have signed up for an academic program that pushes the limit of what even the most efficient and conventionally brilliant students could possibly manage. Of this last scenario, Adrienne was a case in point.

I first met Adrienne in late February of her junior year of high school. When, for the third time, she asked to be excused from class to ride out a panic attack, the counselor at her school passed my name along to her mother. Adrienne's mom and I connected by phone, and she told me that her daughter was an excellent student and a terrific girl who, in her words, was "hard-driving and high-strung." She explained that her seventeen-year-old was eager to get rid of her panic attacks and could get herself to her appointments on her own, so we agreed that I'd meet with her daughter for a couple of sessions. After that, her mother, a single parent, would join us for an appointment.

A few days later, I found myself sitting at my practice across from a dark-haired girl with a sweet, round face. As she started to describe the waves of anxiety that swamped her at school, the tension in her voice made her sound like a world-weary adult, not a fresh-faced high school girl.

When I asked how I could be helpful, she urgently explained, "I have to get rid of these attacks. I'm fine one minute, then I suddenly feel sweaty and dizzy and like I might throw up."

"How long have they been going on?"

"The first one happened during finals, right before winter break. I looked up panic attacks online and knew that I had definitely had one. I didn't have another one until school started again in January. I think I've had three or four since then—they seem to be coming more and more often." While absentmindedly playing with the zipper on her fleece jacket, Adrienne added, "Sometimes I can stay in class and get through it, but lately I feel like I have to leave the room or it will never stop."

I asked Adrienne to describe what her anxiety felt like, and it did indeed sound as though she was having classic panic attacks. I then asked about her life at home, with her friends, and what she liked to do for fun. She explained that she had a brother who was a senior at her same high school. "We get along fine, I guess— we're pretty close as a family because it's just the three of us. I also have great friends," she said while seeming momentarily more at ease, "but I don't get to see them outside of school." The weight of her worries returned as she added, "We just don't have time."

"What do you mean?" I asked, expressing my surprise that she seemed to be suggesting that, at seventeen, she could not squeeze in a social life.

"Well, this is the big year for me college-wise—everybody talks about how bad junior year is, but I didn't really get it." Resigned, Adrienne continued, "But I want to go to Stanford so, you know . . . it's a lot."

"Will you walk me through where your time goes?"

From there, Adrienne told me about her class schedule—she was taking several Advanced Placement courses and Honors Physics—and her membership on the school's speech and debate team. "Right now, we're getting ready for state qualifiers. I do international extemp," she said, referring to an event in which students are given thirty minutes to prepare a seven-minute extemporaneous speech on a current affairs topic. "We're practicing a couple hours after school every day, and I'm also collecting news articles on my own time."

"That sounds really demanding," I offered sympathetically. "I don't see how you're able to fit it all into a twenty-four-hour day."

"I know," she said heavily, "it's pretty bad."

Adrienne explained that her course load left her with as many as six hours of homework a night. "Oh, and I've been studying for the ACT, too. That's a few hours a week, and I also do practice tests that take forever."

My stomach tightened as Adrienne matter-of-factly ticked off all that was on her plate. "I think I want to be a doctor, so one afternoon a week I work in a lab at the Cleveland Clinic. I do that full-time in the summer, but I know that it's important to show that you're really committed to your extracurriculars, so I keep it up all year, too. Except for during track season."

"Track season?" I asked. She could tell that I didn't see how a sport could possibly fit into the picture she was painting.

"Yeah," Adrienne said, now fiddling nervously with the zipper on her jacket. "It starts just a few days after states," she added, referring to the last speech meet of the year.

"So, you mean that when speech and debate team ends, you're not going to get a break?"

"No," she said, while closing her eyes in a way that broadcast a sense of total defeat.

Given that it was only our first session and I wanted Adrienne to be willing to come back, I tried to lighten the mood. Full of hope, I asked, "How about the weekends . . . do you get some downtime then?"

Adrienne, being patient with my ignorance, again replied, "No. That's when we have speech meets. They go all day on Saturday . . . I leave my house by six thirty in the morning and don't usually get home until dinnertime."

"Right!" I said quickly, feeling embarrassed that I'd forgotten about the time-consuming weekly speech team meets. Then I asked cautiously, "How about Sundays—any chance you have time off then?"

"Mostly," she said glumly, "I'm catching up on work I couldn't do on Saturday."

Feeling so overwhelmed by what Adrienne was sharing that I couldn't find a foothold in our conversation, I tried an approach that tends to work well with teenagers: total honesty. "Just *listening* to your schedule," I commiserated, "makes me feel like *I* might have a panic attack. I truly don't know how you do it."

Adrienne appreciated—and accepted—my concern about how much she was juggling. While I wanted to question whether she really *did* need to maintain such a punishing schedule to get into a choice school, I already knew the answer. The admissions landscape for selective colleges has changed dramatically over the last two decades. Today, students with classes and activities like Adrienne's, straight As, glowing recommendations, *and* high scores can apply to many highly competitive colleges and still fail to gain admission to a single one.

"Listen," I said, leaning forward a bit in my seat, "it's great that you are giving high school everything you've got, and I know that if you want a shot at Stanford or a school like it, you're doing what needs to be done. I'm just so sorry that the admissions process has come to such an irrational place."

"Me, too. Sometimes I think that I should just relax about the whole thing and worry less about where I end up." She then added somberly, "But I've worked so hard for so long, I feel like it's dumb to give up now."

"I get it. Honestly, I'm not surprised you're having panic attacks given how much pressure you're under. I'm trusting that they'll ease up when you get through the worst of the college process. In the meantime, I can teach you techniques that will help you get your attacks under control quickly so you won't have to leave class. If that doesn't work, or doesn't work fast enough, we've got some other options to try."

Though Adrienne's schedule was demanding, I've actually heard worse. Some girls also need to have a job or care for their younger siblings while simultaneously managing obligations as exhausting as Adrienne's. It is never my place to tell girls what I think they should do after high school, but it is always my place to stick up for reality. Here's the reality of the college process for choice schools: having a chance of admission requires a superhuman effort. Parents who encourage their daughters to apply to the most competitive schools should be clear-eyed about what they are asking of them. And girls who aspire to attend a highly selective school should be helped to appreciate how very hard they will need to work in high school.

That said, there are some steps we can take to reduce the strain of the competitive college admissions process. First, parents should make sure that they and their daughters share the same expectations. Excellent, in-depth research conducted by social worker Renée Spencer and her colleagues found that girls feel especially stressed when their parents hold higher college ambitions for them than they hold for themselves. If we want our daughters to aim for selective colleges, we should make sure that they want that, too. Though we may be disappointed to learn that we're not on the same page, it's better to have an open conversation—and perhaps negotiation—about college prospects than to proceed as if we're in lockstep when we're not.

Second, parents should do everything they can to keep their daughters from setting their hearts on one or two selective schools. Doing so in the current admissions climate is like setting one's heart on winning the lottery. A girl is much less likely to be disappointed by the outcome of the college admissions process if she's kept an open mind about where she wants to go. College admissions, especially in recent years, often seem to defy all logic. A girl is sometimes accepted by a long-shot college and turned down by a safety school. Or a particular university accepts one classmate while denying admission to another who seemed to be the stronger candidate.

The admissions gamble is often confounded by the financial aid gamble. Few families can afford to pay the full college tuition sticker price, regardless of where their daughter applies. But when financial aid, scholarship, and loan offers come in, they're often all over the map. Ideally, a girl will have some good options to consider when she hears back from colleges. Realistically, she will have no way of knowing at the beginning of the application process what those options are likely to be.

Finally, to the degree that it's possible, we should think seriously about what *else* we ask girls to do when they're trying to get into colleges that accept only a tiny fraction of their applicants. I later learned that Adrienne usually did the household laundry but that her mother had relieved her of that duty until the speech and track seasons ended. In a similar vein, a friend of mine judiciously stopped requiring his daughter to join the nightly family meal during crunch times at school. Instead, he brought a dinner plate to her desk and packed her lunch in the morning so that she could get a little more sleep each day.

Naturally, girls should return to their regular obligations when their schedules downshift from punishing to rational. This may mean waiting until summer to ask your daughter to do substantial chores, or expecting a girl to attend her siblings' band concerts only when her workload abates. But parents should understand that aiming for a highly selective college will require their daughter to work in near-constant service of that goal. There are, of course, young women and their parents who may not want to trade a balanced high school life for the promise of security in adulthood. For them, I have good news. They probably don't have to.

Changing How We Define Success

All parents want their children to grow into adults who have peace of mind. This is a worthy goal, but it is also a distant and vague one that can leave us worrying about the path that will get our girls there. When we want to do something today to calm our nerves about distant tomorrows, it's easy enough to assume that our daughter will feel secure in adulthood if she has enough money, and that she'll have enough money if she's professionally successful, and that she's most likely to be successful in her chosen profession if she attends a competitive college. These assumptions are well meaning, but they are not supported by what we know about fulfillment in midlife.

A 2006 study on the connection between wealth and well-being tells us that happiness in adulthood rises steadily up to the point of having a family income of $50,000. Above that level, making more money has a negligible effect. And research on what *does* contribute to life satisfaction tells us that it pivots on factors that don't necessarily involve being affluent or gaining professional recognition. Adults with high levels of well-being feel good about themselves, have a sense that they are growing and learning, and enjoy healthy, satisfying relationships with other people. Happy grown-ups believe that their life has meaning and direction, they measure themselves against their own standards, and they feel successful in their endeavors.

There is, of course, no universal formula that tells us how to raise girls who will grow up to lead lives of fulfillment. But when we frame adult success in terms of well-being—and not just impressive achievements or earnings—we can improve how we guide our daughters forward. Ultimately, we all want our daughters to feel satisfied and secure as adults, regardless of whether or where they go to college, the professions they choose, or how much money they earn.

In practical terms, it's not always easy for parents to step back from their laser-like focus on their daughter's academic success, especially when so many of us can now monitor girls' daily grades and scores online. But we can change our approach if we change how we think about how girls get from where they are now to where they'll end up.

Swapping Projectiles for Pathways

When I talk with girls and their families about what lies ahead, they often seem to use what I call the "ballistics" model of future success. In this model, the girl is a rocket that will be shot out into the world when she graduates from high school. Her transcript, scores, and extracurricular activities set the coordinates for her launch, and, if she intends to go to college, they are locked in by the fall of her senior year. A girl and her parents can spend high school worrying about what her final trajectory will be, especially as her launch angle shifts from moment to moment with the latest grades and scores. In this model, optimal coordinates (the kind that might shoot her to a highly selective school) suggest that her future will be bright. Less optimal coordinates (perhaps the kind that will send her to a college without a big name) don't put her on such a promising arc.

In truth, this model makes almost no sense. Plenty of people launch themselves to highly competitive colleges and go on to lead miserable lives. And plenty of people with middling high school coordinates go on to lead good, rewarding lives with or without high levels of academic or professional achievement. Indeed, what we all know about how the world really works tells us that we should just about ditch the projectiles model altogether. Instead of regarding school as locking in launch settings, we might better think of it as one early stretch of a long and largely self-determined path. Some girls will follow a straight route, and some will wander; some will zip along while others will advance at a leisurely stroll. In making her way, each girl will make a number of decisions—and that's where parents can come in.

One of my favorite Laurel families had two very different girls graduate from the school. The older daughter was a conventionally excellent student who went on to an impressive college. The younger daughter, by contrast, never enjoyed the basic academic courses that all schools require and got undistinguished grades in all of them except for her design and metalwork classes, which she adored. As a high school student, this younger daughter spent every free moment at school refining her skills in Laurel's art studio, getting decent enough grades in the rest of her classes to attend design school after graduation.

I so admired the girls' parents, whom I got to know well over their many years of being connected to the school, because when we talked about both of their daughters, they always focused on *who,* and never on *what,* their girls would become. During the summers, they encouraged their girls to balance downtime with activities that allowed them to nurture their passions. When their older daughter was dating a guy who jerked her around, they emphasized that her romances and friendships should be warm and trusting, leave her feeling good about herself, and help her grow and change for the better. When they talked with both of their girls about the future, they emphasized that they should find work that felt meaningful, take pride in their efforts, and become adept at something they really cared about. They, as much as any parents I've known, defined success in terms of pursuing well-being, not conventional markers of achievement.

Parents might worry, understandably, that emphasizing long-term life satisfaction over school success will harm their daughter's grades, but research indicates otherwise. Indeed, a recent study gave students a list of values and asked them to rank what they believed to be their parents' priorities. Some of the values had to do with academic and professional achievement and some had to do with nurturing connections with others (which, as we know, contributes to overall well-being). The study tracked the students' grades and the results replicated what other research had found: academic performance *does not suffer* when parents value their children's relationships with others at least as much as they value how their children are doing academically. Importantly, the same study also demonstrated that the students who felt that their parents were highly critical and emphasized academic and professional achievement over everything else were the most stressed.

There may be no better way to make school less taxing and more enjoyable for our daughters than to trade the projectile model for the pathway-to-fulfillment approach. When a girl gets a poor grade—as she inevitably will—she might fear that she has wrecked her trajectory. We can calm her nerves by pointing out that life is all about following a misstep with a course correction. If she worries that she's not measuring up to the students in her class who happen to be academic stars, then we can point out that her ultimate happiness has a lot more to do with feeling good about herself, her relationships, and how she puts her talents to good use than with what she can do in school.

In short, there are a lot of upsides, and no downsides, to reminding our daughters that there's a lot more to succeeding in life than excelling academically. With that in mind, let's turn our attention now to the wider world that surrounds our girls.

. . . .

CHAPTER SIX

Girls in the Culture

OUR CULTURE HOLDS GIRLS AND YOUNG WOMEN TO UNFAIR AND UN-wavering expectations: we want them to be agreeable, forthcoming, and attractive. Each of these ideals exerts pressure on girls. Recognizing these irrational standards to which girls are held is the first step in addressing them. Next, we should become aware of how we unwittingly replicate at home the very same traps our culture sets for girls. Then we must teach our daughters to question destructive social conventions even if, at least from time to time, they still find themselves conforming to them. Finally, we can point our girls toward practical solutions that allow them to navigate the culture without giving up something precious within themselves.

Let's begin by looking at how we can help our daughters learn to protect their time and stick up for their interests.

Acquiescent by Default

A ninth-grade girl named Nikki sat perched on the couch in my practice on a Wednesday afternoon in early October. A gymnast since age four, she held her spine military-straight and eyed me cautiously. We were meeting at her mother's suggestion, and though Nikki had agreed to the appointment, it was clear that actually being in my office made her really nervous. So after we exchanged a few pleasantries, I helped us get started.

"When your mom and I spoke on the phone," I offered, "she told me that you've been feeling so anxious that you're having a hard time sleeping."

Nikki nodded. Her high ponytail bobbed playfully in strange juxtaposition with her drawn expression. She spoke softly. "Yeah, I get to bed by about ten thirty most nights, and even though I'm exhausted, I'm up till two or even three in the morning some-times." Her tone was simultaneously polite, taut, and tired. I know this mixture well, as I hear it so often from the teenage girls who meet with me.

"What's going on in that time?" I wondered aloud. "What are you doing when you're not able to sleep at night?"

Nikki continued haltingly, "Mostly, my mind is just racing. I'm thinking about what happened that day, I'm going over the work I have to do and the conversations I had with my friends." She started to settle in. "I worry that I posted something dumb online or that I might have said something that hurt someone's feelings. I get so wound up that I just can't sleep."

"Have you talked with your folks about this? Do they know about the worries that are keeping you up at night?"

"They know I'm not sleeping, but," she confided, "I don't share what's on my mind because they'll just tell me not to worry. It's not like I can turn off my thoughts . . . when I do fall asleep, it's just because I get so tired that I eventually pass out."

Within a couple of meetings, Nikki was able to take her ten-sion down several notches. In our sessions we practiced relax-ation techniques that helped her clear her head, and we found ways for her to reassure herself that, even if she had hurt some-one's feelings, she could take steps to make things right. Before long she was able to calm down and fall asleep by eleven thirty or midnight most nights.

Nikki soon became more comfortable in our meetings, and on a crisp day in mid-November, she began her appointment by eagerly volunteering, "Things are way better. I'm falling asleep really fast now." I was delighted, but surprised, by her abrupt improvement.

"Really? I'm so glad to hear it. What happened?"

"I have a stress fracture in my foot," she explained, with surprisingly little concern. "The doctor said I have to take six weeks off from gymnastics. That changed everything."

"How so?" I asked.

Nikki matter-of-factly answered, "Well, I'm not freaking out about school all the time."

With our work centered on Nikki's insomnia, we had hardly discussed school. I knew that she was a good student, but when we weren't focused on her sleep problems, we mostly talked about gymnastics or the social drama in her friend group. I was surprised to hear that school was an issue.

"Why were you freaking out about school?"

She then described a typical day to me. Mornings were frantic because Nikki slept in as late as she could to make up for her long nights. She tried to finish her remaining work on the school bus but started most days feeling desperately behind. Once she got home from gymnastics at about nine, Nikki worked as quickly as she could until she was too tired to maintain focus. With the long hours she spent at the gym during the week and on the weekends, it was not actually possible for her to stay on top of her work, and she worried constantly about her grades. "I still manage to do well in school," Nikki explained, "but it's hard with my schedule."

As she talked, I sat there wanting to kick myself. More than twenty years of practicing as a psychologist, and I had just failed Anxiety 101. I should have asked more about the daily context surrounding Nikki's bedtime worries, because her story, now that she had told it in full, fit perfectly with what we know about psychological strain. She was unable to settle down at night because she spent most days pushed to her limit. Ordinary worries felt catastrophic because her nerves were scraped raw before she climbed into bed.

"Would you feel better if you didn't return to gymnastics?" I asked.

"Oh, yeah," she said before adding drily, "but I can't quit."

"Why not?"

"Well . . . I tried to stop . . . but it didn't work out."

I knitted my eyebrows and tilted my head to express that I was both confused and curious about what she meant.

Nikki elaborated, "I'm really close with the woman who runs the gym. At the end of eighth grade I told her that I was worried about how much work I'd have in high school and that I was thinking about stopping gymnastics. I thought it wouldn't be a big deal, but I could tell that her feelings were hurt, and she said that she really didn't want me to give up the sport." From there, Nikki continued, "I didn't want her to be disappointed, so a few days later I told her that I'd changed my mind and that I wanted to stick with it. Right after that, she suggested that I could also help with teaching a class to the younger students, and I just couldn't say no."

"Do your parents see the price you're paying for spending so much time at the gym while trying to be serious about school?" I asked gently.

"They do," she nodded, softening her tone, "and I know that they're concerned about it. My mom and dad tell me that they want me to have more downtime and get more rest. But I really don't want to let my coach down."

Nikki and I both knew that her sleep troubles would come back as soon as she returned to the gym. But she didn't feel that she could quit, and we couldn't add more hours to her day. Nikki looked at me impassively, clearly feeling trapped in an untenable situation. For now, it seemed that the only solution would be to fret her way through three more years of high school.

While Nikki was prepared to live with this possibility, I was not.

We expect that girls will do as asked. Boys, in general, are not held to the same expectation, and evidence for this double standard can be found in the ample vocabulary we have for girls, but not for boys, who turn down requests.

Girls who don't go along with the wishes of others risk being called inconsiderate at best. Depending on the circumstances surrounding a girl's reluctance to do as asked—perhaps a girl who is short on time declines to help with cleaning up a mess she didn't make—she might also be dubbed a diva or a bitch. Even when boys are *actually* inconsiderate, their behavior is often excused because "boys will be boys." The harshest term for a guy who is disagreeable is probably *dick,* but even that seems less damning, less permanent, and somehow more lighthearted than its feminine analogs.

And so our daughters find themselves in an impossible position. It is unsustainable and senseless for girls to agree to do all that is asked of them, and yet they know and fear the disappointment and nasty names they might face should they refuse requests.

No wonder they feel stressed and anxious.

To make matters worse, girls are far more likely than boys to engage in grinding rumination. Whether they are conscious of it or not, many girls (and women) devote valuable energy to a mental channel that constantly, and anxiously, evaluates the impact of small, everyday choices. *Will my friend think I'm being bitchy if I turn down her party to stay home? Did my adviser think I was being self-centered when I said I could do peer tutoring for only one hour this week instead of my usual three?*

Put simply, our daughters have gotten the powerful, if often unspoken, message that they are expected to accommodate others. This leaves many girls feeling as Nikki does: spread thin, strung out, and sorely out of step with their own wishes or interests.

But not all girls feel this way. Through my practice, in my consulting work at Laurel School, and from my talks with girls around the country, I've gotten to know some girls who comfortably turn down requests and don't put themselves through a mental wringer when they pass on a party, cut back on their obligations, or make any other reasonable decision that might happen to disappoint someone else. And I've found they all have something in common: they're less stressed and anxious than most of their peers.

We want our daughters to become self-assured advocates for their own best interests, rather than wasting valuable energy worrying that making rational choices to protect their time will be met with disapproval—especially in circumstances where boys never would. I'm not one to take entrenched cultural forces lightly, and I am not so naïve as to believe that we can, as individual parents, readily reform the sexist world beyond our homes. Nonetheless, there is still much we *can* do to challenge double standards and protect our daughters from their nerve-wracking effects.

Raised to Please

Raising a daughter turns most parents into cultural firefighters. We become acutely aware of sexism, and we don't want our daughter to get burned by its flames. When we overhear our girl and her preschool friends talking about their future lives, we jump in to remind them that they can be *anything they want*. If the neighbor kid teases our daughter about her "boy" haircut, we roll up in our invisible fire truck, uncoil our invisible hose, and douse him with, "Some guys have long hair, some girls have short hair— and she looks great with that haircut!" We aim to raise girls who are resolute and empowered. We want them to have their own point of view and to express it with conviction and, by God, do we mean it!

Right up until we're the ones doing the asking.

We mean it until one of our daughter's third-grade classmates leaves a phone message to invite her over for a playdate, and our girl wrinkles her nose at us and says she doesn't want to go because she doesn't like that kid. Then we say, "Oh, come on . . . she's not *that* bad," or "Do you want to ask her to come over here? Would that make it better?" or "How would you feel if you were in her shoes?"

We work on our daughter to get her to say yes.

Why?

Like it or not, we're also products of our culture, and every one of us, including me, can flip from firefighter to arsonist in a nanosecond. Because as much as girls fear the words that lie in wait for them should they be less than agreeable, we fear those words, too. We don't want to open the door to the possibility that our daughter could be described as rude or inconsiderate, or worse, a mean girl.

Of course there are plenty of things girls *have to do* that they don't want to do, such as going to visit a boring relative. Sometimes they even need to do those things with a smile. We'll soon address those situations and how we should talk with our daughters about them. For now, we should notice that we, too, unwittingly join the chorus that presses girls to acquiesce to requests they don't really need to honor. Instead, we should capitalize on these teachable moments, because they are crucial to our efforts to shield girls from stress and anxiety. Our daughters shouldn't agree to do many of the optional things that make them unhappy, and we shouldn't miss out on opportunities to help them become skilled at saying no. In our culture, however, this turns out to be a surprisingly complex issue.

Speaking While Female

Whether it's learning to say no with confidence or finding other ways to hold their own, our daughters need to know how to stand up for themselves. With a clear picture in my mind of how an empowered young woman should talk, I have, in the past, encouraged girls to always be direct, outspoken, and unapologetic. Over time, however, I have come to appreciate that this guidance—which sounds great and seems to make so much sense—comes with more complications than we tend to acknowledge. Let's address these snags one at a time.

To begin with, the advice that girls should *always* aim to speak boldly and directly rests on the stereotyped view that boys and men are commanding while girls and women are meek. Adopting this premise leads to the natural conclusion that we should encourage our daughters, if they are to establish a more equal place in the world, to speak more like our sons. But anyone who has spent time with girls and boys knows that the underlying caricatures simply aren't true.

Girls are anything but meek. You may have noticed that your

daughter won't hesitate to tell you when she doesn't feel like emptying the dishwasher, wearing that top you like, or taking those dance lessons you're pushing. So long as they are not worried about harming a relationship or causing social backlash, girls are often great at saying no, directly and unapologetically.

And guys aren't always commanding. In fact, most boys and men have ample social skills to politely turn down requests and to be indirect as needed. If asked to join a game of red rover after already committing to freeze tag, plenty of boys will kindly say, "I just told those guys I'd play tag. How about later?" Most men will affably refuse a lunch invitation with something along the lines of, "I'd really like to join you, but I'm swamped. Thanks for asking."

Granted, boys and men—far more than girls and women—are given license to be curt or impolite if they want. I was recently reminded of this point while out on an exercise walk with one of my friends who, like her husband, is a surgeon. We were talking about the double standard for workplace behavior in men and women when she blurted out, "Oh, yeah! I'd be *fired* for saying some of the things my husband tells me he says in the operating room!" After pausing she added ruefully, "Not that he should be saying those things—but he can get away with it."

The critical issue is that we may be off track if our advice to girls on how they *should* be communicating is based on faulty stereotypes of how they and boys are *already* communicating. And then on top of that, even if guys *were* making a universal and unadulterated practice of bluntly asserting themselves, is that an approach we should emulate?

There's another complication with the be-consistently-bold-and-direct advice we give girls beyond the fact that it rests on problematic assumptions: for girls in particular, bluntness can backfire. There's a bumper crop of research showing that women in the workplace are criticized when they act and speak in ways

that are considered to be masculine. A style that is viewed as assertive in men is frequently called pushy in women. The same
behavior that we consider to be direct in men is typically regarded
as abrasive in women. Similarly, expressive men are described as
passionate while expressive women are viewed as emotional.

We have good evidence that our culture can take a harsh stance
toward girls who are perceived to be disagreeable. A study by the
National Women's Law Center that looked at rates of school discipline from a racial angle brought to light the unspoken rules
about how girls are expected to speak. Comparing punishment
for African American and white girls in kindergarten-through-
twelfth-grade public schools, the compelling and disheartening
report found that the African American girls were six times more
likely to be suspended, despite the fact that both groups misbe-
haved at the same rate.

The study's authors chalk up the unequal suspension rates to
an unconscious racial bias (which has been documented in numerous studies) that causes school officials to perceive African
American girls as especially hostile. For example, an African
American girl might be disciplined for openly disagreeing with a
teacher, while a white girl who does the same thing might simply
be ignored or gently corrected. According to the report, black
girls are disproportionately punished because they are seen to
challenge "society's dominant stereotypes of what is appropriate
'feminine' behavior [by] being candid or assertive and speaking
up when something seems unfair or unjust."

Needless to say, we must combat sexist cultural structures that
penalize girls as a group in addition to racist practices that un-
fairly target African American girls. We do this, in part, by encouraging our girls to be assertive and not to pull their verbal punches.
That said, we should not give girls the impression that expressing
their opinions forcefully will always work well for them when we
know that doing so will sometimes come at a high price.

We are most helpful to our daughters when we remember that they have useful options beyond hanging back or expressing themselves bluntly. Indeed, when it comes to communication, our girls are shrewd and versatile tacticians, and we should recognize them as such.

Our daughters *already* see the difference between what they can get away with and what boys can, and we should talk with them about what they have observed. The next time your daughter mentions that a boy at school challenged the teacher or blurted out an answer instead of raising his hand, ask if he was penalized and whether a girl would have been treated differently. Find out what she thinks about the double standards for assertive boys and girls, and for white girls and girls of color. Then find out what she thinks that she, and we, might do about these double standards.

Settle in for a long conversation or, more likely, the first of many conversations on the topic of who can say what and how. The aim of these discussions is not to tell our daughters how to handle themselves. Instead, we want to help our girls recognize and grapple with the inequities they face. From there, they can *decide for themselves* when they want to try to gain ground through a frontal assault and when it might be to their advantage to use a more indirect approach.

Challenging the Language Police

Another problem with making the blanket recommendation that our daughters be more bold and direct is that this guidance rests on a biased critique of how girls speak. It is not unusual to come across articles in the popular press maintaining that females apologize too much, cling to a rising inflection known as uptalk, and undermine their authority by sprinkling sentences with *just*. Not surprisingly, well-meaning advocates for girls and women urge them to drop these verbal habits in order to sound more assertive. For instance, in 2015, feminist Naomi Wolf published an essay admonishing young women to give up these "destructive speech patterns" and reclaim their "strong female voice."

Language scholars, however, have a different perspective on girls and how they talk. In fact, three days after Wolf published her essay, feminist linguist Deborah Cameron (the same one who questioned, in Chapter Four, our standard date-rape prevention advice) published a sharp rejoinder. Cameron noted that when we criticize the speech of a disempowered group, we are simply finding a new way to express an established bias. Specifically, she asserted that Wolf's argument that women undermine their own power with their speech patterns amounted to "back-to-front logic: it's a bit like saying that if only African Americans would stop speaking African American English the police would be less likely to shoot them." According to Cameron, "People may claim that their judgments are purely about the speech, but really they're judgments of the speakers."

Importantly, Cameron also pointed out that the speech patterns we criticize in females are often used equally by males. Cameron does note that young women tend to be at the vanguard of language change, so there are times when they branch out into new linguistic habits ahead of everyone else. Though their innovations are often criticized, it's usually not long before their new ways of talking become mainstream.

Girls may be disparaged, even penalized, for how they (and, allegedly, only they) speak, but that doesn't mean the problem is theirs. In Cameron's words, "Teaching young women to accommodate to the linguistic preferences, a.k.a. prejudices, of the men who run law firms and engineering companies is doing the patriarchy's work for it. It's accepting that there's a problem with women's speech, rather than a problem with sexist attitudes to women's speech."

Cameron and her colleagues in academic linguistics make a convincing argument that it's time to change how we talk about how girls talk. Once we set aside our well-meaning impulse to police girls' language, we can recognize that many of the speech patterns we have been inclined to criticize, such as a girl saying, "I'm *so sorry* that I can't make it to your party, it's *just* that we have too much going on this weekend," follow the culturally bound refusal patterns that every polite person uses. Rather than critiquing how girls speak, we might recognize that they intuitively deploy a sophisticated set of linguistic strategies to turn people down without hurting feelings or damaging a valued relationship.

This is not to say that you must abandon your verbal pet peeves—everyone who cares about language has them. (I, for one, think the use of the word *impactful* should be a felony offense.) But when it comes to how girls speak, let's move from criticism to curiosity. While I was discussing girls' use of language with a high school teacher and several of her students, the instructor lamented, "I just hate how often girls say 'I'm sorry.' I'm always encouraging them to drop it," to which one girl immediately responded, "I know I say it way too much."

I adopted a neutral, curious tone and asked the girl, "Why do you think you use the phrase so often?"

"I'm not sure," she said. "It's not like I'm really sorry. I think that I just use it when I'm not going to do something, like walk to class with someone. I'll say, 'Oh, I'm sorry, but I have to stop by my locker first' or something like that."

"That makes sense," I replied. "You're looking for a way to soften your 'no.' What other phrases could also do the job?"

A girl sitting across from us jumped in. "You could say, 'Oh, I'd love to, but I can't.'"

Another offered humorously, "'Rats! Today won't work.'"

"Oh, yeah," said the reflexive apologist gratefully. She added, "I would totally say both of those things," before thanking her classmates for their useful suggestions.

Let's start with the assumption that there's a logic to how our daughters speak, even when their style rubs us the wrong way. Girls are excellent at reflecting on how they express themselves. We should not hesitate to ask them what's behind their language choices and, if necessary, help them consider other options at their disposal.

The Verbal Tool Kit

Words can be used like a hammer, and sometimes they should. But for communication overall it's usually good to be equipped with something more like a Swiss Army knife, because we need different tools for different contexts. Girls who have varied repertoires for saying no are less likely to go along with other people's wishes or to worry that they will be called names when they turn someone down. As parents, we should help our daughters develop verbal Swiss Army knives that allow them to assert themselves using language that is forceful and direct, or polite and considerate, or whatever else they determine a situation may require.

Though it's not usually my style to set the agenda with my therapy clients, I had a plan in mind for Nikki's next appointment. As soon as we settled in, I said, "I've been thinking about where we left off last time—with your feeling that you couldn't say no to your gymnastics coach." Nikki nodded, definitely wondering where I was headed. "Am I right that you felt stuck because you care about your relationship with her and got the sense that she was hurt when you said you wanted to quit?"

"Yeah," said Nikki. "I've known her a long time and I could tell from the look on her face that she was upset."

"I've got a solution for us to consider. It doesn't come from my work as a psychologist—I learned about it from a scholar who specializes in negotiation. He came up with a really helpful approach for turning people down while actually improving your relationship with them."

Nikki was clearly interested. Dubious, but interested.

From there I explained a simple formula that could help her figure out what she wanted to do and how she wanted to communicate her wishes to her coach. It goes like this: yes, no, yes. The first "yes" reflects the fact that when we decline something, it's because we are trying to say yes to something else. "You," I said to Nikki, "want to quit gymnastics to give yourself more time to do other things. In telling your coach you wanted to quit, you were trying to say yes to getting more sleep and feeling less stressed about school."

Nikki gave me a wistful smile, as if I were describing some unattainable fantasy.

"Your 'no,' the second part of the formula, grows out of that first 'yes.' You're turning your coach down so that you can stop feeling so frantic. From there, you can get to that last 'yes' in the formula—which is what you *can* offer."

"Okay," said Nikki in a businesslike tone, "but what would I actually say to my coach?"

"Now that we've laid out your yes-no-yes, you might actually say something along the lines of, 'I've missed being at the gym since I got injured, but I'm also getting a lot more sleep and feeling better about other stuff. So I won't be returning to competition when my foot heals, but I'd still like to help with the kids' class.'"

Nikki hesitated a moment. "I like that idea, but honestly . . . I'm not even sure that I want to do that last 'yes.' I don't really have time to teach the kids' class."

Grateful for her candor, I took another pass at it. "How about keeping the first part, but adding, 'I won't be returning when my foot heals, but I do want to stay connected. Would it be okay if I came to some meets so that I can see you and cheer for the team?'"

"That," replied Nikki, "I could say," as her face softened and her shoulders relaxed, "and that also *is* something I'd like to do."

Girls care about their relationships, and unless we give them strategies for doing otherwise, they will often sacrifice themselves before damaging a meaningful connection. In addition to the brilliant yes-no-yes formula, I also am quick to encourage girls to use their clever wit. By making a gentle joke (as in, "Rats! Today won't work!"), a girl can say no while simultaneously expressing her playful affection for the person she's refusing.

Perhaps the most effective tool in a girl's verbal Swiss Army knife is her deft use of intonation, which, as we know, sits at the heart of communication. (To put it another way, a melancholy tune with happy lyrics is still a sad song.) As parents, we never run out of opportunities to demonstrate the stupendous power of tone. Revisiting that unwanted playdate invitation, with our girl standing nearby we might call the other parent back and in a style both friendly and firm say, "Thank you for the invitation. Unfortunately, we can't make it work."

The next time your daughter wants to turn something down—perhaps she's up for going to a movie with her friends but would rather skip the socially loaded sleepover—help her find the right words but prioritize helping her find the right tone. Girls can be great at striking different tones and get even better with practice. Once you've got the right phrase—perhaps, "I'm excited about the movie but can't make the sleepover"—have your daughter play with the many tones that could give it a huge range of meanings. The exact same words can be said brusquely, sheepishly, caustically, or—what we're shooting for here—with a gentle confidence that communicates her lack of guilt about her sleepover regrets, and genuine delight in getting to see the movie with her friends.

In general, I've found girls to be highly receptive to guidance on filling out their verbal tool kit with strategies that let them turn people down without hurting feelings or compromising valued connections. All the same, I've had plenty of girls call my attention to a problem with saying no that they consider to be a real stumper: "What should I do," a girl might ask, "if my friend asks *why* I can't come to the sleepover?"

The Transparent Girl

While conducting a workshop with a group of sixth-grade girls about how to turn down unwanted requests, I stumbled into a critical conversation with one of the students in my audience. It began when I asked the entire group how they might handle being invited to hang out with a classmate on a Friday night and not wanting to go. First, we experimented with the yes-no-yes formula (as in, "I can't come over because I want to go to bed early, but can we sit together at lunch on Monday?"). After that, we practiced saying, "How about next Friday?" in a spectrum of tones. Then I threw out another option. "If you wanted to," I suggested, "you could say, 'Thanks for thinking of me, but unfortunately, I've got plans.'"

A hand went up, and I called on its obviously uneasy owner. "But," said the girl, whose limbs were so long and post–growth spurt thin that with her right leg crossed over her left she could comfortably tuck her right foot behind her left calf, "if you don't really have plans that night, well then . . . wouldn't you be *lying*?"

"Oh, no, you're not lying," I responded reassuringly. "Perhaps you have plans to paint your nails, or take *BuzzFeed* quizzes, or maybe your plan is to make no plans at all until you decide what you want to do." My answer made so much sense to me, but it seemed not to convince the girl with the coiled legs. So I continued, "You don't owe your friend a complete accounting of your intentions—you don't have to be an open book if you don't feel like it."

I could tell from the look on the sixth grader's face that she wasn't buying any of what I was selling. At best, my advice seemed to strike the girl as strange. At worst, she may have been wondering why her school had invited a corrupt adult to urge impressionable young women to lie. Long after the workshop ended, our conversation stayed on my mind. I felt sure of the guidance I had offered but was troubled by how obviously uncomfortable it had made the girl. I also knew she wasn't the only student in the room who felt that she didn't have the right to be selective about what personal information she shared with others.

Why did these girls seem to think that full disclosure was always required? The more I weighed this question, the more my attention turned to how we exhort girls to be genuine and how we place authenticity on a lofty pedestal. Of course we are offering well-intentioned guidance when we encourage girls to be "real" and "true." We are urging them to follow their hearts, not to shape themselves for others. But this does not seem to be what our daughters are hearing. More than we realize, girls understand us to be saying that they must always be utterly and completely forthright.

That's a problem, especially when we combine it with the cultural injunction to be agreeable. A girl can't actually accomplish both because, like any other human, every girl contains a world of complicated thoughts and feelings. She cannot possibly be simultaneously see-through and utterly pleasing to others.

Having negative thoughts and feelings is not inherently problematic, since thinking, feeling, and doing operate independently of one another. We can't easily control—and rarely need to control—what we think and feel. We must only regulate how we actually conduct ourselves. Sometimes, of course, our thoughts and feelings helpfully guide our actions, such as when we happily accept an invitation to spend time with someone we really like. But in order to be civil members of society, adults routinely detach what we think and feel from what we do. This is exactly what's happening when we make polite small talk with a colleague we can't stand when there's no one else on our elevator.

For girls who believe that their thoughts, feelings, and actions must be in full agreement, simply *having* a negative sentiment triggers anxiety. An everyday annoyance, such as being assigned to work on a group project with an irritating classmate, leaves the girl who assumes she should be utterly transparent with two—and only two—untenable options. To be completely "honest," she must make no attempt to hide her irritation and suffer the consequences. Or, the girl must feel ashamed of her irritation and fretfully search for a way to purge her heart (and mind and behavior) of any unpleasantness.

But really, how have girls *not* gotten the memo that it's often okay to think one thing and show another? If they want to decline an invitation, why would they worry about saying that they're already busy? Kind, decent adults do both of these things all the time, and boys certainly don't seem to lose sleep over these concerns the way girls do. How did our daughters get the impression that they've got a problem on their hands as soon as they have a thought or feeling they wouldn't want to broadcast?

Well, my fellow arsonists, we have some soul-searching to do. In the constant, garden-variety exchanges that make up parenting, there are times when we attempt to legislate what happens in our daughters' hearts and minds. I can tell you how this usually goes down in my home. Often, we're sitting at dinner on a week-night when one of my girls gripes about a classmate or teacher. At these times, I can be quick to minimize or dismiss her complaint with, "Well, that kid probably has something hard going on. Your job is to be kind." Or, "I'm sure your teacher is very busy and will hand back your assignment soon."

Sometimes, I'm sure, I respond abruptly simply because I am tired from my own long day. At other times, I may shut my daughter down because I know that our culture counts on girls, more than boys, to be accommodating and polite. Regardless of what's behind a brusque response on any given evening, it's all too easy for my girl to hear me saying, "Your negative thoughts and feelings are unacceptable."

Full Disclosure Is Not Required

Poets, philosophers, and social scientists have long articulated what every one of us knows to be true: we reveal different parts of ourselves under different conditions. We can think about this phenomenon in theatrical terms by noting that when we are "front stage" (at school, at work, and so on) our actions are guided, in part, by the presence of an audience. When we are "back stage" (at home, alone) we can let our hair down and more freely be ourselves.

As parents, we sometimes forget that our girls have, and should have, front and back stages. When I shut down my daughter's complaints, I'm neglecting the fact that she really does know the difference between what we say at home and what we say or do in public. I'm worrying, unnecessarily, that allowing her to gripe about her classmate or teacher might be taken as permission to *act* on her grievance by being rude or unpleasant at school. Both of my daughters are smarter than that, and your daughter is, too. Giving our girls the anxiety relief that comes with embracing the whole of their inner lives can be as simple as adjusting how we respond to the grousing that often happens at the end of the day.

My younger daughter has very strong opinions and freely speaks her mind. If she likes something, she will let you know, and if she doesn't like something, you'll hear about that, too. In kindergarten, a particular classmate rubbed my daughter the wrong way, and on many afternoons she came home overflowing with complaints about her. Once I became committed to teaching my own daughters about their front and back stages, I started to respond, "Yes, that sounds pretty aggravating. You are absolutely allowed to be *brain annoyed* with her. But, remember, we expect you to be *behavior polite.*" This advice made perfect sense to my daughter and served as a useful introduction to the idea that she, like the rest of us, has both a public and a private self.

In a similar vein, when my older daughter first encountered the high social drama of middle school, we let her know that she could use our home to air her grievances about any nonsense she encountered during the day. We promised not to share what she told us unless someone's safety was in question. Our condition for giving her ample room to complain freely and confidentially was that we expected her to leave her griping with us and be a solid citizen at school.

This is not to say that my daughters are flawlessly behaved. They are as real and whole and imperfect as any of us are. It *is* to say, however, that we've gone out of our way to clarify for our girls that they, like the rest of us, have space within themselves (and within our home) where they can be open and honest and curious about what they truly think and feel. I'm all for encouraging our girls to be genuine and authentic. To me, a genuine and authentic girl is one who feels that she can really get to know herself.

We may worry that giving girls plenty of latitude to express negative thoughts and feelings will lead to bad behavior, but the reality is usually the opposite. Every adult knows that having a safe place to vent our true feelings usually makes it easier to be on good behavior around people we don't like. Unloading our displeasure can also clear the path toward finding constructive strategies for dealing with difficult relationships. In truth, I sometimes wonder if the girls who routinely engage in sneaky or indirect meanness are the ones who have been denied permission to have negative thoughts and feelings. The more you squelch a sentiment, the more likely it is to come out sideways.

If necessary, we can remind our daughters that there's a big difference between expressing unpleasant sentiments and acting like a jerk. Imagine, for example, a scenario in which a parent tells his daughter that part of an upcoming holiday will be spent visiting a great-aunt. The girl responds, "Ugh, you are the worst dad ever for making us do that over break—it's like paying a two-hour visit to a tree stump." While her feelings may be legitimate (visiting a great-aunt may not be at the top of her vacation to-do list), what the girl said needs a serious overhaul.

To lay down some lines without shaming his daughter, the father might respond, "I get it that you're frustrated with me and that you find these visits boring. You have a right to your viewpoint, but it's not okay for you to get ugly. You'll need to find a kinder way to say what's on your mind. Also, during the visit, I do expect you to be your utterly charming self, regardless of how you feel."

An interaction like this one accomplishes three important things at once: it reminds girls that they can't mistreat anyone, even their parents; it affirms that girls should feel perfectly free to think one thing and show another; and, to return to the topic of girls being pleasers, it gives us a way to talk about the times when our daughters must go along with a plan they dislike. Every one of us runs into situations when we have to do something we really don't want to do. It's helpful for our daughters to know that there's nothing wrong with faking enthusiasm (or at least polite acceptance) when the circumstances require as much.

Don't be surprised if it takes your daughter some time to learn what belongs on her front and back stage. Most of us, girls included, make mistakes along the way when deciding what we share with others (and how we share it) and what we want to keep to ourselves. All the same, we should support our girls as they explore and establish their public and private personas, as we want them to regard themselves as nuanced and complex. Indeed, our home conversations should always be grounded in the assumption that there's much more to our daughters than meets the eye. Because when it comes to girls and young women, our culture tends to think the opposite.

Looks Matter . . . Too Much

It may actually be impossible to overstate how much girls' and young women's lives are saturated with signals that their looks *really* matter. Though you may not need convincing on this point, here are a few examples just in case. Even when speaking about infants, adults comment on girls' appearance far more than on boys'. The cosmetic and body product industry spends $13 billion each year on advertisements suggesting to girls and women that they need to do something about how they look. Beauty pageants are still a thing. Nearly every woman showcased in the popular media—from magazines to Disney television shows to news anchors—is objectively pretty, while many of the men in the same contexts look like people we actually know. The media remains persistently preoccupied with the clothing, hair, and looks of powerful, accomplished women who are in positions that have absolutely nothing to do with their clothing, hair, or looks.

In short, we have two problems. First, cultural forces constantly signal to our daughters that how they look just might be more important than *anything else*. Second, our culture promotes a Bambi-eyed, pearly-toothed, smooth-and-lustrous-haired, flawless-skinned, fit-but-thin-but-curvy beauty ideal that is actually impossible for most girls and young women to replicate.

As to the first problem, we should recognize that it is fundamentally anxiety-provoking for girls to feel that so much of their value rides on the genetic lottery of outward appearance and not on qualities they can actually control, such as how creative, kind, smart, funny, diligent, and all kinds of awesome they are. Furthermore, our preoccupation with girls' appearance does more than draw attention away from what really matters about them. It actually *undermines* what matters.

In fact, one remarkable study found that simply commenting on a young woman's appearance can temporarily erode her intellectual abilities. To investigate the impact of highlighting how girls look, a team of psychologists invited college students to take part in what was billed as a study of hiring strategies. Participants were asked to submit a résumé along with a photo of themselves. Once the researchers had time to "review" the résumés and pictures, they gave the women identical comments about their materials. But for half of the women, they included an extra sentence: "I can see from your picture that your look is very presentable, and looking good is an advantage in the employment market." After receiving their feedback, the research participants took a difficult math test.

The women who read comments about their appearance did significantly worse on the math test than the women whose pictures were never discussed. Remarkably, this was true even for the participants who themselves placed a low priority on their looks. Focusing on young women's superficial qualities can keep them from showing us just how substantial they really are.

As parents, we should try to downplay the importance of our daughters' surface features and showcase the importance of everything else about them. Sometimes, this can be pleasant and easy. When my girls were young and strangers would compliment them on their cuteness, I got into the habit of responding cheerfully, "She's even *better* on the inside!" But at other times, the conversations we have with our daughters about how they look start in a very painful place.

Shortly after eleven on a Wednesday morning, my cellphone buzzed with a call from one of my dearest college friends. I was a little surprised to be hearing from her in the middle of the workday, as she's a high-powered attorney, but I gladly picked up.

"Hey, do you have a minute?" she asked quickly. I could hear that something was weighing heavily on her mind.

"Of course. What's up?"

"Cammie," her fourth-grade daughter, "was *so* upset last night." My friend shared that Cammie had seemed tense through dinner and then burst into tears at bedtime. As her mom tucked her in, she explained that girls at school had been taunting her about her looks.

"I guess that they were telling her that her nose is too pointy and asking why she didn't shave the dark hair on her legs." Scornfully, my friend added, "I'm so pissed that they went after her like that. I told her that they were being mean and that she should ignore them, but I could tell this morning that what they said had really gotten under her skin."

We talked through the possibility of reaching out to the teacher or the other girls' parents and agreed that Cammie should be consulted before her mom took either step. In the meantime, I wanted to try to help my friend and her sweet, hurting girl.

"Tonight, when things are quiet," I began, "find some time to sit down with her. Bring some paper and a pen, and tell her you want to make the 'Pie Chart of Cammie.'" Though smiles don't make sounds, I could tell that my friend was amused on the other end of the line. From there I explained that the title of her daughter's pie chart should be "What *Matters* about Cammie."

"Draw a tiny little sliver of pie in the circle, and tell her that it stands for how she looks on the outside. Then work with her to fill the rest of the circle with words that describe the qualities that make her the amazing kid she is."

"She'll love it," said my friend, "and it will make sense to her right away. She's got so much going for her . . . so much to feel confident about."

I got an email from my friend the next day letting me know how things went. She told me that Cammie caught on even faster than expected and delighted in filling her pie chart with words describing the many things she likes about herself. My friend added that once Cammie finished filling in her circle, she took it upon herself to draw a second chart. She told her mom that this one represented "what the mean girls in my class think is important," and made it the inverse of her own pie chart, with most of the circle assigned to "looks" and only a tiny sliver assigned to "everything else." The best part, her mother wrote, was that Cammie ended the evening by pointing to the second circle and declaring, "and *that's* why I don't hang out with them."

If your daughter has already aged out of the pie chart exercise, there are still plenty of ways to help her to cast a skeptical eye on our culture's preoccupation with girls' and women's outsides. For example, we can observe with our daughters how often the world focuses on the surface features of women who are known for their accomplishments. We might say, "Why is the Internet talking about how pretty that singer looks without her makeup instead of what it took for her to become one of the most skilled performers of her generation?" Or "That woman is in charge of America's foreign policy—what does it tell us when the press chooses to cover her latest hairstyle?" Though it ought to go without saying, we should make a point of admiring our girls' earned accomplishments—such as their hard work at school, their burgeoning athletic skills, their positive contributions to their social group—at *least* as much as (if not a whole lot more than) we admire their exteriors. We reduce girls' anxiety when we help them derive their worth from qualities they can cultivate and control.

"Everyone's Beautiful" Can Backfire

Girls get the message that their looks count for much of their value. As if that weren't destructive enough, they also come to understand that our culture idealizes a *very* narrowly defined form of female beauty. Thanks to that, we have truckloads of research documenting the fact that simply looking at media-portrayed paragons increases how uneasy girls feel about their own appearance. At best, our daughters can spend too much time obsessing about their perceived flaws. At worst, they sometimes engage in unhealthy and dangerous practices—such as turning to severe dieting or excessive exercise—in an effort to force their bodies to better match an unattainable ideal.

To this I should add that there has never been a generation as steeped in pictures as the girls we are raising today. In addition to viewing traditional media, they consume hundreds, if not thousands, of photos posted online by their friends. And what do they see in a lot of those posts? Girls showcasing their appearance, seeking to replicate the perfected look of professional models, and doing what they can to run up the likes each photo will receive.

We have our work cut out for us. We need to help our girls feel good about themselves in a culture that leaves many of them feeling bad about the way they look. To do this, we often turn to the age-old practice of reassuring our girls that they *are* beautiful. This is a well-meaning strategy that my mom used with me and that moms everywhere use to comfort their girls. Lately, however, I've started to wonder if we should reconsider our approach.

I'm behind any effort to celebrate the full range of human beauty and to teach our girls that "attractive" comes in an infinite number of forms, but we need to recognize that telling our girls that beauty comes in every variety doesn't always leave them feeling less worried about how they look. First off, many girls just don't buy it. Our daughters can see with their own eyes that our culture celebrates some physical forms and denigrates others. In truth, most adult women don't believe the "everyone is beautiful" message, either. A large-scale survey of a diverse sample of adult American women found that 91 percent reported that they disliked the shape of their bodies. We really shouldn't expect girls and young women to rebuff absurd beauty standards when grown women can't even do it.

It is important to note that research consistently demonstrates that African American girls and women report feeling quite a bit better about their appearance than their white, Hispanic, or Asian American counterparts. Paradoxically, however, African American girls (and Hispanic, Asian American, and Native American girls) are just as likely to have experimented with unhealthy dieting practices as white girls. Put simply, the slim prototype of female beauty shapes how women of all ages, races, and ethnicities regard their own looks, however much we wish it didn't.

When I think about the call that came from Cammie's mom, I realize that I had to squelch my own impulse to say, "Please let Cammie know that I *love* her nose! Tell her that she's as beautiful as can be." These are all very kind things to say, but I worry that rushing to reassure our self-conscious daughters that they really are gorgeous risks underscoring the harmful premise that it's very important to *be* attractive.

Of course, most parents tell their daughters that they're beautiful. Because to us, they truly are. In my own home, I'll sometimes say to my girls, "You look so lovely!" when the moment strikes me, and I don't want to stop sharing my spontaneous, affectionate admiration of them. So from time to time I make a point of adding: "But regardless of how you look, you and I both know that your appearance is the most trivial thing about you. It matters so much more that you are the fun, considerate, and hardworking girl that you are." Ten times out of ten, my daughters roll their eyes in response to my addendum, but I don't mind. I simply welcome their eye rolls as confirmation that they heard what I said.

We don't want our girls to feel bad about their looks, yet we should aim to balance the enthusiasm we express about their appearance with our enthusiasm about the rest of what they have to offer the world. Think of it this way: if a girl derives an enormous amount of self-esteem from thinking that she's a stunner, is that really the outcome we were hoping for? I would never want to deny a girl the joy of feeling pretty—and there are real pleasures to be had in dressing in flattering clothes, playing with makeup, and doing one's hair—but we should bear in mind that to take pride in one's physical form is to take pride in one's most superficial quality. And thankfully, there are healthy ways for our daughters to feel good about their bodies that have nothing to do with appearance.

Celebrating Physical Function, Not Form

Research consistently demonstrates that participating in sports improves how girls feel about their bodies. These results are encouraging, but they've long been tempered by an important question: Do athletic girls feel good about themselves only because being fit helps them to more closely resemble our cultural ideal? To address this possibility, a large-scale study asked teenage girls how they felt about how their bodies looked and, separately, how they felt about what their bodies could do.

Here's what the researchers found: girls who participated in organized activities, such as team sports, took more pride in the *functional* aspects of their bodies than girls who simply exercised regularly or girls who were sedentary. In other words, structured athletic programs that involve skill building, cooperation, and shared goals help girls to take pleasure in what their bodies can accomplish. It's important to note that the study also found that girls who participated in activities that include a heavy emphasis on the physical form, such as dance and gymnastics, took *less* pride in what their bodies could do than girls who played sports that focus on speed, strength, or skill. This result echoes other research showing that participating in sports with an aesthetic component can actually leave girls feeling worse about their physiques.

What's the takeaway from this research? In short, we can help our daughters feel good about what their bodies can do by encouraging them toward skill-building physical activities, assuming we have the time, money, energy, and other needed resources to do so. If we're on the fence between volleyball and ballet, or between swimming and gymnastics, studies suggest that we should lean toward the team activities and away from the appearance-oriented ones. The research also demonstrates that even if your daughter doesn't want to make an ongoing commitment to a sport, you should help her find ways to be physically active. It will improve how she feels about her body in addition to being good for her health.

Happily, there's yet another way for a girl to value her body: by appreciating that it often *feels* good. Parents aren't always comfortable celebrating their daughters' emerging awareness of sensual enjoyment because doing so can seem awfully close to the more-awkward-than-it-should-be topic of girls' sexuality. So let's start small. The next time you reach for a luscious hand lotion, enjoy with your daughter how wonderful it smells and how great it feels on your skin and, if she's interested, hers. Really savor the tastes of your favorite foods, and encourage her do to the same. Find ways to celebrate the sensation of snuggling up under heavy blankets on a cold day, or of exercising, or of running a hairbrush through one's hair. There's no need to feel weird or make a big deal about it: just bear in mind that we *want* our daughters to find lots of ways to feel happy both in and about their bodies.

Fundamentally, it falls to parents to combat our culture's pervasive message that appearance really matters. For starters, we can go out of our way to emphasize the substantial, as opposed to superficial, qualities in girls and women. We can make a point of showing our daughter the article about the scientific work done by a Nobel Prize winner and of skipping the article about the outfit the scientist wore while accepting her award. As our daughters age, we can grab that article about the scientist's outfit and help our girl appreciate its absurdity. When we do talk about girls' physiques, we might focus on what girls' bodies can *do* and the great ways they can *feel* instead of addressing how they look.

In my ideal world, we'd stop judging girls—and girls would

stop judging themselves—by their outward appearance. For now, this remains a challenge that all of us need to work continuously to address. But in truth, the weight of this problem, like so many others, is not distributed equally among all of the girls and young women in our culture.

The Headwinds of Prejudice

Girls and young women who belong to racial or ethnic minority groups contend with every single one of the stressful and anxiety-provoking situations raised in this book. But unlike Caucasian girls, they do so while also fighting the headwinds of discrimination.

At times, they face the raw gales of slurs, harassment, threats, or worse. Frequently, too, they are buffeted by gusts of subtle bias that may or may not be intentional. For example, bright minority students can tell that some of their teachers are surprised by their academic prowess. Asian American girls encounter teachers who seem to be surprised if they are *not* gifted mathematicians. Strangers ask American-born minority girls, "Where are you *really* from?" Store owners watch some minorities closely as they shop. Yet the constant, taxing, lived experience of being non-white is dismissed by those expressing well-meaning sentiments such as, "I just don't see color."

Scholars have documented in detail the chronic emotional and physiological stress that comes with living in the windstorm of prejudice. While it's not surprising that outright racism or xenophobia triggers fear and terror, research tells us that exposure to less overt bias also takes a heavy toll. Being told, "Everyone can succeed if they really try," or asked, "How can I be racist? Many of my friends are black!" often leaves minority girls and young women putting a lot of mental energy into trying to make sense of such interactions and figuring out how to respond to them.

My work with Kendra, an African American girl, better familiarized me with many of the wearing, low-grade slights experienced by minorities. I first met Kendra when she was nine years old and her folks sought my help after the heart attack death of her forty-year-old uncle. She was close with her father's brother, and she understandably became extremely frightened that her dad would suddenly die the same way.

We worked through Kendra's fears and then continued to touch base at her request in the years that followed. When she was in eighth grade, Kendra asked her parents if we could have a few meetings to talk through how she might gracefully extricate herself from a difficult friendship that had run its course. In the midst of those sessions, she arrived to one of our late-afternoon meetings looking unusually glum. Kendra had just come from playing soccer with her middle school team. She was wearing black track pants and a pink sweatshirt and had her hair pulled back in braids. The look on her face was serious, yet pained, in a way I did not remember having seen before.

"Are you okay?" I asked her as soon as she'd gotten settled.

"I don't know," she answered hesitantly. Then, after a long pause, she explained, "It's just that we have this assistant coach at soccer who keeps calling me by the name of one of the other black girls on the team."

I was glad that she felt willing to introduce the issue of race in our sessions, and was eager to let her know that I thought I could support her on this topic, even as a white woman.

Neutrally, I asked, "I take it that your coach is white?"

"Yeah," said Kendra, "and she's nice and all. I just don't know what to do. I feel like I should correct her, but I'm trying to figure out how to do it without sounding disrespectful."

We spent the rest of the session kicking around ideas for what she might say. While the coach's behavior was almost certainly unintentional, it left Kendra feeling far less valued than her white teammates. To make matters worse, Kendra also felt that *she* was the one responsible for finding an effective, yet diplomatic, solution to the problem. Ultimately, we decided that she'd politely but firmly say, "I'm Kendra," the next time her coach called her by the wrong name. That option did not feel altogether comfortable, but it was still better than anything else we could come up with.

Later on, when she was in high school, Kendra talked with me about having to start from scratch with each AP course she took that was taught by a teacher she didn't already know.

"They assume the white kids are smart, but it's like I have to prove myself every time, even though I've never gotten below an A." Advanced Placement classes are hard enough. For Kendra they also came with the charge of feeling that she needed to demonstrate that she even had a right to be in the room.

Kendra's smarts and hard work secured her a spot at Princeton. Over winter break of her freshman year, she stopped by my office for a visit.

"How are things?" I asked, feeling very glad to see her. It's a funny thing to be a therapist: I become devoted to my clients but only get updates on their lives when they choose to share them.

"They're okay. It's really good on the academic side. I like my classes a lot and was really well prepared for them." Her tone then became more melancholy. "The social side has been complicated. I've found some really good friends—several black friends and a few white—the kind of people I think I'll stay close with for years."

"But . . ." I offered.

"But . . . I've been surprised by how often people treat me like I don't quite belong. Or as though I was only accepted because

I'm black. It's subtle, but I can feel it. Honestly, I thought that getting into Princeton would change things—I thought I'd be taken more seriously. How can I get this far and *still* have to put up with this stuff?"

For minority girls, having a supportive family waiting at home helps to buffer some of the negative effects of bigotry. Though I wish she didn't need it, I was happy to know that Kendra had kind, thoughtful parents—and now a solid group of friends—who could support her along the way. All the same, we should recognize that, to a great degree, the work of addressing discrimination sits squarely on the shoulders of those in the cultural majority.

Anyone in that boat needs to recognize how we contribute to the headwinds of bias, even if that is not at all our intention. Past that, we also ought to find ways to act as tailwinds to ease the journey of those who walk through the world as minorities. This requires a willingness to engage with the painful realities of prejudice, which, I appreciate, is a charged and sensitive subject. In truth, I feel anxious even addressing it here: I worry that I cannot do the topic justice and fear that I will be unwittingly offensive.

More than a little of me wants to turn away from thinking about discrimination, and, as a member of the dominant culture, that is an option I can exercise at will. But if writing this book has taught me anything, it's that we should not run from discomfort. When we confront what makes us uneasy—and help our daughters do the same—we find that anxiety is usually a warning that something is amiss, and that stress is inherent to growth and change.

Conclusion

. . . .

CHALLENGES COME AT OUR DAUGHTERS FROM ALL SIDES. OUR GIRLS worry about their relationships with us and with their friends; they step into the unsteady world of romance; they face sometimes overwhelming demands at school; and they wrestle with the broader culture's expectations that they be compliant, transparent, and attractive. These difficulties aren't new. But they now play out in the context of modern technology that straps girls onto a speeding social media roller coaster from which they rarely dismount. They happen in the midst of a dizzying twenty-four-hour news cycle that keeps even the mellowest among us on edge. And they take place at a moment in time when the world around our daughters seems to move more quickly than ever before.

Under so much pressure, under such constant siege, it's no surprise that our girls come to us feeling nervous and upset. For parents, there's nothing worse than having a child who is in distress. At these times, we want to do *anything* we can to help our daughters feel better. Our instincts may tell us to rescue our girl from the source of her discomfort, to shelter her from what makes her uneasy.

If following these instincts worked, I wouldn't have written this book and you wouldn't be reading it. Tension and turmoil, we find, are strange creatures. They don't die down when our daughters avoid them. In fact, when we shrink from pressure and fear, they just take on new, harrowing proportions.

Stress and anxiety can be addressed only when faced head-on. We're most useful to our girls when we help them confront, and sometimes even embrace, these two fundamental aspects of everyday life. They should ask, "*What* is the source of all this stress?" and "*Why* am I anxious?" These are the questions that will help girls master the challenges they face, because the answers put them back in control.

Stress, it turns out, rises when our daughters are pushed to operate at the edge of their capacities. It almost always helps girls grow. So long as our daughters know how to restore themselves, and aren't faced with demands that far exceed their emotional and intellectual resources, they should come to recognize that being stretched beyond familiar limits cultivates strength and durability.

Anxiety, as we now know, often arrives as a well-meaning messenger. It alerts your daughter that something's not right, or that it would be smart for her to stay on her toes. There are, of course, girls whose nerves won't stop talking though they have nothing useful to say. But most of the time we, and our daughters, should regard anxiety as an ally, not an enemy, and find out what it wants us to know.

The world asks more of our daughters than it ever has before, and it now offers them more, too. As parents, we're at our best when we help our girls advance, not retreat, in the face of the challenges and opportunities they will inevitably encounter.

Because girls who learn to face their fears find out just how brave they can be.

Acknowledgments

· · · · · · · · · · ·

THIS BOOK WOULD NOT HAVE COME ABOUT WITHOUT THE KEEN AND steadfast efforts of my agent, Gail Ross, and the wisdom and diligence of my editor, Susanna Porter. I am the lucky beneficiary of their exceptional talents and those of their dynamite teams at Ross Yoon Agency and Random House.

The final form of this manuscript was greatly improved by early feedback from several friends and colleagues. Thanks go to Daniel and Jennifer Coyle, Lisa Heffernan, Davida Pines, and Amy Weisser for generously offering their time and insights. An extra measure of gratitude is reserved for Amanda Block, my outstanding research assistant who, with unflagging care, helped to polish this book and the scholarly citations within it.

My thinking has been enriched and refined by ongoing conversations with psychologists Aarti Pyati, Erica Stovall White, and especially Tori Cordiano, who provided excellent comments on early drafts and who, as my officemate, patiently tolerates my constant interruptions to discuss topics ranging from the professional to the personal to the simply playful. I am likewise buoyed by my work at Laurel School, a bastion of love and respect for girls, where Head of School Ann V. Klotz's dedication to educating the minds and hearts of young women energizes the entire school community. Of this community I could not be more thankful or proud to count myself a member.

Extraordinary friends, including Hetty Carraway, Anne Curzan, Alice Michael, and Carol Triggiano, and my loving family—especially my marvelous parents and daughters—have encouraged me throughout. No one has loaned more tireless support to this project than Darren, my dear husband. He is not only the most devoted partner—and father to our daughters—I could ask for, but he also nimbly executes the many additional roles I call on him to serve: cheerleader, sounding board, and close reader. I aspire to deserve him.

My training as a psychologist was provided by remarkable clinicians and scholars, and I am indebted to every one of them for shepherding me into the only career I can imagine having. In this book my own ideas are integrated with excellent work done by others, and I have aimed to acknowledge everyone whose work has informed my thinking. Any errors or omissions are mine alone.

Finally, I am boundlessly grateful to the girls and young women I have met through my work as a psychologist. Their decency, vitality, and depth never cease to impress and inspire me.

Notes

. . . .

Epigraph

ix **It is not the presence** Freud, A. (1965). *Normality and Pathology in Child-hood: Assessments of development.* Madison, WI: International Universities Press, pp. 135–36.

For the ease of the reader, I twice removed the term *ego* from this quotation as it has an idiosyncratic meaning in psychoanalytic texts, and removing it does not alter the meaning of Ms. Freud's words.

Introduction

xvi **symptoms of chronic tension** Anderson, N. B., Belar, C. D., Breckler, S. J., et al. (2014). *Stress in America™: Are teens adopting adults' stress habits?* (Rep.). Washington, DC: American Psychological Association.

xvi **experiencing emotional problems** Collishaw, S. (2015). Annual research review: Secular trends in child and adolescent mental health. *Journal of Child Psychology and Psychiatry* 56 (3), 370–93.

Mojtabai, R., Olfson, M., and Han, B. (2016). National trends in the prevalence and treatment of depression in adolescents and young adults. *Pediatrics* 138 (6), e20161878.

xvi **anxious is on the rise** Calling, S., Midlov, P., Johansson, S-E., et al. (2017). Longitudinal trends in self-reported anxiety. Effects of age and birth cohort during 25 years. *BMC Psychiatry* 17 (1), 1–11.

Tate, E. (2017, March 29). Anxiety on the rise. Retrieved from inside highered.com/news/2017/03/29/anxiety-and-depression-are-primary-concerns-students-seeking-counseling-services.

xvii **psychological stress and tension** Burstein, M., Beesdo-Baum, K., He, J.-P., and Merikangas, K. R. (2014). Threshold and subthreshold generalized anxiety disorder among US adolescents: Prevalence, sociodemographic, and clinical characteristics. *Psychological Medicine* 44 (11), 2351–62.

Merikangas, K. R., He, J., Burstein, M., et al. (2010). Lifetime prevalence of mental disorders in US adolescents: Results from the national comorbidity study—adolescent supplement (NCS-A). *Journal of the American Academy of Child and Adolescent Psychiatry* 49 (10), 980–89.

Kessler, R. C., Avenevoli, S., Costello, E. J., et al. (2012). Prevalence, persistence, and sociodemographic correlates of *DSM-IV* disorders in the national comorbidity survey replication adolescent supplement. *Archives of General Psychiatry* 69 (4), 372–80.

xvii **31 percent of girls** Calling, S., Midlov, P., Johansson, S-E., et al. (2017). Longitudinal trends in self-reported anxiety. Effects of age and birth cohort during 25 years. *BMC Psychiatry* 17 (1), 1–11.

The gender ratios reported by Calling and colleagues are echoed in the study by Kessler and colleagues, which finds that anxiety disorders are between 1.5 and 2.5 times more likely to occur in girls than in boys.

xvii **symptoms of psychological strain** Anderson, Belar, Breckler, et al. (2014).

xvii **jumped by 55 percent** Fink, E., Patalay, P., Sharpe, H., et al. (2015). Mental health difficulties in early adolescence: A comparison of two cross-sectional studies in England from 2009–2014. *Journal of Adolescent Health* 56 (5), 502–7.

xvii **faster pace in girls** Calling, Midlov, Johansson, et al. (2017).

Van Droogenbroeck, F., Spruyt, B., and Keppens, G. (2018). Gender differences in mental health problems among adolescents and the role of social support: Results from the Belgian health interview surveys 2008 and 2013. *BMC Psychiatry* 18 (1), 1–9.

xvii **from thirteen to seventeen** Mojtabai, R., Olfson, M., and Han, B. (2016). National trends in the prevalence and treatment of depression in adolescents and young adults. *Pediatrics* 138 (6), e20161878.

xvii **three times more likely** Breslau, J., Gilman, S. E., Stein, B. D., et al. (2017). Sex differences in recent first-onset depression in an epidemiological sample of adolescents. *Translational Psychiatry* 7 (5), e1139.

xvii **43 percent more likely** American College Health Association. (2014). *American College Health Association—National College Health Assessment II: Reference group executive summary.* Hanover, MD: American College Health Association.

xviii **seeing something new** Collishaw. (2015).

xviii **simply more willing** MacLean, A., Sweeting, H., and Hunt, K. (2010). "Rules" for boys, "guidelines" for girls. *Social Science and Medicine* 70 (4), 597–604.

xviii **doing in school** Giota, J., and Gustafsson, J. (2017). Perceived demands of schooling, stress and mental health: Changes from grade 6 to grade 9 as a function of gender and cognitive ability. *Stress and Health* 33 (3), 253–66.

xviii **how they look** Zimmer-Gembeck, M., Webb, H., Farrell, L., and Waters, A. (2018). Girls' and boys' trajectories of appearance anxiety from age 10 to 15 years are associated with earlier maturation and appearance-related teasing. *Development and Psychopathology* 30 (1), 337–50.

xviii **to be cyberbullied** Kessel Schneider, S., O'Donnell, L., and Smith, E. (2015). Trends in cyberbullying and school bullying victimization in a regional census of high school students. *The Journal of School Health* 85 (9), 611–20.

xviii **dwell on the emotional injuries** Paquette, J. A., and Underwood, M. K. (1999). Gender differences in young adolescents' experiences of peer victimization: Social and physical aggression. *Merrill-Palmer Quarterly* 45 (2), 242–66.

xviii **age of puberty for girls** Biro, F. M., Galvez, M. P., Greenspan, L. C., et al. (2010). Pubertal assessment method and baseline characteristics in a mixed longitudinal study of girls. *Pediatrics* 126 (3), e583–90.

xix **thongs and push-up bikini tops** Zurbriggen, E. L., Collins, R. L., Lamb, S., et al. (2007). *Report on the APA task force on the sexualization of girls. Executive summary.* Washington, DC: American Psychological Association.

Abercrombie and Fitch sells push-up bikini tops to little girls. (2011, March 28). Retrieved from parenting.com/article/abercrombie-fitch-sells-push-up-bikinis-to-little-girls.

Chapter One: Coming to Terms with Stress and Anxiety

4 **demonstrate higher-than-average** Wu, G., Feder, A., Cohen, A., et al. (2013). Understanding resilience. *Frontiers in Behavioral Neuroscience* 7 (10), 1–15.

7 **three distinct domains** Psychologists also recognize the important category of traumatic stress, which applies to overwhelming, upsetting events that completely outmatch an individual's coping abilities, a critical topic that exceeds the scope of this book.

7 **event that requires adaptation** Buccheri, T., Musaad, S., Bost, K. K., et al. (2018). Development and assessment of stressful life events subscales—A preliminary analysis. *Journal of Affective Disorders* 226, 178–87.

8 **daily hassles triggered** Johnson, J. G., and Sherman, M. F. (1997). Daily hassles mediate the relationship between major life events and psychiatric symptomatology: Longitudinal findings from an adolescent sample. *Journal of Social and Clinical Psychology* 16 (4), 389–404.

8 **Enduring chronic stress** Kim, P., Evans, G. W., Angstadt, M., et al. (2013). Effects of childhood poverty and chronic stress on emotion regulatory brain function in adulthood. *Proceedings of the National Academy of Sciences* 110 (46), 18442–47.

8 **two grave and persistent** Compas, B. E., Desjardins, L., Vannatta, K., et al. (2014). Children and adolescents coping with cancer: Self- and parent reports of coping and anxiety/depression. *Health Psychology* 33 (8), 853–61.

Compas, B. E., Forehand, R., Thigpen, J., et al. (2015). Efficacy and moderators of a family group cognitive-behavioral preventive intervention for children of depressed parents. *Journal of Consulting and Clinical Psychology* 83 (3), 541–53.

17 **Almost simultaneously** Actually, there's an extremely long-running debate in the history of psychology about where emotions come from. In the late 1800s William James, a man dubbed the "Father of American Psychology" (and whom you might also know as the brother of the novelist Henry), proposed that we make decisions about what we are feeling based on our physical sensations or, in his words, "organic changes, muscular and visceral" [James, W. (1894). The physical basis of emotion. *Psychological Review* 1 (7), 516–29]. Put simply, when our heart starts to gallop, we realize that we must feel afraid.

Since then, several modifications to James's theory have been proposed. Some psychologists have argued that our physical and emotional reactions occur simultaneously, not in sequence, while others have pointed out that we often rely on situational cues to decide what to make of our physical sensations [Moors, A. (2009). Theories of emotion causation. *Cognition and Emotion* 23 (4), 625–62]. For instance, a girl who is exercising will likely interpret her pounding heart as a sign that she's getting a good workout. But if her heart starts racing when she's next up to give a speech, she may conclude that she's feeling anxious. Theoretical debates aside, all psychologists agree that physical and emotional experiences are closely intertwined, and that our *interpretation* of our physical reactions can determine whether we experience anxiety ("I'm panicking! I'm gonna blow this speech!") or another emotion altogether ("Wow, I must be very excited about giving this speech!").

19 **a cardiac event** Fleet, R. P., Lavoie, K. L., Martel, J., et al. (2003). Two-year follow-up status of emergency department patients with chest pain: Was it panic disorder? *Canadian Journal of Emergency Medicine* 5 (4), 247–54.

19 **nearly 30 percent** Kessler, R. C., Chiu, W. T., Jin, R., et al. (2006). The epidemiology of panic attacks, panic disorder, and agoraphobia in the national comorbidity survey replication. *Archives of General Psychiatry* 63 (4), 415–24.

19 **we diagnose panic disorder** You may have noted that obsessive-compulsive disorder (OCD) and post-traumatic stress disorder (PTSD) are not included among the anxiety disorders addressed here. Though anxiety is a critical feature of both disorders, they are no longer classified with the anxiety disorders as of the publication of the fifth edition of the *Diagnostic and Statistical Manual* (*DSM-5*) in 2013. PTSD now belongs to a new category, trauma and stressor-related disorders, and OCD belongs to another new category, obsessive-compulsive and related disorders. The relocation of these diagnoses highlights two important facts.

First, psychological and psychiatric diagnosis does not "cleave nature at its joints," as Carl Linnaeus, an eighteenth-century scholar, hoped scientific taxonomies might do. The boundaries between the various psychological disorders are often blurry and the decision to locate a diagnosis with one group or another can be somewhat arbitrary. For example, anorexia nervosa is housed, not surprisingly, with the feeding and eating disorders, but the argument is occasionally made that it has more in common with obsessive-compulsive phenomena (e.g., the obsessive belief that one is overweight and the accompanying behavioral compulsion to diet and/or exercise to excess).

Second, anxiety is a component in a great number of disorders that make their home outside of the anxiety disorders section of the *DSM-5*. Given that anxiety alerts us when something is amiss, it makes sense that anxiety appears on the symptom lists for distressing afflictions such as depression with anxious distress, illness anxiety disorder (hypochondria in layperson's terms), and borderline personality disorder. Even when anxiety doesn't play the lead role in a diagnosis, it often has a supporting part.

20 **can run in families** We know that some anxiety disorders are more likely to run in families than others and that genes appear to play an especially potent role in panic disorder.

Reif, A., Richter, J., Straube, B., et al. (2014). MAOA and mechanisms of panic disorder revisited: From bench to molecular psychotherapy. *Molecular Psychiatry* 19 (1), 122–28.

21 **tailored and systematic approach** Stewart, R. E., and Chambless, D. L. (2009). Cognitive-behavioral therapy for adult anxiety disorders in clinical practice: A meta-analysis of effectiveness studies. *Journal of Consulting and Clinical Psychology* 77 (4), 595–606.

21 **outside of our awareness** Göttken, T., White, L. O., Klein, A. M., et al.

(2014). Short-term psychoanalytic child therapy for anxious children: A pilot study. *Psychotherapy* 51 (1), 148–58.

24 **twice as likely as boys** McLean, C. P., and Anderson, E. R. (2009). Brave men and timid women? A review of the gender differences in fear and anxiety. *Clinical Psychology Review* 29 (6), 496–505.

25 **premenstrual hormonal shifts** Farange, M. A., Osborn, T. W., and McLean, A. B. (2008). Cognitive, sensory, and emotional changes associated with the menstrual cycle: A review. *Archives of Gynecology and Obstetrics* 278 (4), 299–307.

25 **drop in estrogen** Kaspi, S. P., Otto, M. W., Pollack, M. H., et al. (1994). Premenstrual exacerbation of symptoms in women with panic disorder. *Journal of Anxiety Disorders* 8 (2), 131–38.

25 **sustain or exacerbate** Nillni, Y. I., Toufexis, D. J., and Rohan, K. J. (2011). Anxiety sensitivity, the menstrual cycle, and panic disorder: A putative neuroendocrine and psychological interaction. *Clinical Psychology Review* 31 (7), 1183–91.

25 **passed down to daughters** Genetic models also help to explain why girls are especially anxiety-prone, though research in this area still has a lot of room to grow. For now, we know that the genetic vulnerability to anxiety disorders likely involves several genes working in concert.

　　Hettema, J. M., Prescott, C. A., Myers, J. M., et al. (2005). The structure of genetic and environmental risk factors for anxiety disorders in men and women. *Archives of General Psychiatry* 62 (2), 182–89.

　　Carlino, D., Francavilla, R., Baj, G., et al. (2015). Brain-derived neurotrophic factor serum levels in genetically isolated populations: Gender-specific association with anxiety disorder subtypes but not with anxiety levels or Val66Met polymorphism. *PeerJ* 3:e1252.

25 **prescription drugs can help** Wehry, A. M., Beesdo-Baum, K., Hennelly, M. M., et al. (2015). Assessment and treatment of anxiety disorders in children and adolescents. *Current Psychiatry Reports* 17 (7), 1–19.

25 **medication is in use** Otto, M. W., Tuby, K. S., Gould, R. A., et al. (2001). An effect-size analysis of the relative efficacy and tolerability of serotonin selective reuptake inhibitors for panic disorder. *The American Journal of Psychiatry* 158 (2), 1989–92.

25 **mindfulness practices have emerged** Borquist-Conlon, D. S., Maynard, B. R., Esposito Brendel, K., and Farina, A. S. J. (2017). Mindfulness-based interventions for youth with anxiety: A systematic review and meta-analysis. *Research on Social Work Practice*. doi.org/10.1177/1049731516684961.

26 **one of my favorite colleagues** K. K. Novick, personal communication, September 1998.

28 **brain to the lungs** Streeter, C. C., Gerbarg, P. L., Saper, R. B., et al. (2012). Effects of yoga on the autonomic nervous system, gamma-aminobutyric-acid, and allostasis in epilepsy, depression, and post-traumatic stress disorder. *Medical Hypotheses* 78 (5), 571–79.

28 **hack her own nervous system** Just as we can voluntarily control our breath to help the brain calm down, we can deliberately reverse the physiological effects of anxiety by tensing and relaxing our muscles. Systematic muscle relaxation—deliberately contracting and releasing muscle groups in sequence—effectively reduces the amount of cortisol in the bloodstream. Cortisol is a stress hormone that the body releases as part of the fight-or-flight response, and research finds that the simple act of squeezing and then releasing muscle groups reduces cortisol far more than simply sitting quietly [Pawlow, L. A., and Jones, G. E. (2005). The impact of abbreviated progressive muscle relaxation on salivary cortisol and salivary immunoglobulin A (sIgA). *Applied Psychophysiology and Biofeedback* 30 (4), 375–87].

Chapter Two: Girls at Home

38 **girls' school in Dallas** I am indebted to the counseling staff at Ursuline Academy of Dallas for sharing their wisdom with me.

38 **spectacular renovation project** Wenar, C., and Kerig, P. (2006). *Developmental Psychopathology*, 5th ed. Boston: McGraw-Hill.

39 **brain's emotional centers** Casey, B. J., Jones, R. M., and Hare, T. A. (2008). The adolescent brain. *Annals of the New York Academy of Science* 1124 (1), 111–26.

45 **managing intractable stress** Compas, B. E., Desjardins, L., Vannatta, K., et al. (2014). Children and adolescents coping with cancer: Self- and parent reports of coping and anxiety/depression. *Health Psychology* 33 (8), 853–61.

Compas, B. E., Forehand, R., Thigpen, J., et al. (2015). Efficacy and moderators of a family group cognitive-behavioral preventive intervention for children of depressed parents. *Journal of Consulting and Clinical Psychology* 83 (3), 541–53.

47 **read our reactions** Nolte, T., Guiney, J., Fonagy, P., et al. (2011). Interpersonal stress regulation and the development of anxiety disorders: An attachment-based developmental framework. *Frontiers in Behavioral Neuroscience* 5 (55), 1–21.

48 **very nervous themselves** Borelli, J. L., Rasmussen, H. F., John, H. K. S.,

et al. (2015). Parental reactivity and the link between parent and child anxiety symptoms. *Journal of Child and Family Studies* 24 (10), 3130–44.

Esbjørn, B. H., Pedersen, S. H., Daniel, S. I. F., et al. (2013). Anxiety levels in clinically referred children and their parents: Examining the unique influence of self-reported attachment styles and interview-based reflective functioning in mothers and fathers. *The British Journal of Clinical Psychology* 52 (4), 394–407.

50 **more war-ridden now** Roser, M. (2018). War and peace. Retrieved from ourworldindata.org/war-and-peace.

50 **concerns about personal safety** American Psychological Association. (2017). Stress in America: Coping with change, part 1.

50 **rates of violent crime** Gramlich, J. (2017). Five facts about crime in the U.S. Pew Research Center.

Uniform Crime Reporting, Federal Bureau of Investigation. (2016). Crime in the United States, Table 1A.

51 **teens of past generations** Centers for Disease Control and Prevention. (2015). Trends in the prevalence of marijuana, cocaine, and other illegal drug use. National youth risk behavior survey: 1991–2015.

Centers for Disease Control and Prevention. (2015). Trends in the prevalence of alcohol use. National youth risk behavior survey: 1991–2015.

51 **bike helmets and seatbelts** Centers for Disease Control and Prevention. (2015). Trends in the prevalence of behaviors that contribute to unintentional injury. National youth risk behavior survey: 1991–2015.

51 **they do have sex** Ibid.

51 **more common among adults** National Institute on Drug Abuse. (2017). Monitoring the future survey: High school and youth trends.

Han, B., Compton, W. M., Blanco, C., et al. (2017). Prescription opioid use, misuse, and use disorders in U.S. adults: 2015 national survey on drug use and health. *Annals of Internal Medicine* 167 (5), 293–301.

56 **Food and Drug Administration actually forbids** Food and Drug Administration. (2017). Full-body CT scans—what you need to know.

60 **research on daily hassles** Johnson, J. G., and Sherman, M. F. (1997). Daily hassles mediate the relationship between major life events and psychiatric symptomatology: Longitudinal findings from an adolescent sample. *Journal of Social and Clinical Psychology* 16 (4), 389–404.

62 **poverty causes unrelenting stress** Vliegenthart, J., Noppe, G., van Rossum, E. F. C., et al. (2016). Socioeconomic status in children is associated with hair cortisol levels as a biological measure of chronic stress. *Psychoneuroendocrinology* 65, 9–14.

62 **rates of emotional problems** Luthar, S., Small, P., and Ciciolla, L. (2018). Adolescents from upper middle class communities: Substance misuse

and addiction across early adulthood. *Development and Psychopathology* 30 (1), 315–35.

　　Luthar, S. S., and Becker, B. E. (2002). Privileged but pressured? A study of affluent youth. *Child Development* 73 (50), 1593–610.

62 **more likely to suffer** Luthar, S. Speaking of psychology: The mental price of affluence. American Psychological Association, 2018, apa.org/research/action/speaking-of-psychology/affluence.aspx.

62 **intense achievement pressures** Luthar, S. S., and Latendresse, S. J. (2005). Children of the affluent: Challenges to well-being. *Current Directions in Psychological Science* 14 (1), 49–53.

62 **physical and psychological distance** Luthar, S. S., and D'Avanzo, K. (1999). Contextual factors in substance use: A study of suburban and inner-city adolescents. *Development and Psychopathology* 11 (4), 845–67.

62 **Terese Lund and Eric Dearing** Lund, T., and Dearing, E. (2013). Is growing up affluent risky for adolescents or is the problem growing up in an affluent neighborhood? *Journal of Research on Adolescence* 23 (2), 274–82.

Chapter Three: Girls Among Girls

68 **one of three categories** Shiner, R. L., Buss, K. A., McClowry, S. G., et al. (2012). What is temperament *now*? Assessing progress in temperament research on the twenty-fifth anniversary of Goldsmith et al. (1987). *Child Development Perspectives* 6 (4), 436–44.

69 **landmark research conducted** Kagan, J. (1998). Biology and the child. In N. Eisenberg (Ed.), *Handbook of Child Psychology*, vol. 3: *Social, emotional, and personality development*, 5th ed. New York: Wiley, pp. 177–236.

69 **brain wave patterns** Calkins, S. D., Fox, N. A., and Marshall, T. R. (1996). Behavioral and physiological antecedents of inhibited and uninhibited behavior. *Child Development* 67 (2), 523–40.

72 **become more flexible** Putman, S. P., Samson, A. V., and Rothbart, M. K. (2000). Child temperament and parenting. In V. J. Molfese and D. L. Molfese (Eds.), *Temperament and Personality Across the Life Span*. Mahwah, NJ: Erlbaum, pp. 255–77.

72 **identified the critical factor** Chen, X., Hastings, P., Rubin, K., et al. (1998). Child-rearing attitudes and behavioral inhibition in Chinese and Canadian toddlers: A cross-cultural study. *Development and Psychology* 34 (4), 677–86.

　　Chen, X., Rubin, K., and Li, Z. (1995). Social functioning and adjustment in Chinese children: A longitudinal study. *Development and Psychology* 31 (4), 531–39.

Chess, S., and Thomas, R. (1984). *Origins and Evolution of Behavior Disorders*. New York: Brunner/Mazel.

72 **one or two solid friendships** Waldrip, A. M., Malcolm, K. T., and Jensen-Campbell, L. A. (2008). With a little help from your friends: The importance of high-quality friendships on early adolescent development. *Social Development* 17 (4), 832–52.

The research on this topic is complex, and there is certainly evidence that having a large social network improves the likelihood of having strong dyadic (one-on-one) friendships [Nagle, D. W., Erdley, C. A., Newman, J. E., et al. (2003). Popularity, friendship quantity, and friendship quality: Interactive influences on children's loneliness and depression. *Journal of Clinical Child and Adolescent Psychology* 32 (4), 546–55]. However, Waldrip, Malcolm, and Jensen-Campbell (2008, p. 847) found that "an adolescent who has at least one friend who offers support, protection, and intimacy is less likely to display problems after controlling for other important relationships as well as the number of friends. Based on these findings, it appears that friendship quality is indeed a unique predictor of an adolescent's adjustment."

74 **girls are more empathic** Van der Graaff, J., Branje, S., De Weid, M., et al. (2014). Perspective taking and empathic concern in adolescence: Gender differences in empathic changes. *Development and Psychology* 50 (3), 881–88.

Rueckert, L., Branch, B., and Doan, T. (2011). Are gender differences in empathy due to differences in emotional reactivity? *Psychology* 2 (6), 574–78.

75 **three forms of unhealthy** This terrific terminology was shared with me by Jacqueline Beale-DelVecchio, a middle school teacher at Sacred Heart Academy in Chicago, after I presented to her middle school students on the topic of being assertive (as opposed to being passive or aggressive). I have since used the terminology Ms. Beale-DelVecchio shared with me in dozens of workshops with girls on how to handle conflict. They immediately latch on to the evocative metaphors and can put them to good use.

81 **opponent off balance** Thanks go to the brilliant Elizabeth Stevens, an educator and aikido black belt, for sharing her martial arts expertise with me regarding this point.

82 **threw a problem** This piece of wisdom was shared with me by the thoughtful educator Daniel Frank. He learned it from his grandmother, Martha Rahm White.

83 **stunted screen-zombies** Livingstone, S. (2018). Book review. iGen: Why today's super-connected kids are growing up less rebellious, more tolerant, less happy—and completely unprepared for adulthood. *Journal of Children and Media* 12 (1), 118–23.

83 **enthralled by the peers** (2014, March 11). Teens and Social Media? "It's Complicated." Retrieved February 3, 2018, from remakelearning.org/blog/2014/03/11/teens-and-social-media-its-complicated/.

86 **authorized their friends** Deborah Banner, who teaches English at Marlborough School in Los Angeles, shared this excellent solution with me.

87 **less sleep than boys** Maslowsky, J., and Ozer, E. J. (2014). Developmental trends in sleep duration in adolescence and young adulthood: Evidence from a national United States sample. *Journal of Adolescent Health* 54 (6), 691–97.

87 **sleep phase delay** Ibid.

The reasons for the pubertal shift in the circadian cycle are not altogether clear. Experts note that this pattern is common among mammals and speculate that there may be an evolutionarily driven reproductive benefit to "staying up late socializing with peers . . . at a time of day that is not dominated by older individuals." [Hagenauer, M. H., and Lee, T. M. (2012). The neuroendocrine control of the circadian system: Adolescent chronotype. *Frontiers in Neuroendocrinology* 33 (3), 211–29, 225.]

87 **around age twelve** Stöppler, M. C. Puberty: Stages and signs for boys and girls. Retrieved from medicinenet.com/puberty/article.htm.

87 **nine hours of sleep** Johnson, E. O., Roth, T., Schultz, L., and Breslau, N. (2006). Epidemiology of DSM-IV insomnia in adolescence: Lifetime prevalence, chronicity, and an emergent gender difference. *Pediatrics* 117 (2), e247–e256.

88 **frazzled and brittle** Shochat, T., Cohen-Zion, M., and Tzischinsky, O. (2014). Functional consequences of inadequate sleep in adolescents: A systematic review. *Sleep Medicine Reviews* 18 (1), 75–87.

88 **emitted by backlit screens** Higuchi, S., Motohashi, Y., Liu, Y., et al. (2003). Effects of VDT tasks with a bright display at night on melatonin, core temperature, heart rate, and sleepiness. *Journal of Applied Physiology* 94 (5), 1773–76.

Kozaki, T., Koga, S., Toda, N., et al. (2008). Effects of short wavelength control in polychromatic light sources on nocturnal melatonin secretion. *Neuroscience Letters* 439 (3), 256–59.

89 **incoming text messages** Van den Bulck, J. (2003). Text messaging as a cause of sleep interruption in adolescents, evidence from a cross-sectional study. *Journal of Sleep Research* 12 (3), 263.

Adachi-Mejia, A. M., Edwards, P. M., Gilbert-Diamond, D., et al. (2014). TXT me I'm only sleeping: Adolescents with mobile phones in their bedroom. *Family and Community Health* 37 (4), 252–57.

89 **access to a phone** Vernon, L., Modecki, K. L., and Barber, B. L. (2018).

Mobile phones in the bedroom: Trajectories of sleep habits and subsequent adolescent psychosocial development. *Child Development* 89 (1), 66–77.

90 **viewing the social media** Vogel, E., Rose, J., Roberts, L., and Eckles, K. (2014). Social comparison, social media, and self-esteem. *Psychology of Popular Media Culture* 3 (4), 206–22.

90 **result of their online** Nesi, J., and Prinstein, M. J. (2015). Using social media for social comparison and feedback-seeking: Gender and popularity moderate associations with depressive symptoms. *Journal of Abnormal Child Psychology* 43 (8), 1427–38.

93 **show the "highlights reel"** Walsh, J. (2018). *Adolescents and Their Social Media Narratives: A digital coming of age*, 1st ed. London: Routledge, p. 26.

93 **agenda behind the image** Walsh, J. (2016, August 10). For teenage girls, swimsuit season never ends [Interview by L. Damour]. *The New York Times.*

Chapter Four: Girls Among Boys

103 **half of all eighth-** Axelrod, A., and Markow, D. (2001). *Hostile Hallways: Bullying, teasing, and sexual harassment in school* (Rep.). AAUW Educational Foundation: aauw.org/files/2013/02/hostile-hallways-bullying-teasing-and -sexual-harassment-in-school.pdf.

108 **not heterosexual are subjected** Williams, T., Connolly, J., Pepler, D., and Craig, W. (2005). Peer victimization, social support, and psychosocial adjustment of sexual minority adolescents. *Journal of Youth and Adolescence* 34 (5), 471–82.

108 **lower levels of self-esteem** Ormerod, A. J., Collinsworth, L. L., and Perry, L. A. (2008). Critical climate: Relations among sexual harassment, climate, and outcomes for high school girls and boys. *Psychology of Women Quarterly* 32 (2), 113–25.

108 **outcomes are intensified** Gruber, J. E., and Fineran, S. (2008). Comparing the impact of bullying and sexual harassment victimization on the mental and physical health of adolescents. *Sex Roles* 59 (1–2), 1–13.

108 **protective school climate** Espelage, D. L., Aragon, S. R., Birkett, M., and Koenig, B. W. (2008). Homophobic teasing, psychological outcomes, and sexual harassment among high school students: What influence do parents and schools have? *School Psychology Review* 37 (2), 202–16.

109 **likely to be bullied** Fekkes, M., Pijpers, F. I. M., and Verloove-Vanhorick, S. P. (2004). Bullying: Who does what, when and where? Involvement of children, teachers and parents in bullying behavior. *Health Education Research* 20 (1), 81–91.

Wang, J., Iannotti, R. J., and Nansel, T. R. (2009). School bullying among U.S. adolescents: Physical, verbal, relational, and cyber. *Journal of Adolescent Health* 45 (4), 368–75.

109 **rarely target guys** Guerra, N. G., Williams, K. R., and Sadek, S. (2011). Understanding bullying and victimization during childhood and adolescence: A mixed methods study. *Child Development* 82 (1), 295–310.

109 **girls are disproportionately blamed** Wang, J., Iannotti, R. J., and Nansel, T. R. (2009).

110 **undermine their academic performance** Gruber, J., and Fineran, S. (2016). Sexual harassment, bullying, and school outcomes for high school girls and boys. *Violence against Women* 22 (1), 112–33.

110 **other way around** Goldstein, S. E., Malanchuk, O., Davis-Kean, P. E., and Eccles, J. S. (2007). Risk factors for sexual harassment by peers: A longitudinal investigation of African American and European American adolescents. *Journal of Research on Adolescence* 17 (2), 285–300.

110 **reveals that girls harass** Gruber, J., and Fineran, S. (2016).

110 **their own admission** Reed, L. A., Tolman, R. M., and Ward, M. L. (2017). Gender matters: Experiences and consequences of digital dating abuse in adolescent dating relationships. *Journal of Adolescence* 59, 79–89.

111 **feeling more threatened** Ormerod, A. J., Collinsworth, L. L., and Perry, L. A. (2008). Critical climate: Relations among sexual harassment, climate, and outcomes for high school girls and boys. *Psychology of Women Quarterly* 32 (2), 113–25.

Reed, L. A., Tolman, R. M., and Ward, M. L. (2017).

112 **something along these lines** Fine, M., and McClelland, S. I. (2006). Sexuality education and desire: Still missing after all of these years. *Harvard Educational Review* 76 (3), 297–338.

113 **boys usually get a different** Ott, M. A. (2010). Examining the development and sexual behavior of adolescent males. *Journal of Adolescent Health* 46 (4 Suppl), S3–11.

114 **derogatory sexualized term** *Dog* is also an entrant into the category of words sometimes used to describe males who pursue meaningless flings with multiple partners. The term, however, seems not to be widely used at present, and its potency as a derogatory term for males is diminished by the multiple uses to which it is also put. For example, it is sometimes used as a term of familiarity among men (as in, "What's up, Dog?") and at other times used to describe an unattractive woman.

114 **report aptly titled** Lippman, J. R., and Campbell, S. W. (2014). Damned if you do, damned if you don't . . . if you're a girl: Relational and normative contexts of adolescent sexting in the United States. *Journal of Children and Media* 8 (4), 371–86.

114 **This study, like others** Temple, J. R., Le, V. D., van den Berg, P., et al. (2014). Brief report: Teen sexting and psychosocial health. *Journal of Adolescence* 37 (1), 33–36.

115 **"virtually immune from criticism,"** Lippman, J.R., and Campbell, S.W. (2014), p. 371.

115 **two-thirds of girls** Thomas, S. E. (2018). "What should I do?": Young women's reported dilemmas with nude photographs. *Sexuality Research and Social Policy* 15 (2), 192–207, doi.org/10.1007/s13178-017-0310-0.

115 **"develop meaningful relationships"** Damour, L. (2017, January 11). Talking with both daughters and sons about sex. *The New York Times*. Retrieved from nytimes.com/2017/01/11/well/family/talking-about-sex -with-daughters-and-sons.html.

120 **likely to make compromises** Tolman, D. L. (1999). Femininity as a barrier to positive sexual health for adolescent girls. *Journal of the American Medical Women's Association* 53 (4), 133–38.

Kettrey, H. H. (2018). "Bad girls" say no and "good girls" say yes: Sexual subjectivity and participation in undesired sex during heterosexual college hookups. *Sexuality and Culture* 22 (3), 685–705, doi.org/10.1007/s12119 -018-9498-2.

120 **less likely to use contraception** Impett, E. A., Schooler, D., and Tolman, D. L. (2006). To be seen and not heard: Feminist ideology and adolescent girls' sexual health. *Archives of Sexual Behavior* 35 (2), 131–44.

Zurbriggen, E. L., Collins, R. L., Lamb, S., et al. (2007). Report on the APA task force on the *Sexualization of Girls, Executive Summary*, American Psychological Association, Washington, DC.

120 **rates of teen pregnancies** Schalet, A. (2004). Must we fear adolescent sexuality? *Medscape General Medicine* 6 (4), 44.

120 **sexual educations and attitudes** Brugman, M., Caron, S. L., and Rade- makers, J. (2010). Emerging adolescent sexuality: A comparison of American and Dutch college women's experiences. *International Journal of Sexual Health* 22 (1), 32–46.

121 **"made a plan together"** Ibid., p. 39.

121 **"girl is a slut"** Ibid., p. 43.

124 **elaborate norms for refusals** Eslami, Z. (2010). Refusals: How to develop appropriate refusal strategies. In A. Martínez-Flor and E. Usó-Juan (Eds.), *Speech Act Performance: Theoretical, empirical and methodological issues (Language Learning and Language Teaching 26*, Amsterdam: John Benjamins), pp. 217–36.

124 **people decline requests** Allami, H., and Naeimi, A. (2011). A cross-linguistic study of refusals: An analysis of pragmatic competence development in Iranian EFL learners. *Journal of Pragmatics* 43 (1), 385–406.

Cameron, D. (2008). *The Myth of Mars and Venus*. Oxford: Oxford University Press.

125 **women in the study** Kitzinger, C., and Frith, H. (1999). Just say no? The use of conversation analysis in developing a feminist perspective on sexual refusal. *Discourse and Society* 10 (3), 293–316, pp. 304–5.

125 **Language scholars note** Ibid.

125 **a feminist linguist** Cameron, D. (2008), p. 96.

127 **compared to young people** Monto, M. A., and Carey, A. G. (2014). A new standard of sexual behavior? Are claims associated with the "hookup culture" supported by general survey data? *Journal of Sex Research* 51 (6), 605–15.

127 **most recent generation** Ibid.

127 **had *no* sex since** Twenge, J. M., Sherman, R. A., and Wells, B. E. (2017). Sexual inactivity during young adulthood is more common among U.S. millennials and iGen: Age, period, and cohort effects on having no sexual partners after age 18. *Archives of Sexual Behavior* 46 (2), 433–40.

128 **reported being virgins** Centers for Disease Control and Prevention. (2015). Trends in the prevalence of sexual behaviors and HIV testing. National youth risk behavior survey: 1991–2015.

Centers for Disease Control and Prevention. (2017). Youth Risk Behavior Survey Data. Available at cdc.gov/yrbs. Accessed on June 20, 2018.

128 **When asked to estimate** Weissbourd, R., Anderson, T. R., Cashin, A., and McIntyre, J. (2017). *The talk: How adults can promote young people's healthy relationships and prevent misogyny and sexual harassment* (Rep.). Retrieved from mcc.gse.harvard.edu/files/gse-mcc/files/mcc_the_talk_final.pdf.

128 **63 percent of men** Garcia, J. R., Reiber, C., Merriwether, A. M., et al. (2010a, March). Touch me in the morning: Intimately affiliative gestures in uncommitted and romantic relationships. Paper presented at the Annual Conference of the NorthEastern Evolutionary Psychology Society, New Paltz, NY.

Garcia, J. R., Reiber, C., Massey, S. G., and Merriwether, A. M. (2012). Sexual hookup culture: A review. *Review of General Psychology* 16 (2), 161–76.

128 **remaining 84 percent** Weissbourd, R., Anderson, T.R., Cashin, A., and McIntyre, J. (2017).

129 **drive-by physical encounter** LaBrie, J. W., Hummer, J. F., Ghaidarov, T. M., et al. (2014). Hooking up in the college context: The event-level effects of alcohol use and partner familiarity on hookup behaviors and contentment. *Journal of Sex Research* 51 (1), 62–73.

129 **further things are likely** Owen, J., Fincham, F. D., and Moore, J. (2011). Short-term prospective study of hooking up among college students. *Archives of Sexual Behavior* 40 (2), 331–41.

129 **drinking is more closely** Owen, J., and Fincham, F. D. (2010). Effects of gender and psychosocial factors on "friends with benefits" relationships among young adults. *Archives of Sexual Behavior* 40 (2), 311–20.

129 **feel less inhibited** Owen, J., Fincham, F. D., and Moore, J. (2011).

131 **93 percent of boys** Sabina, C., Wolak, J., and Finkelhor, D. (2008). The nature and dynamics of Internet pornography exposure for youth. *Cyber-Psychology and Behavior* 11 (6), 691–93.

131 **"mainstream commercial pornography"** Sun, C., Bridges, A., Johnson, J. A., and Ezzell, M. B. (2016). Pornography and the male sexual script: An analysis of consumption and sexual relations. *Archives of Sexual Behavior* 45 (4), 983–84, p. 983.

131 **decreased enjoyment of real-life** Ibid.

131 **practices that are common** Lim, M. S., Carrotte, E. R., and Hellard, M. E. (2016). The impact of pornography on gender-based violence, sexual health and well-being: What do we know? *Journal of Epidemiology and Community Health* 70 (1), 3–5.

131 **frequency of anal sex** Stenhammar, C., Ehrsson, Y. T., Åkerud, H., et al. (2015). Sexual and contraceptive behavior among female university students in Sweden—repeated surveys over a 25-year period. *Acta Obstetricia et Gynecologica Scandinavica* 94 (3), 253–59.

131 **"common in pornography"** Ibid., p. 258.

131 **negative or painful experience** Stulthofer, A., and Ajdukovic, D. (2013). A mixed-methods exploration of women's experiences of anal intercourse: meanings related to pain and pleasure. *Archives of Sexual Behavior* 42 (6), 1053–62.

Chapter Five: Girls at School

137 **statistics show that girls** Voyer, D., and Voyer, S. D. (2014). Gender differences in scholastic achievement: A meta-analysis. *Psychological Bulletin* 140 (4), 1174–204.

137 **As high school students** Livingston, A., and Wirt, J. *The Condition of Education 2004 in Brief* (NCES 2004–076). U.S. Department of Education, National Center for Education Statistics (Washington, DC: U.S. Government Printing Office, 2004).

Office for Civil Rights. (2012, June). *Gender equity in education: A data snapshot.* U.S. Department of Education. Retrieved from ed.gov/about/offices/list/ocr/docs/gender-equity-in-education.pdf.

137 **in college, women** Autor, D., and Wasserman, M. (2013). *Wayward Sons:*

The emerging gender gap in labor markets and education (Rep.). Washington, DC: Third Way. Retrieved from economics.mit.edu/files/8754.

Bauman, K., and Ryan, C. (2015, October 7). Women now at the head of the class, lead men in college attainment. Retrieved from census.gov/ newsroom/blogs/random-samplings/2015/10/women-now-at-the-head -of-the-class-lead-men-in-college-attainment.html.

Digest of Education Statistics—National Center for Education Statistics. (2015, September). Bachelor's, master's, and doctor's degrees conferred by postsecondary institutions, by sex of student and discipline division: 2013-14. Retrieved from nces.ed.gov/programs/digest/d15/ tables/dt15_318.30.asp?current=yes.

137 **feeling stressed by school** Murberg, T. A., and Bru, E. (2004). School-related stress and psychosomatic symptoms among Norwegian adolescents. *School Psychology International* 25 (3), 317-22.

138 **study people's mindsets** Crum, A. J., Salovey, P., and Achor, S. (2013). Rethinking stress: The role of mindsets in determining the stress response. *Journal of Personality and Social Psychology* 104 (4), 716-33.

139 **close friend move away** Park, D., Yu, A., Metz, S. E., et al. (2017). Beliefs about stress attenuate the relation among adverse life events, perceived distress, and self-control. *Child Development*. doi.org/10.1111/cdev.12946.

139 **bodily response to stress** Jamieson, J. P., Nock. M. K., and Mendes, W. B. (2012). Mind over matter: Reappraising arousal improves cardiovascular and cognitive responses to stress. *Journal of Experimental Psychology: General* 141 (3), 417-22.

142 **more time fretting** Giota, J., and Gustafsson, J. (2017). Perceived demands of schooling, stress and mental health: Changes from grade 6 to grade 9 as a function of gender and cognitive ability. *Stress and Health* 33 (3), 253-66.

Murberg, T. A., and Bru, E. (2004).

Silverman, W. K., La Greca, A. M., and Wasserstein, S. (1995). What do children worry about? Worries and their relation to anxiety. *Child Development* 66 (3), 671-86.

142 **take to heart** Roberts, T. (1991). Gender and the influence of evaluations on self-assessments in achievement settings. *Psychological Bulletin* 109 (2), 297-308.

142 **Years of research confirm** Burnett, J. L., O'Boyle, E. H., VanEpps, E. M., et al. (2013). Mind-sets matter: A meta-analytic review of implicit theories and self-regulation. *Psychological Bulletin* 139 (3), 655-701.

143 **care more about pleasing** Pomerantz, E. M., Altermatt, E. R., and Saxon, J. L. (2002). Making the grade but feeling distressed: Gender differences

in academic performance and internal distress. *Journal of Educational Psychology* 94 (2), 396–404.

Pomerantz, E. M., Saxon, J. L., and Kenny, G. A. (2001). Self-evaluation: The development of sex differences. In G. B. Moskowitz (Ed.), *Cognitive Social Psychology: On the tenure and future of social cognition.* Mahwah, NJ: Erlbaum, pp. 59–74.

Pomerantz, E. M., and Ruble, D. N. (1998). The role of maternal control in the development of sex differences in child self-evaluative factors. *Child Development* 69 (2), 458–78.

143 **attuned to our moods** McClure, E. B. (2000). A meta-analytic review of sex differences in facial expression processing and their development in infants, children, and adolescents. *Psychological Bulletin* 126 (3), 424–53.

143 **unwittingly signal disappointment** Levering, B. (2000). Disappointment in teacher-student relationships. *Journal of Curriculum Studies* 32 (1), 65–74.

145 **hand-wringing students** Hewitt, P. L., Flett, G. L., and Mikail, S. F. (2017). *Perfectionism: A relational approach to conceptualization, assessment, and treatment.* New York: The Guilford Press, p. 22.

149 **girls are more disciplined** Duckworth, A. L., and Seligman, M. E. P. (2006). Self-discipline gives girls the edge: Gender in self-discipline, grades, and achievement scores. *Journal of Educational Psychology* 98 (1), 198–208.

155 **sounds uncannily like** Kay, K., and Shipman, C. (2014, May). The confidence gap. *The Atlantic.* Retrieved from theatlantic.com/magazine/archive/2014/05/the-confidence-gap/359815/.

155 **willingness to overprepare** Credit for connecting the dots between how girls operate at school and how they later operate in the workplace goes to Nancy Stickney, a member of my community who attended a local talk where I addressed the importance of helping girls take a tactical approach to their schoolwork. Ms. Stickney reached out to me afterward to note that she'd seen the exact same phenomenon among women in her corporate career.

156 **put themselves forward** Kay, K., and Shipman, C. (2014). *The Confidence Code: The science and art of self-assurance—what women should know.* New York: HarperCollins.

157 **effective learning techniques** Dunlosky, J., Rawson, K. A., Marsh, E. J., et al. (2013). Improving students' learning with effective learning techniques: Promising directions from cognitive and educational psychology. *Psychological Science in the Public Interest* 14 (1), 4–58.

158 **half of the students** Office for Civil Rights. (2012, June).

Voyer, D., and Voyer, S. D. (2014). This large-scale survey of the available research found that, for math and science courses, elementary school girls get the same grades as boys in math and get better grades in science; middle and high school girls get better grades than boys in both fields; college-aged women get better grades in math and the same grades in science.

158 **teachers believe math** Riegle-Crumb, C., and Humphries, M. (2012). Exploring bias in math teachers' perceptions of students' ability by gender and race/ethnicity. *Gender and Society* 26 (2), 290–322.

158 **students in biology classes** National Science Board. (2018). *Undergraduate education, enrollment, and degrees in the United States* (Rep.). Science and Engineering Indicators.

158 **men in those courses** Grunspan, D. Z., Eddy, S. L., Brownell, S. E., et al. (2016). Males underestimate academic performance of their female peers in undergraduate biology classrooms. *PLoS ONE* 11 (2): e0148405.

159 **evaluate application materials** Moss-Racusin, C. A., Dovidio, J. F., Brescholl, V. L., et al. (2012). Science faculty's subtle gender biases favor male students. *PNAS* 109 (41), 16474–79.

159 **discriminated against at school** Nguyen, H. D., and Ryan, A. M. (2008). Does stereotype threat affect test performance of minorities and women: A meta-analysis of experimental evidence. *Journal of Applied Psychology* 93 (6), 1314–34.

160 **talking about the biases** Johns, M., Schmader, T., and Martens, A. (2005). Knowing is half the battle: Teaching stereotype threat as a means of improving women's math performance. *Psychological Science* 16 (3), 175–79.

160 **false negative stereotype** McGlone, M. S., and Aronson, J. (2007). Forewarning and forearming stereotype-threatened students. *Communication Education* 56 (2), 119–33.

161 **elevated rates of anxiety** Nelson, J. M., and Harwood, H. (2011). Learning disabilities and anxiety: A meta-analysis. *Journal of Learning Disabilities* 44 (1), 3–17.

161 **second and third graders** Shaywitz, S. E., Shaywitz, B. A., Fletcher, J. M., and Escobar, M. D. (1990). Prevalence of reading disability in boys and girls: Results of the Connecticut longitudinal study. *Journal of the American Medical Association* 264 (8), 998–1002.

161 **likely to be inattentive** Rucklidge, J. J. (2010). Gender differences in attention-deficit/hyperactivity disorder. *Psychiatric Clinics of North America* 33 (2), 357–73.

Biederman J., Mick, E., Faraone, S. V., et al. (2002). Influence of gender on attention deficit hyperactivity disorder in children referred to a psychiatric clinic. *The American Journal of Psychiatry* 159 (1), 36–42.

166 **fail to gain admission** Stanford, for instance, admitted 16 percent of its applicants in 1996 and only 4.7 percent in 2017.

Stanford University, News Service. (1996, June 3). *Stanford's 'yield rate' increases to 61.4 percent* [Press release]. Retrieved from news.stanford.edu/pr/96/960605classcentu.html.

Stanford University. (2017, August). *Our selection process.* Retrieved from admission.stanford.edu/apply/selection/profile.html.

As admission rates have dropped, more and more students enroll in more and more Advanced Placement courses in order to gain a competitive edge. In 1997, 566,720 students took a total of 899,463 AP exams. In 2017, 2,741,426 students took a total of 4,957,931 AP exams.

College Board. (1997). *AP data—archived data* (Rep.). Retrieved from research.collegeboard.org/programs/ap/data/archived/1997.

College Board. (2017). *Program summary report* (Rep.). Retrieved from secure-media.collegeboard.org/digitalServices/pdf/research/2017/Program-Summary-Report-2017.pdf.

167 **Renée Spencer and her colleagues** Spencer, R., Walsh, J., Liang, B., et al. (2018). Having it all? A qualitative examination of affluent adolescent girls' perceptions of stress and their quests for success. *Journal of Adolescent Research* 33 (1), 3–33.

169 **A 2006 study** Kahneman, D., Krueger, A. B., Schkade, D., et al. (2006). Would you be happier if you were richer? A focusing illusion. *Science* 312 (5782), 1908–10.

169 **Happy grown-ups believe** Ryff, C. D., and Keyes, L. M. (1995). The structure of psychological well-being revisited. *Journal of Personality and Social Psychology* 69 (4), 719–27.

171 **a list of values** Ciciolla, L., Curlee, A. S., Karageorge, J., and Luthar, S. S. (2017). When mothers and fathers are seen as disproportionately valuing achievements: Implications for adjustment among upper middle class youth. *Journal of Youth and Adolescence* 46 (5), 1057–75.

171 **replicated what other research** Luthar, S. S., and Becker, B. E. (2002). Privileged but pressured? A study of affluent youth. *Child Development* 73 (50), 1593–610.

Chapter Six: Girls in the Culture

177 **less damning, less permanent** To be sure, guys contend with their own set of threatening words. Boys, unfortunately, are encouraged by our culture to conform to ultra-macho ideals. They learn to aggressively enforce

this standard by questioning one another's masculinity and heterosexuality with slurs such as *pussy, fag, homo,* and so on. Boys also use *bitch* as a provocative insult, but the term takes on a different meaning when traded between boys than when leveled at a girl. Specifically, when one boy calls another a bitch, the slur falls somewhere between likening him to a girl and to a submissive girlfriend (as in, "being someone's bitch").

177 **engage in grinding rumination** Jose, P. E., and Brown, I. (2008). When does the gender difference in rumination begin? Gender and age differences in the use of rumination by adolescents. *Journal of Youth and Adolescence* 37 (2), 180–92.

181 **bumper crop of research** There's a robust research literature supporting my friend's point that women are often punished in professional settings when they engage in the "assertive" behavior that is rewarded, or at least not considered to be problematic, in men. For example:

Salerno, J. M., and Peter-Hagene, L. (2015). One angry woman: Anger expression increases influence for men, but decreases influence for women, during group deliberation. *Law and Human Behavior* 39 (6), 581–92.

Rudman, L. A., Moss-Racusin, C. A., Phelan, J., and Nauts, S. (2012). Status incongruity and backlash effects: Defending the gender hierarchy motivates prejudice against female leaders. *Journal of Experimental Social Psychology* 48 (1), 165–79.

Phelan, J. E., Moss-Racusin, C. A., and Rudman, L. A. (2008). Competent yet out in the cold: Shifting criteria for hiring reflect backlash toward agentic women. *Psychology of Women Quarterly* 32 (4), 406–13.

182 **documented in numerous studies** For example, Sagar and Schofield found that ambiguously hostile behaviors were rated by preadolescents as more "mean and threatening when the perpetrator was black than when he was white." Similarly, Hugenberg and Bodenhausen found that some European Americans "are biased to perceive threatening affect in Black but not White faces, suggesting that the deleterious effects of stereotypes may take hold extremely early in social interaction."

Sagar, H. A., and Schofield, J. W. (1980). Racial and behavioral cues in black and white children's perceptions of ambiguously aggressive acts. *Journal of Personality and Social Psychology* 39 (4), 590–98.

Hugenberg, K., and Bodenhausen, G. V. (2003). Facing prejudice: Implicit prejudice and the perception of facial threat. *Psychological Science* 14 (6), 640–43.

182 **According to the report** Onyeka-Crawford, A., Patrick, K., and Chaudhry, N. (2017). *Let her learn: Stopping school pushout for girls of color* (Rep.). Washington, DC: National Women's Law Center, p. 3.

183 **apologize too much** Crosley, S. (2015, June 23). Why women apologize and should stop. *The New York Times*. Retrieved from nytimes.com/2015/06/23/opinion/when-an-apology-is-anything-but.html.

183 **known as uptalk** Fendrich, L. (2010, March 12). The valley-girl lift. *The Chronicle of Higher Education*.

183 **sprinkling sentences with** *just*. Leanse, E. P. (2015, June 25). Google and Apple alum says using this word can damage your credibility. *Business Insider*.

184 **Naomi Wolf published** Wolf, N. (2015, July 24). Young women, give up the vocal fry and reclaim your strong female voice. *The Guardian*. Retrieved from theguardian.com/commentisfree/2015/jul/24/vocal-fry -strong-female-voice.

184 **published a sharp rejoinder** Cameron, D. (2015, July 27). An open letter to Naomi Wolf: Let women speak how they please. *In These Times*. Retrieved from inthesetimes.com/article/18241/naomi-wolf-speech-uptalk -vocal-fry.

185 **colleagues in academic linguistics** High-rising terminal declarative, eh? (1992, January 19). *The New York Times*. Retrieved from nytimes .com/1992/01/19/opinion/l-high-rising-terminal-declarative-eh-061992 .html.

187 **"improving your relationship"** Ury, W. (2007). *The Power of a Positive No: How to say no and still get to yes*. New York: Bantam.

188 **damaging a meaningful connection** Of course boys care about their relationships, too, and though guys, far more than girls, can be rude without consequence, why should they be allowed this margin? We should, of course, raise our sons to have polite and adept verbal Swiss Army knives, too.

192 **have long articulated** The humanities are replete with the theme of the divided self. Horace (65–8 BC), the Roman poet, wrote a particularly amusing satire describing his efforts to be polite to a clingy and cloying fan whom he wanted to tell off:

> By chance I was strolling the Sacred Way, and musing,
> As I do, on some piece of nonsense, wholly absorbed,
> When up runs a man I know only by name, who grabs
> Me by the hand, crying: 'How do you do, dear old thing?'
> 'Fine, as it happens,' I answer, 'and best wishes to you.'
> As he follows me, I add: 'You're after something?'
> He: 'You should get to know me better, I'm learned.'
> I: 'I congratulate you on that.' Desperately trying

To flee, now I walk fast, now halt, and whisper a word
In the ear of my boy, as the sweat's drenching me
Head to foot. While the fellow rattles on, praising
Street after street, the whole city, I silently whisper,
'Oh Bolanus, to have your quick temper!' Since I'm not
Replying, he says: 'You're dreadfully eager to go:
I've seen that a while: but it's no use: I'll hold you fast:
I'll follow you wherever you're going.' 'No need
For you to be dragged around: I'm off to see someone
You don't know: he's ill on the far side of Tiber,
Near Caesar's Garden.' 'I've nothing to do, I'm a walker:
I'll follow.' Down go my ears like a sulky donkey,
When the load's too much for his back.

> *Satires:* Book I, Satire IX (Translated by A. S. Kline)

192 **phenomenon in theatrical terms** Social scientist Erving Goffman also worked with the analogy of a front and back stage in his highly intelligent and historically bound treatise *The Presentation of the Self in Everyday Life* (1959) (New York: Anchor Books). Goffman's elaborate dissection of human interaction goes far beyond my simple likening of our public and private personas to the activity of the front and back stage.

195 **comment on girls' appearance** Karraker, K. H., Vogel, D. A., and Lake, M. A. (1995). Parents' gender-stereotyped perceptions of newborns: The eye of the beholder revisited. *Sex Roles* 33 (9/10), 687–701.

  Rubin, J. Z., Provenzano, F. J., and Luria, Z. (1974). The eye of the beholder: Parents' views on sex of newborns. *American Journal of Orthopsychiatry* 44 (4), 512–19.

195 **industry spends $13 billion** Advertising spending in the perfumes, cosmetics, and other toilet preparations industry in the United States from 2010 to 2017 (in million U.S. dollars). (2017). Retrieved from statista.com/statistics/470467/perfumes-cosmetics-and-other-toilet-preparations-industry-ad-spend-usa/.

195 **remains persistently preoccupied** Rogers, K. (2016, August 18). Sure, these women are winning Olympic medals, but are they single? *The New York Times.* Retrieved from nytimes.com/2016/08/19/sports/olympics/sexism-olympics-women.html.

  Fahy, D. (2015, March 16). Media portrayals of female scientists often shallow, superficial. Retrieved from blogs.scientificamerican.com/voices/media-portrayals-of-of-female-scientists-often-shallow-superficial/.

196 **erode her intellectual abilities** Kahalon, R., Shnabel, N., and Becker, J.

C. (2018). "Don't bother your pretty little head": Appearance compliments lead to improved mood but impaired cognitive performance. *Psychology of Women Quarterly* 42 (2), 136–50.

199 **"looks without her makeup"** Capon, L. (2016, November 21). Alicia Keys has stopped wearing makeup and is killing it. *Cosmopolitan.*

199 **"America's foreign policy"** White, T. (2006, March 28). Rice loosens up her locks and her image. *The Baltimore Sun.* Retrieved from articles .baltimoresun.com/2006-03-28/features/0603280057_1_rice-head-of-hair -condoleezza.

Rosen, J. (2013, June 14). Hillary Clinton, hair icon. *Town and Country.*

199 **simply looking at media-portrayed** Monro, F., and Huon, G. (2005). Media-portrayed idealized images, body shame, and appearance anxiety. *International Journal of Eating Disorders* 38 (1), 85–90.

200 **disliked the shape** Runfola, C. D., Von Holle, A., Trace, S. E., et al. (2013). Body dissatisfaction in women across the lifespan: Results of the UNC-SELF and Gender and Body Image (GABI) Studies. *European Eating Disorders Review: The Journal of the Eating Disorders Association* 21 (1), 52–59.

200 **feeling quite a bit better** Grabe, S., and Shibley Hyde, J. (2006). Ethnicity and body dissatisfaction among women in the United States: A meta-analysis. *Psychological Bulletin* 132 (4), 622–40.

Kelly, A. M., Wall, M., Eisenberg, M. E., et al. (2005). Adolescent girls with high body satisfaction: Who are they and what can they teach us? *Journal of Adolescent Health* 37 (5), 391–96.

Duke, L. (2000). Black in a blonde world: Race and girls' interpretations of the feminist ideal in teen magazines. *Journalism and Mass Communication Quarterly* 77 (2), 367–92.

200 **experimented with unhealthy dieting** Neumark-Sztainer, D., Croll, J., Story, M., et al. (2002). Ethnic/racial differences in weight-related concerns and behaviors among adolescent girls and boys: Findings from project EAT. *Journal of Psychosomatic Research* 53 (5), 963–74.

202 **participating in sports** Hausenblas, H. A., and Downs, D. S. (2001). Comparison of body image between athletes and non-athletes: A meta-analytic review. *Journal of Applied Sport Psychology* 13 (3), 323–39.

202 **a large-scale study** Abbott, B. D., and Barber, B. L. (2011). Differences in functional and aesthetic body image between sedentary girls and girls involved in sports and physical activity: Does sport type make a difference? *Psychology of Sport and Exercise* 12 (3), 333–42.

202 **sports with an aesthetic component** Slater, A., and Tiggman, M. (2011). Gender differences in adolescent sport participation, teasing, self-objectification and body image concerns. *Journal of Adolescence* 34 (3), 455–63.

204 **gusts of subtle bias** Sue, D. W., Capudilupo, C. M., Torino, G. C., et al. (2007). Racial microaggressions in everyday life: Implications for clinical practice. *American Psychologist* 62 (4), 271–86.

204 **Scholars have documented** Zeiders, K. H., Doane, L. D., and Roosa, M. W. (2012). Perceived discrimination and diurnal cortisol: Examining relations among Mexican American adolescents. *Hormones and Behavior* 61 (4), 541–48.

Jackson, L., Shestov, M., and Saadatmand, F. (2017). Gender differences in the experience of violence, discrimination, and stress hormone in African Americans: Implications for public health. *Journal of Human Behavior in the Social Environment* 27 (7), 768–78.

Brody, G. H., and Lei, M. (2014). Perceived discrimination among African American adolescents and allostatic load: A longitudinal analysis with buffering effects. *Child Development* 85 (3), 989–1002.

Berger, M., and Sarnyai, Z. (2014). "More than skin deep": Stress neurobiology and mental health consequences of racial discrimination. *Stress: The International Journal on the Biology of Stress* 18 (1), 1–10.

205 **a lot of mental energy** Sellers, R. M., Copeland-Linder, N., Martin, P. P., and Lewis, R. L. (2006). Racial identity matters: The relationship between racial discrimination and psychological functioning in African American adolescents. *Journal of Research on Adolescence* 16 (2), 187–216.

207 **having a supportive family** Brody, G. H., Chen, Y., Murry, V. M., et al. (2006). Perceived discrimination and the adjustment of African American youths: A five-year longitudinal analysis with contextual moderation effects. *Child Development* 77 (5), 1170–89.

Elmore, C. A., and Gaylord-Harden, N. K. (2013). The influence of supportive parenting and racial socialization messages on African American youth and behavioral outcomes. *Journal of Child and Family Studies* 22 (1), 63–75.

Brody, G. H., Miller, G. E., Yu, T., et al. (2016). Supportive family environments ameliorate the link between racial discrimination and epigenetic aging. *Psychological Science* 27 (4), 530–41.

207 **engage with the painful realities** Irving, D. (2014). *Waking Up White, and Finding Myself in the Story of Race.* Cambridge, MA: Elephant Room Press.

Bergo, B., and Nicholls, T. (Eds.) (2015). *"I Don't See Color": Personal and critical perspectives on white privilege.* University Park: Pennsylvania State University Press.

Recommended Resources

. . . .

Chapter One: Coming to Terms with Stress and Anxiety

For Parents:

Foa, E., and Andrews, L. W. (2006). *If Your Adolescent Has an Anxiety Disorder: An Essential Resource for Parents.* New York: Oxford University Press.

Rapee, R., Wignall, A., Spence, S., et al. (2008). *Helping Your Anxious Child: A step-by-step guide for parents.* Oakland, CA: New Harbinger.

For Girls:

Huebner, D., and Matthews, B. (2005). *What to Do When You Worry Too Much: A Kid's Guide to Overcoming Anxiety.* Washington, DC: Magination Press.

Schab, L. M. (2008). *The Anxiety Workbook for Teens: Activities to help you deal with anxiety and worry.* Oakland, CA: Instant Help Books.

Stahl, B., and Goldstein, E. (2010). *A Mindfulness-Based Stress Reduction Workbook.* Oakland, CA: New Harbinger.

Chapter Two: Girls at Home

For Parents:

Dell'Antonia, K. J. (2018): *How to Be a Happier Parent: Raising a Family, Having a Life, and Loving (Almost) Every Minute of It.* New York: Avery.

Kabat-Zinn, J. (2007). *Arriving at Your Own Door: 108 Lessons in Mindfulness.* New York: Hyperion.

Lythcott-Haims, J. (2015). *How to Raise an Adult: Break Free of the Overparenting Trap and Prepare Your Kid for Success.* New York: St. Martin's Press.

Wilson, R., and Lyons, L. (2013). *Anxious Kids, Anxious Parents: 7 Ways to Stop the Worry Cycle and Raise Courageous and Independent Children.* Deerfield Beach, FL: Health Communications.

For Girls:

Sedley, B. (2017). *Stuff That Sucks: A Teen's Guide to Accepting What You Can't Change and Committing to What You Can.* Oakland, CA: Instant Help Books.

Chapter Three: Girls Among Girls

For Parents:

Boyd, D. (2015). *It's Complicated: The Social Lives of Networked Teens.* New Haven, CT: Yale University Press.

Cain, S. (2013). *Quiet: The Power of Introverts in a World That Can't Stop Talking.* New York: Crown.

Simmons, R. (2011). *Odd Girl Out: The Hidden Culture of Aggression in Girls.* New York: First Mariner Books.

Wiseman, R. (2009). *Queen Bees and Wannabes: Helping Your Daughter Survive Cliques, Gossip, Boyfriends, and the New Realities of the Girl World.* New York: Three Rivers Press.

For Girls:

Criswell, P. K., and Martini, A. (2003). *A Smart Girl's Guide to Friendship Troubles: Dealing with Fights, Being Left Out & the Whole Popularity Thing.* Middletown, WI: Pleasant Company.

Chapter Four: Girls Among Boys

For Parents:

Orenstein, P. (2017). *Girls and Sex: Navigating the Complicated New Landscape.* New York: HarperCollins.

Siegel, D. J. (2013). *Brainstorm: The Power and Purpose of the Teenage Brain.* New York: Jeremy P. Tarcher/Penguin.

Tolman, D. L. (2005). *Dilemmas of Desire: Teenage Girls Talk About Sexuality.* Cambridge, MA: Harvard University Press.

For Girls:

Bialik, M. (2017). *Girling Up: How to be Strong, Smart and Spectacular.* New York: Philomel Books.

Fonda, J. (2014). *Being a Teen: Everything teen girls and boys should know about relationships, sex, love, health, identity & more.* New York: Random House.

Chapter Five: Girls at School

For Parents:

Dweck, C. S. (2006). *Mindset: The new psychology of success.* New York: Ballantine.

Orenstein, P. (1994). *Schoolgirls: Young Women, Self-Esteem, and the Confidence Gap.* New York: Doubleday.

Silver, L. B. (2006). *The Misunderstood Child: Understanding and coping with your child's learning disabilities,* 4th ed. New York: Three Rivers Press.

Simmons, R. (2018). *Enough as She Is: How to Help Girls Move Beyond Impossible Standards of Success to Live Healthy, Happy, and Fulfilling Lives.* New York: HarperCollins.

For Girls:

Kay, K., and Shipman, C. (2018). *The Confidence Code for Girls: Taking risks, messing up, & becoming your amazingly imperfect, totally powerful self.* New York: HarperCollins.

Chapter Six: Girls in the Culture

For Parents:

Lamb, S., and Brown, L. M. (2006). *Packaging Girlhood: Rescuing our daughters from marketers' schemes.* New York: St. Martin's Press.

Orenstein, P. (2011). *Cinderella Ate My Daughter: Dispatches from the Front Lines of the New Girly-Girl Culture.* New York: HarperCollins.

Simmons, R. (2010). *The Curse of the Good Girl: Raising Authentic Girls with Courage and Confidence.* New York: The Penguin Press.
Tatum, B. D. (2017). *Why Are All the Black Kids Sitting Together in the Cafeteria: And other conversations about race.* New York: Basic Books.

For Girls:

Paul, C. (2016). *The Gutsy Girl: Escapades for Your Life of Epic Adventure.* New York: Bloomsbury.

Index

. . . .

About the Author

. . . .

LISA DAMOUR, PH.D., is the *New York Times* bestselling author of *Untangled,* as well as the monthly Adolescence columnist for *The New York Times.* Dr. Damour has also written numerous academic papers related to education and child development. After graduating with honors from Yale University and working for the Yale Child Study Center, she received her doctorate in clinical psychology at the University of Michigan. Dr. Damour directs Laurel School's Center for Research on Girls, maintains a private psychotherapy practice, consults and speaks internationally, and is a Senior Advisor to the Schubert Center for Child Studies at Case Western Reserve University. She and her husband have two daughters and live in Shaker Heights, Ohio.

drlisadamour.com
Facebook.com/lisadamourphd
Twitter: @LDamour

About the Type

• • • • • • • • • • •

This book was set in Legacy, a typeface family designed by Ronald Arnholm (b. 1939) and issued in digital form by ITC in 1992. Both its serifed and unserifed versions are based on an original type created by the French punchcutter Nicholas Jenson in the late fifteenth century. While Legacy tends to differ from Jenson's original in its proportions, it maintains much of the latter's characteristic modulations in stroke.